THE GREEN[illegible]

Gideon Haigh's other books for Auru[illegible] accounts of the last two Ashes series, *Ashes 200*[illegible] and *Downed Under* (2006–07); *Mystery Spinner,* his biography of the forgotten Australian Test spinner Jack Iverson, which was voted Cricket Society Book of the Year, shortlisted for the William Hill Sports Book of the Year and hailed as 'a classic' by the *Sunday Times*; *The Big Ship,* his biography of the Australian Test captain Warwick Armstrong, whose side achieved the 1920s Ashes whitewash; *Many a Slip,* his diary of a club cricket season; and *Peter the Lord's Cat,* his collection of the most unexpected and eccentric obituaries from the pages of *Wisden Cricketers' Almanack.* He covered the last two Ashes series for the *Guardian, Wisden Cricketer* and cricinfo.com. He lives in Melbourne, Australia.

'The star writer of the moment and the latest in a blue-blooded lineage, reaching back to Neville Cardus through C.L.R. James and Matthew Engel, whose allusions soar beyond the boundaries of normal cricket journalism into music, politics and literature. Haigh's analyses are brilliant.'

CHRISTOPHER DOUGLAS, WISDEN CRICKETER

THE GREEN AND GOLDEN AGE

Writings on Modern Cricket

Gideon Haigh

First published in Great Britain 2008
by Aurum Press Ltd, 7 Greenland Street, London NW1 0ND
www.aurumpress.co.uk

Published by arrangement with Black Inc., an imprint of Schwartz Publishing Pty Ltd

A catalogue record for this book is available from the British Library.

ISBN 978 1 84513 338 2

10 9 8 7 6 5 4 3 2 1
2012 2011 2010 2009 2008

Book design: Thomas Deverall
Printed by CPI Bookmarque, Croydon, Surrey

CONTENTS

INTRODUCTION *The (Green and) Gold Standard* ix

THE BAGGY GREEN MACHINE

MARK TAYLOR *Safe Hands* 3

STEVE AND MARK WAUGH *A Lovely Waugh* 8

STEVE WAUGH *Comfort Stop* 11

WAUGH'S FAREWELL *Over and Out* 15

RICKY PONTING *Heir Today* 17

RICKY PONTING *Little Big Man* 20

ADAM GILCHRIST *Rocket Man* 27

ADAM GILCHRIST *The Exclamation Mark* 33

DAMIEN MARTYN *The Step-Up* 36

DARREN LEHMANN *Afternoon Light* 45

JO ANGEL *Look Homeward* 51

CRICKET BOOKS OF 2004 *Our Heroes and Others* 53

THE WARNE AGE

SHANE WARNE *The Young Veteran* 67

SHANE WARNE *The Comeback Kid* 75

WARNE'S RETURN *He's Back* 79

WARNE AND MURALI *Long Playing Records* 82

SHANE WARNE *Bad Boy, Bad Book* 86

SHANE WARNE *Genius?* 89

A CLUTCH OF CHARACTERS

BELINDA CLARK *The Little Mistress* 95

DANIEL VETTORI *Sebastian Flight* 103

MATTHEW MAYNARD *Lost and Found* 105

BRIAN LARA *First among Unequals* 108

Billy Bowden *Billy the Kidder* 110

Darrell Hair *The Lightning Rod* 112

A PACKET OF MATCHES

Perth 1997 *Nasty, Brutish and Short* 117

The 1997 Ashes *The View from Couch Central* 120

World Cup 1999 *One-Day Best* 124

Day 5 The Oval 2001 *As Good as It Gets* 128

Melbourne 2001 *Luck's a Fortune* 131

Melbourne 2004 *Boxing Day Massacre* 133

Super Series Game 1 *Super Snooze* 136

Super Series *Back to the Future* 139

Super Test *Defeat without Honour* 142

South Africa in Australia 2005–06 *Payback Time* 145

WINNING AND LOSING

The West Indies 2000 *Decline and Fall* 151

The Return of the All-Rounder *Queue Jumpers* 160

Test Cricket *125 Not Out?* 169

Australia in 2004 *Success and its Discontents* 177

Injuries *Please Try Harder* 180

Jaques v Katich *Lightweight Clash* 183

Champions Trophy 2006 *According to Taste* 185

World Cup 2007 *Runneth Over* 188

World Cup 2007 *The Dying Game* 192

Malcolm Speed *The Case for the Defence* 195

MANAGEMENT AND MISMANAGEMENT

James Sutherland *Taking Charge* 199

Match-Fixing *Fallen Idols* 214

Match-fixing *The Fix is In* 216

Match-fixing *Who Fixes the Fixers?* 221

MATCH-FIXING *So Far, So Bad* 224
MATCH-FIXING *Caught* 227
THE LAWS OF CRICKET *Spirited Debate* 230
THE AKHTAR CASE *Thrown to the Wolves* 232
CROWDS *Patriot Games* 234
LORD'S *Cricket's Fawlty Towers* 237
COACHES *Moores: The Pity* 239
ZIMBABWE *Out of Africa* 243
TWENTY20 2005 *The Shape of Things to Come* 247
TWENTY20 2006 *The Excitement Machine* 249
TWENTY20 2007 *The Balloon Goes Up* 251

INTRODUCTION
The (Green and) Gold Standard

Cricket is hardly alone in having a golden age; there are golden ages in cultural phenomena from comic books and detective fiction to arcade games and dancehall music. Cricket, though, is uncommonly susceptible to golden age thinking: the cast of mind that burnishes past time and character, usually to the detriment of the present. It has an outsized sense of inheritance and tradition; it has pauses and longueurs that invite reflection and reminiscence; it requires a time and space that savours of past luxuries, of peace and of plenty.

As the owner of a cat called Trumper, I'm hardly entitled to denounce this thinking. On the other hand, it is as much a trap as the assumption that all is for the best in this best of all possible worlds. The blessings of this era are abundant and manifest. If you're an Australian, this last decade has been as good as it gets, a pageant of success, with just enough disappointment along the way to make the highlights worth cherishing; a procession of players as good as any ever seen, including a trio of first-rate captains in Mark Taylor, Steve Waugh and Ricky Ponting. Shane Warne or Glenn McGrath or Adam Gilchrist could have defined an era on their own. I wonder sometimes if the rest of my cricket-watching life is not going to be rather anti-climactic.

Like any *belle époque,* this one has also known its discontents, some transitory, some abiding – to the extent, indeed, that it has sometimes felt like a relief to write about cricket, rather than politics, commerce, corruption, or all three at once. On the other hand, I've never felt this a useless process. An era defines itself not only by its deeds, but by what it won't stand for. No issue has shocked me more than match-fixing. I recall the satisfaction with which I wrote in the first edition of *The Cricket War* (1993): 'No team has yet "thrown" a game.' I recall the disgust with which I had to cut the line from the second edition in 2000. All the same, it was consoling that many people shared that disgust; that, amid so much contrivance and so many cheap thrills in sport, cricket's integrity still mattered.

Thus this book, *The (Green &) Golden Age,* which samples some of my writings since 1997 on modern cricket and cricketers, mainly Australian. It is a record of the achievements and dissatisfactions of the moment, most of the pieces having been written quickly, to tight word limits and deadlines, for papers, magazines, books and blogs. The first was written on the day Mark Taylor retired; the last to plug a late-opening hole in *Inside Sport.* There is the short piece I composed for the *Australian* on the day that Warne and Mark Waugh admitted their misadventures with John the Bookie – I can still remember my shock and sorrow. There are some match reports for the *Guardian* from 2005's Super Series, which was like being sent to review *Plan 9 from Outer Space.* There are interviews, blog posts, columns and critiques, including of Steve Waugh's 2-kilogram autobiography, which I had a weekend to read then describe in 1400 words – the things I do for cricket …

In some ways, if it doesn't sound pretentious, it is also a record of the genre, of the different ways we are increasingly challenged to write about cricket in particular and sport in general. The coverage of sport is one area in which newspapers and magazines have improved radically over the last twenty-five years; it is broader and deeper and richer and more varied than when I took my first steps in the trade. There is too much, of course – hell, there is too much of everything. And if you're not bored occasionally in this line of work, you're probably lacking imagination. But creatively, analytically, technologically, professionally, these are good days to be a journalist in sport – as good, in fact, as they are bad in other areas. Find yourself a paper or a cricket magazine from 1982 and see if you don't agree with me. The past wasn't all Cardus and Ray Robinson. There were always plenty of ghosted columns, and none of them was as unintentionally funny as Steve Harmison's.

I can genuinely thank my editors for *The (Green &) Golden Age*; without them, none of it would have been written. They include David Frith, Stephen Fay, John Stern, Christian Ryan, Sambit Bal, Graem Sims, Sally Warhaft, Ben Clissitt and Adam Sills. Latterly, it was a pleasure to work with Chris Feik, Morry Schwartz, Denise O'Dea and their Black Inc. colleagues. *The (Green &) Golden Age* is dedicated to Jim Schembri and Wendy Tuohy: friends since our first day as reporters together.

Gideon Haigh
Melbourne 2007

THE BAGGY GREEN MACHINE

MARK TAYLOR

Safe Hands

'Does no-one have a bad word to say about him?' an English cricket journalist asked me of Mark Taylor a month or so ago. He was genuinely baffled that anyone, especially in the squalid and scandal-wracked world of sport, could be so uniformly respected and bereft of enemies.

It was impossible to enlighten him. Taylor may have his flaws. He does seem to chew with his mouth open. He may not floss regularly. Yet Australia's thirty-ninth captain and its latest Australian of the Year is assuredly a rare figure, even among athletes. Cricketers in Australia have been admired, revered, even worshipped. Seldom have they been so plainly and completely liked, as sportsman and as civilian.

Taylor led Australia in fifty consecutive Tests and to twelve series victories in fifteen starts, including three Ashes rubbers; he oversaw, too, the recapture and retention of the Frank Worrell Trophy. If his form was spasmodic over the past three years, he was at the conclusion of his career the highest-scoring Test batsman still playing, at a time when international new ball talent was abundant. In his first year in Test cricket, he absorbed bowling like a black hole absorbs light, averaging 70 in his initial fourteen Tests. If he regressed to the mean in his remaining ninety Tests, he still averaged a handy 40 doing so. He was also one of the outstanding slip fielders of his generation, with a simple technique and fly-paper palms.

Yet it was thanks to his attitude as much as his achievement that he finished his playing days with so many fans, great captains being rarer in cricket even than great all-rounders. He reminded me always of the man at the bar who absorbs all the saloon talk and, when the hubbub dies, offers an insight so pertinent that one wonders what all the preliminary argument was about. Sir Donald Bradman once expressed the challenge of captaining a cricket team as a set of balances: 'A good captain will be a fighter; confident but not arrogant, firm but not obstinate, able to take criticism without letting it unduly disturb him.' Taylor mastered all these balances and more. There was dignity without solemnity, charm without unction, wholesomeness without sickly sweetness.

Curiously, Taylor's first experience of wielding authority was not in Australia but in England, while playing as 'pro' with Greenmount in the Bolton League, near Manchester, just over a decade ago. Taylor made a record 1300 runs at 70 and led the team to a championship, but the experience that left its mark was that of taking charge. As he recalled to author Jack Egan soon after:

> The first two weeks I was a bit nervous about it, and then there was a training session a week or so later that was going rather poorly; everyone was sort of doing their own thing and one bloke walked past me and said: 'This is an absolute shambles.' I thought: 'It's time for me to step in here.' So I said: 'Right, you, you and you bowl, you pad up, you bat and the rest of you over here with me.' From there it went well because they could see I was starting to get serious about it.

While his initial Test-run glut attracted public attention in 1989–90, Taylor's ability to 'get serious' also left a forceful impression on critics and colleagues. His skipper Allan Border noted in February 1990: 'He's a very astute young man. He gets on very well in a group situation but he's also the kind of bloke who can come down hard now and then, as all captains need to. His tactics on the field are impressive. He thinks about it and knows what's going on.' Australia's selectors took such praise seriously enough to trial Taylor as skipper of an Australia B-team touring

Zimbabwe in September 1991, and he left favourable impressions on a squad vice-captained by Steve Waugh and including future Test men Shane Warne, Stuart Law, Peter McIntyre and Paul Reiffel. Appointment as Border's national vice-captain followed a year later.

Good deputies are seldom remembered. No-one's written a book called *Great American Vice-Presidents*. Withal Taylor did leave an impression. He seems the sort of fellow one would appreciate around an office: the reliable but thoughtful kind who organises flowers if someone is off sick, or passes round the card when someone has a baby. The sort, in other words, with that intuitive sense of the day-to-day niceties that keep a group of people functioning contentedly. It was noticeable how much Australia missed Taylor's pacific temperament when illness ruled him out of the First Test at Wanderers in February 1994. As Warne and Merv Hughes rose to the bait of a hostile crowd, Taylor was an onlooker. Knowing better than most the pressures inherent in a hasty rise to prominence, he made a point of counselling Warne when he stood in for Border during the match against Boland. 'We just had a chat about where he was going in cricket,' Taylor explained. 'I was merely pointing out to him that I didn't think he was enjoying his cricket as much as before and I was trying to find out why.'

The key word in that remark is 'enjoy'. Taylor assumed Australia's captaincy a couple of months later, and it was a word I don't think I've heard a sporting figure use more often. I remember in particular a press conference in Perth at the end of Mark Taylor's first Ashes series as captain. England's Mike Atherton had grumbled miserably about the congestion of the international cricket calendar, to a sympathetic hearing. Yet when Taylor was presented with the proposition that Australia might also be playing too much, he would have none of it. 'No way,' he said. 'I think I speak for all the blokes. I love Test cricket.' As an antidote to the purse-mouthed professionalism of the age – that talked about cricket as 'going to work', that classified losing as 'a bad day at the office' – Taylor's unalloyed pleasure in the game never failed to refresh.

When it comes to recalling Taylor as captain, the on-field moments will come to mind most readily: the innovative bowling changes, the counter-intuitive strategies. But it was this ability to convey enthusiasm for the game, and incubate that ineffable spirit of comradeship and interdependence, that made him. With Warne, for example, he remained paternal, but never paternalistic. I remember a cameo in the Boxing Day Test of 1994 when Atherton edged to second slip, where Warne took it on the bounce: a possible appeal died in the young man's throat before he could open his mouth, for Taylor was already gesturing to the umpire to void the catch.

Discussing Bradman, R. C. Robertson-Glasgow proposed: 'Great captaincy begins off the field. True leadership springs from affection even more than from respect.' In Taylor's case, this was never seen more clearly than when Australia defeated the West Indies in 1995. The world champions had not been beaten at home for twenty-two years, but their house was divided. Australia had lost their previous Worrell Trophy Test in seven sessions, but were happy and close-knit, and in Taylor had a captain as resourceful as the last to bring the silverware home. Just as Ian Chappell had taken the 1972–73 series despite losing his two top pace-men, Dennis Lillee and Bob Massie, Taylor won while manipulating an attack minus Craig McDermott and Damien Fleming that had few pretentions but deep discipline. Just as Chappell had made only two forced changes to his Test side during the series, Taylor stuck to the same XI throughout. Fittingly it was Taylor who threw the ball towards the ionosphere after taking the catch to clinch the decisive Test by an innings and 53 runs.

Taylor's sternest interrogation was his protracted spell on batting skid row in 1996–97: 26 innings worth just 614 runs. Taylor continued to lead not just ably but unselfishly. On the first morning of the Old Trafford Test in July 1997, for example, he won the toss under a mackerel sky and on a pitch promising ample sideways movement, but also long-term deterioration. Taylor could easily have bowled and spared himself the immediate ordeal of batting, but gambled on the harder option. He again failed with the bat, but succeeded in the scenario-planning when Australia prevailed by 326 runs. Four months later the thin thickened in two innings in three weeks at the Gabba: 124 against Queensland and 112 against New Zealand. Centuries to stymie South Africa at Adelaide and out-do India at Bangalore ensued; the 334 not out at Peshawar was merely rich icing on an already plump cake.

Taylor often pointed out during his wretched run that having to give the game away would 'not be the end of the world'. He would be disappointed to cease playing a game he loved on such a note, but his world would not stop turning. Observing Justin Langer's sorrow at parting from his six-week-old child as the Australians left for England in May 1997, Taylor told his comrade: 'Mate, the only thing you can be sure of is that it only gets tougher the older you get.' Not for nothing was Australia's thirty-ninth captain also New South Wales' thirty-ninth father of the year. 'I try to stay as relaxed as I possibly can and remember that it's just a game,' he said – always knowing that this was more easily said than done.

Observing the fuss surrounding Taylor's valediction, some will chastise the media for devoting such lavish space and airtime to encomiums to a cricketer on his retirement. What's best about Taylor is that he wouldn't object to such a reaction: he always seemed sensibly disinclined to imbue cricket with life-or-death significance. John Arlott once paid Mike Brearley the compliment: 'The best thing about you, Mike, is that you're the only England captain who knows it doesn't *really* matter.' Mark Taylor knew it too.

The Australian February 1999

STEVE AND MARK WAUGH

A Lovely Waugh

Justin Langer, having retired hurt on Thursday, was available to bat at the Oval yesterday, but within half an hour of play's commencement was about as likely to appear as Bernhard Langer. A day of utterly routine slaughter impended, and there was a sense in which even the bowlers and fielders could feel it coming.

Steve and Mark Waugh duly brought it all to pass. Steve was on one leg, but both were of one mind. They are playing what will probably be their last Test in England, and their hundreds yesterday were almost certainly their final innings. But there were no Bradman-like ducks to leave us toasting cricket's glorious uncertainty; there was a lot of rather grinding certainty instead, and no breath left among the fielders for three cheers.

Steve Waugh's mood was immediately clear. In the first few overs, he played two extravagant slashes at Ormond. Both times, he bowed his head penitentially and cupped a glove to the side of his helmet visor, shutting out intruding thoughts and gearing himself for a long entrenchment. The second time, Steve went down the pitch to talk to his brother, though only briefly. 'Do as I say not as I do' may have been the message. It was almost certainly not: 'Do you remember that time when we were nine years old that I stuck your head down the dunny?' The twins aren't conversationalists: Waugh-Waugh entails very little Jaw-Jaw.

About half an hour from lunch, Steve began feeling the tear in his calf sustained at Trent Bridge, and limping a little. But there was no sign of strain when he went down on his haunches to slog-sweep Tufnell for six – the stroke with which he reached 50 – or drove inside-out down the ground. He simply husbanded his energies and sauntered his singles, like a slightly gouty laird strolling round his estate.

In Adelaide five years ago, after he had made his usual fat hundred, two Sri Lankan players sought Steve Waugh out. 'Do you meditate?' they asked. 'Because you look like you are in a trance when you bat.' Australia's captain sent them away disappointed – the closest he comes to meditation is chewing his gum a little harder – but there is no doubt he has reserves of concentration granted to few players in history.

In the early days of his career, Mark Waugh also suggested a trance-like state when at the crease, though more because his economy of movement sometimes implied an economy of thought. He batted as if for his own amusement. Dismissal was pleasure deferred rather than pleasure denied. Nowadays he is more hardened. He knows he has received the selectors' indulgence in recent years, and is prepared to bat beyond the point where it has probably ceased to entertain him, for achievement and for the statistical exchequer. Not everything has changed, as one saw yesterday. Mark still plays delightful strokes, including that signature flick to leg with a glance over his shoulder, like a teenager on his bike sneaking a look at a pretty girl. He also retains some idiosyncratic weaknesses, particularly the ball on his body which he doesn't quite play yet also doesn't quite avoid. But he now usually manages to stave off boredom, delaying it yesterday until after his twentieth Test hundred had accrued. Only then did he gift Gough his wicket, his head as high in the air as the bowler's was low.

It's sometimes considered strange that the Waughs have not been more productive in harness, Sabina Park '95 and Sydney '99 being notable exceptions to a pattern of fairly modest partnerships spaced over many Tests together. This may have more to do with the lore and mystique associated with twins than with cricket sense – it wouldn't occur to anyone to ask why Steve Waugh has not made more of his allegiances with, say, Justin Langer – but it does relate something of their differences as individuals.

There's a story attached to the world fifth-wicket record that the twins share: 464 in Perth for New South Wales just over ten years ago. It ended only when their captain declared. It's said that Mark was heard afterwards expressing his thankfulness, as he was quite tired, and Steve his annoyance, as he had thought them good for several hundred more.

As then, so yesterday: while Mark put his feet up, Steve's feet showed even less sign of budging than usual. Though Inzamam-ul-Haq would have beaten him over a hundred yards, Australia's captain took his average against England to the far side of 60, and his average in England to the far side of 70. He received a smaller round of applause than Bradman after his last Test innings at the Oval, but spectators by then probably felt they'd applauded him enough.

The Guardian September 2001

STEVE WAUGH

Comfort Stop

Eight-hundred-and-one pages; 300,000 words; 1.9 kilograms. In this statistically minded age, it is the dimensions of Steve Waugh's autobiography that first command attention. He has, again, swept the field. Bradman disposed of his life in 316 pages, Hobbs in 320, Allan Border in a paltry 270. And this after ten tour diaries, an album of photographs, and three biographies. The man's a machine.

The hackneyed sportspeak of the title isn't for nothing either. This is not a comfortable book to hold, let alone read. Most sport memoirs are slight, perfunctory and produced with little care. *Out of My Comfort Zone* is beset with the opposite problem. The stupendous act of will and effort of documentation involved in its production oozes from every page, almost every passage. Waugh's manuscript apparently ran to scores of hand-written exercise books, and he writes as he batted, in thrall to the idea that the man with the most pages wins. Unable to determine what is important, he has convinced himself that everything is equally so. Some have accused Waugh of an act of vanity in producing a chronology so exhaustive. I do not see it this way. Waugh is simply incapable of thinking small or expressing himself succinctly. If Waugh the batsman saw an easy-paced wicket, he immediately began planning his 150 not out; Waugh the writer looks on all those unfilled pages as another opportunity for a long entrenchment.

Batting and writing, of course, are not the same activities, and it is a shame that Penguin, his publishers, were unable to disabuse

---

A review of *Out of My Comfort Zone* by Steve Waugh (Penguin, 2005)

him of the assumption that they are. For there are hints here of genuine self-disclosure, of the drive that made Waugh the cricketer he was, and of the frailties contained by his tight-wound personality. 'For me,' he explains, 'the hardest part about not doing well was that I began to think I was a failure not just as a player but as a person too.' And elsewhere, because he is inclined to repetition: 'Failure was not just a scoreboard thing – in those blurred moments, I felt personally inadequate as well.'

Waugh agrees that he tended to look after number one: 'Life as a full-time professional teaches you to be selfish in many ways.' But he was innately self-sufficient in any respect, not to mention a practised bottler-up of his emotions, even with brother Mark. Waugh recalls a poignant heart-to-heart conversation they shared amid the worst of his twin's travails during the match-fixing mess: 'Before we parted, we had one of those moments where you know you should let your guard down and just do something. I'm sure we both sensed it – the notion that we should embrace and reassure each other it was going to be okay. But we didn't.' Another golden moment of understatement is shared between Waugh and Mark Taylor in a urinal in Bulawayo. 'I'm going to be a father, Tugga,' says Taylor casually; this, believes Waugh, 'strengthened our bonds of mateship'. This chapter might well have been entitled 'Out of My Comfort Station'.

Beneath the surface, there were more things going on. Waugh is the voice of anxious suggestibility when he enumerates his host of superstitions. The famous red rag was only the start – the sight of a ladybird, for example, he took as a good omen. Captaincy, it turned out, was an even lonelier business than playing: 'A captain can tell he's skipper the moment he sits down to a team dinner at a restaurant and the chairs on either side are vacant for longer than they have been in the past.' He got nervous, and would sometimes suffer 'a mild anxiety attack' at the coin toss. By the end of his career, his only confidante was his wife, Lynette, to whom he 'let all my pent-up emotions gush out and bawled like a baby' when he was retrenched as one-day skipper.

Perhaps it was this understanding of his own vulnerabilities that made him so shrewd in exploiting those of others. There are many intriguing vignettes of the England teams of his era, with glimmers of their lack of cohesion and conviction. 'Regularly on tour we would walk into a restaurant as a group of ten or fifteen and make eye contact with two or three English players having a quiet meal together,' Waugh recalls. 'You could tell they were uneasy about our team spirit and their contrasting lack of togetherness.' Sometimes Waugh is openly contemptuous, as when Alec Stewart says before a one-day international that England are 'just hoping to compete'; Waugh gives the translation: 'We are shit-scared and hope we don't make fools of ourselves.'

Funnily enough, the clearest glimpse of Waugh the character is not his own. It is in the postscript penned by Lynette, who describes the uncompromisingly male environment from which Waugh and his three brothers emerged, where when sport was not being played it was being consumed: 'Sport so dominated the TV that a cricket bat leant against the on/off switch to ensure it stayed on.' Dinner at the Waughs', she says, was an almost Darwinian affair, with the television's background blare a substitute for conversation: 'The plates had barely touched the table when there was a flurry and a clash of forks with food going everywhere ... There was this frantic pace to meals, every meal, as if they'd not eaten for a week. Along with the unbelievable speed they could eat was the noise – the sounds of chomping almost drowned out the TV.' This, perhaps, is the Waugh 'comfort zone': not merely small but also heavily fortified.

Waugh's book would have benefited from more such detached observation. The author himself isn't really capable of it. Just when Waugh seems about to open up, to really unburden himself, the demands of serving the chronology of events impel him onward; he is drawn to the comfort of cliché ('An overwhelming sense of anticipation on top of the comforting knowledge that this was an Australian cricketer's ultimate sporting adventure stirred me as we gathered at Sydney airport in readiness for my second Ashes tour') and the safety of stats ('I performed okay in our other matches, playing in all eight games and finishing fourth in the Australian batting aggregates ... and equal second in the wicket-taking stakes'). The book ends on the day of Waugh's retirement, as though life itself ended with cricket; there are no reconsiderations, or ruminations, or even second thoughts.

Waugh is also prone to descriptions that are like literary slog-sweeps: batting on an awkward pitch is like 'being a wildebeest crossing a swollen African creek bed, knowing that eventually a submerged crocodile will sink its fangs into your flesh'; batting in a cap means that 'the security blanket of a protective helmet wasn't there as a backstop'; fielding under pressure has the 'adrenaline zipping round like a Scalextric race-car and threatening to overload your thought processes'; using criticism as a spur is inspired by 'the way a sewage-treatment works can ultimately extract drinking water from effluent'. As for his contemporaries, Michael Bevan is 'a "pyjama Picasso", creating masterpiece after masterpiece to the point that his genius became mundane when people were spoiled by his continued brilliance'; Gavin Robertson 'once had the classic textbook technique but it somehow metamorphosed into a batting stance that resembled a badly constipated individual with a "headless chook" approach'; Ricky Ponting and Matt Hayden cause him to muse that 'instead of a pit bull terrier and a Labrador playing ball, the guide dog had been replaced by a Rottweiler.' Follow that, if you can.

Both Waughs have now produced books that are subtly revelatory of themselves, Mark relying on an overactive author to do all the work, and Steve doing it all himself to an exhaustive and exhausting degree: if Steve has managed to demonstrate that more can mean less, Mark has already shown that less can mean almost nothing. Steve's title, however, is misleading. His book might concern him leaving his comfort zone; his writing finds him well within it.

The Wisden Cricketer January 2006

WAUGH'S FAREWELL

Over and Out

First, a disclaimer: I did not see Steve Waugh's last Test innings live, nor did I see it on television except as a replay. I am thus unable to testify to the atmosphere at the Sydney Cricket Ground on 6 January 2004, or to provide any of those stirring anecdotes that grant the teller a personal place in history.

'Well, it's now or never, Gids, old chum,' said Steve as he picked up his bat. 'Go to it, Tugga,' I replied simply ...

That afternoon, instead, I was at practice at my cricket club, with about twenty-five of my team-mates. It was hot and muggy. There was, as usual, a lot of banter. But the banter died down every time Steve Waugh faced a ball. We had parked a car behind the nets, and turned the radio up as loud as it would go, so that the ABC commentary on the Test provided a soundtrack to our exertions.

When Waugh, with 4 overs left, miscued a slog-sweep off Anil Kumble, and the ball hung in the air over Sachin Tendulkar in the shadow of the Brewongle Stand, everyone froze in their tracks. Would he stay? Would he go? Could this, after 10,927 runs in 500 hours of Test batting, really be it? Waugh c Tendulkar b Kumble 80. As he retreated to a standing ovation in Sydney, my team-mates and I broke likewise into spontaneous applause.

The Border–Gavaskar Trophy of 2003–04 had not been one of Waugh's great series. Because his valediction had been foreshadowed at the start of summer in order to tamp down speculation about his future, almost everyone who'd wanted to had been afforded a glimpse of the great man on his appointed round. But the Waugh Index had fluctuated. The man who'd done everything in cricket discovered in Brisbane that he hadn't, with an ignominious hit-wicket duck that also included running his partner out. In Australia's Melbourne win, he spent two hours *hors de combat* after his elbow bore the brunt of a lifter from Ajit Agarkar.

Some cricket columnists seemed to write about nothing but Waugh all summer. One Sydney newspaper turned his totemic red rag into mass-merchandised sentiment, offering replicas to readers for waving when he walked to the wicket. One half-expected a twenty-one-gun salute every time he took guard. To his credit, Waugh looked slightly embarrassed by the palaver, and was hungrier for runs than anything else; it may be simply an impression, but he seemed more relieved than triumphant when it was all over.

That afternoon at my home ground we kept practising into the twilight, then repaired to the clubrooms for beers, a little talk of Waugh, then selection for our next round of games. And, perhaps curiously, it has been Test-cricket business as usual here since, the baton of leadership snug in the knapsacks of Ricky Ponting and Adam Gilchrist. In fact, despite the maudlin talk of sad days and ending eras at the time, Waugh's has proven a very Australian farewell – when it was over, it was over, and the game abided.

Wisden Asia December 2004

RICKY PONTING

Heir Today

To concerns about the demoralising and deadening effects of the grind of international cricket, there could be no more effective riposte than Ricky Ponting. Too many games? Too much travel? Bring them on! In 2003, tackling every challenge with unfailing enterprise, he set the tempo of the world's best Test and one-day teams – and in Australia's undefeated World Cup campaign the tactics too.

Ponting's calendar year featured eleven hundreds, five among 1154 one-day runs at 46.16, and six in 1503 Test runs at 100.2, including three that became doubles. Yet as impressive as his run-pile's height was the energy with which it was scaled. Ponting hits his attacking shots hard, and his defensive strokes barely less hard: even at his most restrained and responsible, he impresses one as barely contained, brimful of confidence, ready any moment to bust loose.

For almost its entirety, the same has been thought of Ponting's career; it has been hampered not by doubts about his ability but by certainties. Born in Tasmania's Prospect, he quickly became it. His grandmother dressed four-year-old Ricky in a T-shirt bearing the legend: 'Inside this shirt is an Australian Test cricketer'. He had his first equipment deal with Kookaburra at the age of twelve, represented his state at seventeen, his country at twenty, and his maiden Test hundred at Headingley in July 1997 suggested not so much a coming man as an arriving and disembarking one.

For the next four years, however, Ponting's career was of the coming-and-going kind: there was more coming than going, as a

Test average a tick over 40 from his first forty-five Tests suggests, but questions remained about his staying power, especially when it was devoted to staying out late and causing commotions in nightclubs in Calcutta and Sydney. Thirty subsequent Tests in which he has averaged 77.83 have answered every interrogatory, plus a few not even asked. His restless cricket intelligence forced him to the forefront of candidates to succeed Steve Waugh as Australian captain; his marriage to Rianna Cantor, an arts–law graduate from the University of Wollongong, provided domestic serenity.

Few issues in Australian cricket have caused such public discontent as the cultivation of separate Test and one-day teams. When Waugh's limited-overs commission was rescinded, one Sydney newspaper ran mug shots of the country's selectors beneath the headline 'Wanted: For Incompetence'. Some, doubtless, wished their prejudices justified when Ponting was appointed Waugh's one-day successor just over two years ago; he did not oblige them. The worst mishap when Australia began its World Cup defence in February 2003 befell them before they took the field, and Ponting so sedulously contained the morale damage from the Shane Warne drug drama that the miscreant was barely missed. With 114 (109 balls) in the first Super Six game against Sri Lanka and 140 not out (121 balls) in the final against India, he was Australia's highest scorer of the tournament.

As if to make his own statement about the relationship between the game's two forms, Ponting then set about bringing to Test cricket some of his one-day vim. Three Tests against the West Indies yielded 523 at 130.75. Series against Zimbabwe and Bangladesh then warmed him up for a rematch with India, who'd had Australia's and his measure thirty months earlier. While again more than matching Australia, India had this time to go round Ponting rather than through him. He sold his wicket not just dearly but, with 242 (352 deliveries, 31 fours) at Adelaide and 257 (458 deliveries, 25 fours) in Melbourne, exorbitantly.

While Ponting's appointment as Waugh's Test successor in January 2004 was welcomed for restoring the five- and one-day leaderships to a single custodian, it reasserted some other old Australian cricket values too: that a team's most complete batsman should bat at number three and that the captain is chosen from a team's best eleven cricketers. Departures from both customs have been countenanced in recent years – not without sound reason – but Ponting seems to fit as snugly into the traditions of his office as any of his predecessors. And, as for 'the grind', Ponting seems quite content for it to continue – preferably with Australia doing much of the grinding.

Wisden Cricketers' Almanack 2004

RICKY PONTING

Little Big Man

When Ricky Ponting arrived in international cricket, he used always to keep an eye on Mark Waugh. Waugh was the Australian team's resident Joe Cool, making cricket look easy, doing everything with time to spare. For a new kid on the blockhole, there was no more obvious benchmark.

A decade or so on, and Ponting has assumed that role. The runs and records that peal from his bat are only part of the story. He personifies Australian cricket: busy, industrious, confident, aggressive, combative, sometimes truculent, always in the thick of the action. His predecessor Steve Waugh used to monitor developments from the gully, masticating inscrutably, extemporising almost inaudibly. Ponting fields as close to the bat as circumstances permit, close enough for the batsman to feel his spiky aura, and for umpires to sometimes bear the brunt of his quick temper.

Standing only 1.78 metres, Ponting casts a shadow of disproportionate length. He was named *Wisden*'s inaugural number one cricketer in the world in 2004. He became ICC Player of the Year in November 2006. He is batting in the form of his life: not one Test bowler managed to hit his stumps last year. Two rivals to the title, Mohammed Yousuf and Kevin Pietersen, regard him as clearly the best batsman in the world. If Ponting continues at his recent rate of productivity, he should have passed 12,000 Test runs by the end of next year, surpassing not just the Australian record of Allan Border (11,174) but Brian Lara's new Test marker (11,953).

Ponting's appeal isn't confined to his own generation: Richie

Benaud recently nominated him to lead his best Ashes team of the last thirty years. Nor is it confined to his own country: a host of players in this year's *Cricketers' Who's Who* in England name him as their most admired cricketer, from New Zealander Scott Styris to Middlesex's highly-thought-of prodigy Eoin Morgan.

In Australia, his abilities sometimes seem more obvious in their absence. So unexpected are his occasional failures that you can hear the hasty rip of Velcro from the dressing-room. An Australian batting order without Ponting at number three looks like INXS without Michael Hutchence, or series four of *Monty Python* (the one without John Cleese). When Ponting sat out the Chappell–Hadlee Trophy in February, his team was monstered by New Zealand in three consecutive matches. Suddenly, sage judges were deeming the World Cup wide open. In hindsight, it slammed shut with the dressing-room door behind Ponting on his return. He calmly pronounced his team favourite for the World Cup, and did more than anyone to make the billing stick.

As other teams bumbled, stumbled, played too little, drank too much, derided their schedules and defenestrated their coaches, Ponting kept his men focused and in fighting trim. Australia's first successful World Cup campaign twenty years ago came from nowhere; its second, in 1999, came back from nowhere; under Ponting, its third and fourth have only been heading one way, free not merely of defeat but of doubt. Outgoing coach John Buchanan admitted before the final in Bridgetown to having become an auxiliary: 'The perfect team is the one that keeps wanting to be better day in and day out. I've been basically a passenger for the last three years or so. I get there [to practice], put the gear out and bring it back in again.' No-one disagreed.

In the West Indies, Ponting exuded enormous pleasure at winning; the more so because the winning was by a lot, and accompanied by the sense that 'no-one touched us'. It was the Australians who did the touching, and none too gently, their trophy needing a silversmith's attention after featuring in the post-final horseplay. Of course, everyone loves winning. But in Ponting's case, this love co-exists with a loathing of losing intense even for an Australian captain. Allan Border merely feared failure; Ponting seethes with hatred for it.

Even after giving up the Border–Gavaskar Trophy in 2001, Steve Waugh could profess pride at having participated in such a series; he eagerly took his cricketers to Gallipoli, partaking of the legend of that bravest of defeats. It is hard to imagine Ponting doing the same: he prefers his victories on an overwhelming scale. When Australia lost that delirious one-day, one-wicket, one-spare-ball game of 870 runs against South Africa in February last year, he was 'distraught and angry'. When Australia lost the VB Series finals to England a year later, he was 'disappointed and angry'. When he thought Duncan Fletcher was enjoying his discomfiture just a little too much at Trent Bridge two years ago, of course, Ponting discharged a spitball no less acidic for mostly ending up in his own face.

Bizarrely, Ponting was criticised for the Australians being too pally with Michael Vaughan's Englishmen during that series when the Ashes so briefly changed hands. Bizarrely, because his diary suggests a rich vein of anger throughout. For example, he describes complaining to Vaughan about wayward English throwing at Lord's and threatening retaliation: 'If you hang around here for a while you can expect your fair share flying around too.' He describes chipping Ashley Giles about commenting on an umpiring decision: 'Telling him how to do the umpiring too now, is it, mate?' While 'mate' usually incarnates Aussie affability, with an icy edge it is among the most menacing words in the national vernacular.

Nor was his own team spared the sharp edge of Ponting's tongue. He describes bawling out his XI at Edgbaston: 'What is the point of us having meetings and agreeing on strategies if everything goes out the window when we get on the field?' He records a tirade at Brett Lee when the bowler blamed a ridge in his run-up for his persistent overstepping: 'You knew what the conditions would be before we started, so it is no good making excuses now.'

He recounts dropping Andrew Symonds for his night out at Taunton: 'If this is the way you're going to behave, I don't want you in the side.' When the sullen Symonds was slow with the necessary contrition, Ponting exploded: 'Don't encourage me!' To Gilchrist, he roared: 'He can go home then!'

Most conspicuous of all in that series, unfortunately, were his interactions with officials, reminiscent of the candy-store kibbitzer Biderman baiting the umpire Dr Wolfenberg in the baseball scenes of *Portnoy's Complaint*. In his own diary, Ponting documents such episodes as remonstrating with Billy Bowden for not giving Simon Jones out LBW at Edgbaston ('What was wrong with that?') and admonishing Steve Bucknor for giving Damien Martyn out LBW at Old Trafford ('That was a diabolical decision. He's smashed that.'). In his own book on the series, Fletcher thought he saw a deliberate Australian strategy at work: 'Whenever a decision went against Australia during the series, did you notice how Ponting would invariably walk straight up to the umpire and challenge his decision using overbearing body language.' To call it a strategy may be giving it too much credit; it is probably more a habit, and one that Ponting has struggled so far to break, twice skirmishing with umpires in the Champions Trophy. Neville Cardus once asked Don Bradman if complaints about umpiring usually came from defeated teams. Bradman corrected him: complaints, he said, *always* came from defeated teams. Ponting, it seems, is intent on proving the Don wrong.

The Australian captain's tendency to truculence stands out all the more because he has otherwise kept conspicuously free of trouble. No profile of him is complete without an allusion to his misadventures in the Bourbon & Beefsteak, the Sydney night-haunt from which Ponting staggered with a black eye in January 1999. In its way, this is a kind of tribute. If the most colourful anecdote retailed about you is more than eight years old, you've done a fair job of keeping your private life limelight-free. On that occasion, too, Ponting was unlucky. His contretemps came immediately after the Australian Cricket Board's cover for Shane Warne and Mark

Waugh was blown. Ponting didn't get away with reciting a screed about his naïvety and stupidity; he had to field questions at a full-scale press conference, confess to a problem with alcohol, acquiesce to counselling and submit to a suspension. Curiously, the episode can be seen as a vindication of exemplary justice. Once humiliated, twice shy. English cricket will be hoping that the experience is similarly therapeutic for Andrew Flintoff.

Sunil Gavaskar, today cricket's most self-righteous rent-a-quote, assailed the Australians at the World Cup for being 'awful in the way they have sometimes behaved on the field, much to the chagrin of the traditional fans of the game'. Ponting almost immediately rose to the bait by picking a fight with Kevin Pietersen in Antigua, and waxing impenitent afterwards: 'I jumped all over the top of him. It wasn't great leadership as far as I was concerned. But I am not sorry I did it.' All the same, Cricket the Ponting Way is not usually so crude; it is less about belittling or vilifying opponents than about provoking them to play on Australia's terms. The team doesn't so much lob shells as detonate depth charges. The most conspicuous victim of late has been South Africa's endlessly obtuse captain Graeme Smith, who allows the Australians to set the terms of every engagement, reacting to anything and everything. In the Cape Town Test last March, for example, Smith even embroiled himself in a slanging match over pitch repairs, made at the instigation of the ICC referee, which Ponting began cheekily prodding with his bat. Smith went blue in the mouth complaining that the Australians 'weren't playing the game fairly'. Ponting simply smirked: 'We get inside your head don't we?' After the tour, Smith admitted to his rival: 'Sixth months cricket against you blokes. It's just too hard.' It certainly is if you ceaselessly bang your head against them.

The Ponting ascendancy is being consolidated by trends in the game. The convergence of technique, tactics and tone between Test and one-day cricket has made it easier for one man to do both captaincy jobs for Australia. Where Mark Taylor and Steve Waugh were diminished as Test skippers the moment they lost the continuity of being Australia's limited-overs leader, Ponting benefits from being the master of all he surveys.

Cricket Australia, too, has fostered a backroom atmosphere of maximum congeniality towards its main man. Manager Steve Bernard was a selector when Ponting was picked for Australia. New coach Tim Nielsen is well known to Ponting from his years as John Buchanan's assistant, but having no Test experience will naturally defer to his captain. His role will be chiefly to bed down the new players Australia expects to graduate to Test status in the next three years, many of whom he has worked with at the Centre of Excellence in Brisbane. Ponting, the arrangement implies, should be free to do what he does best.

Bowling coach Troy Cooley, meanwhile, was sixteen years a first-grade fast bowler for Ponting's Mowbray club in Launceston, for quite a lot of that time working as a diesel mechanic before setting out his stall as a Level III coach a decade ago; he was on the committee at Mowbray when the boy Ponting took his first trip to the AIS Cricket Academy. There are now two Tasmanians among the four selectors too: David Boon and Jamie Cox, both of whom captained Ponting at Sheffield Shield level.

Ponting came into Australian cricket so young, making his first-class debut a month before he was entitled to vote, that he is achieving the same kind of legendary status within his own team that Steve Waugh achieved in his last few years. Although Matthew Hayden actually made his Test debut eighteen months earlier than his captain, Ponting has pervaded the Australian summers of the twenty-first century as no other cricketer: almost the first man picked in any class of cricket, apparently impervious to injury, and almost free from the ebb and flow of form. The next generation of Australian players – Clarke, Tait, Johnson, Voges, Cosgrove, Watson, Cullen – first glimpsed him on television when they were cricket-crazy boys. Television tending to gild its subjects with a cathode-ray halo, he is someone they have in a way always wanted to be: not a bad attribute for any leader.

Ponting's other great attribute as captain is one that Victor

Richardson once attached to Bradman: his own prowess as a player. And the cricketer who once sought a benchmark against which to measure himself has in a sense become his own.

Cricinfo Magazine July 2007

ADAM GILCHRIST

Rocket Man

For the first few weeks of the Australian season, the Ian Healy question was an index of sporting sentimentality among local cricket devotees. Granted, the great keeper's powers may have waned. But surely those beastly selectors could have granted him a last hurrah, and fans the opportunity in a Test or three for a farewell salute. You heard it a lot, and not only from Queenslanders. Though Aussies like to be regarded as a ruggedly practical lot, they can grow wistful and rheumy-eyed where sporting heroes are concerned.

One thing Aussies like even more than the last sporting hero, however, is the next. And it required precisely 268 minutes and 163 balls for the Healy question to be answered forever: the time it took successor Adam Gilchrist to belt a match-winning 149 not out at Bellerive Oval against Pakistan. At 5 for 126 in the fourth innings chasing 369 for victory, an English XI would have been bringing forward their flight time. But when Gilchrist came out to bat, his partner Justin Langer confided: 'You never know.' A touch of Wilf Rhodes, George Hirst and 'we'll get 'em in singles', even if Gilchrist had nothing so mean as singles in mind: he struck 13 fours and a six. Harmonising like the Mormon Tabernacle Choir, Gilchrist and Langer added 238. 'This is one for the true believers', Prime Minister Paul Keating said famously after his 1993 election in the face of apparently insuperable odds. 'You never know', might become a similar antipodean watchword.

As the teams crossed the continent to Perth the next day for their series' final instalment, Gilchrist and Langer were thronged by dizzy well-wishers at every step of their journey. Gilchrist, having woken to seventy-four salutations on his mobile-phone message bank, can have returned few; some of the more hysterical scenes appeared to have been inspired by *A Hard Day's Night*. A Test cricketer for less than three weeks, Gilchrist found his photo in the strapline above the masthead of Melbourne's *Age* newspaper with the poser: 'Australia's Next Captain?'

Gilchrist is, however, anything but a momentary pop sensation. He's built on classically Australian lines: tall, fit enough to run the Melbourne Cup, and with ears as big as the webbing on his keeping gauntlets. Twenty-eight on the eve of the Second Test, he's spent perhaps a decade becoming an overnight success.

Like Mark Taylor and Merv Hughes in recent years, Gilchrist comes from a family that travelled extensively while he was growing up. At various times in his boyhood, young Adam found himself in Dorrigo, Junee, Deniliquin and Lismore. Perhaps the experience of rebuilding networks of friends at regular intervals was formative: Gilchrist has the unfussy affability characteristic of the self-sufficient. But one can take such speculation too far. Asked if being the youngest of four children might have inculcated in him unusual reserves of patience, he laughs: 'I don't know about that. I was always told that the youngest was the most spoiled!'

Father Stan was an accomplished first-grade cricketer in Sydney for ten years, later a coach, and Gilchrist followed in his footsteps ten years ago by joining Gordon. His first season, at seventeen, marked him out as an unusual talent: he scored 297 runs at 49.5 and claimed 15 dismissals in what proved the team's first premiership for thirty-two years.

In those embryonic days Gilchrist was only a reserve stumper: Gordon's Phil Emery was state keeper. And such was Gilchrist's authority with the bat that many sage judges urged him to forsake the gloves altogether. Gilchrist himself was ambivalent. He enjoyed uninterrupted custody of the keeping role on an Australian under-nineteen tour of England in August 1991, executing 47 dismissals to complement 1122 runs at 80. He also managed to combine the role of keeper–batsman with captaincy when he led an AIS Cricket

Academy XI tour of South Africa in March 1992. Yet it wasn't until the end of the 1993–94 season – by which time he'd become a fringe state batsman – that Gilchrist finally made his ambit claim to be considered keeper cum frontline striker.

The decisive influence was Academy head coach Rod Marsh. Gilchrist regards the former Australian keeper as a touchstone. They both bat left-handed and play golf right-handed. They're both Scorpios. Marsh even shares a birthday with Gilchrist's brother. Spooky, huh? Gilchrist thought so. He also thought that keeping enhanced his sense of security: 'I always feel more relaxed when I'm playing as a keeper and not entirely reliant on my batting to hold my place in a team.' That entailed relocating to Marsh's former state of Western Australia. It was not a lay-down *misère*: incumbent Tim Zoehrer enjoyed a hearty local following. But Gilchrist scored a timely hundred in a trial game, and Zoehrer was packed off, muttering darkly about conspiracies.

Gilchrist may detect some irony in the *West Australian* banner headline after his Hobart heroics with Langer: 'We Did It'. For Gilchrist has seen the flipside of that chauvinism; after three ducks in his first five first-class innings for WA, Perth's more parochial pundits wondered aloud if his ticket from Sydney was a return one. He won them over nonetheless. In his first two seasons, Gilchrist accumulated 115 dismissals and 1233 runs, including an undefeated 189 from 187 deliveries at Adelaide Oval in the Sheffield Shield final of March 1996. That earned a national call-up seven months later when Healy's hamstring twanged during the Titan Cup; then first shot at the title, as it were, when Australia's selectors formalised a policy of picking a specialist one-day team two years ago.

Gilchrist likes one-day cricket; none of this fuddy-duddy stuff about it not being the real McCoy from him. And he should like it, because it likes him. Gilchrist was halfway through a bowl of ice-cream during the break between innings in a CUB Series game against New Zealand in January 1998 when Steve Waugh invited him to open the batting. He almost dropped his spoon. But he responded simply: 'Yeah, I'll give it a go.' 'Go' proved the operative word.

Gilchrist had a taste for opening, another legacy from Marsh. 'I remember that Rod Marsh told me when I was at the academy that I should try and open at least for my grade side. Even if I batted down the order at a higher level, the keeper often had to face the second new ball, so experience of that environment and those conditions would be good for me.' Fulfilling such a conspicuous role, too, wasn't so much of a burden when Gilchrist realised how keeping to an international attack added polish to his glovework. He says: 'Keeping is one of those things, I suppose like leg-spin bowling, where you get better the more you do of it – especially playing at a higher level, being exposed to the best bowlers. I know I've certainly improved my keeping since I started playing first-class cricket, and keeping to Warney, Pigeon and Bevo has been a great benefit to me since.'

Rarely can a suggestion made over a bowl of Royal Vanilla have been so richly rewarded. Gilchrist is already among Australia's top ten run-scorers in the abbreviated game, and by some distance the most rapid. His first hundred dismissals, too, have come with an understated ease that would not have disgraced his predecessor. The only setback along his journey was the World Cup. Tipped as one of its likely stars, Gilchrist found himself hemmed-in by fast bowlers from round the wicket and armed with the helpful white Duke ball. Excluding half-centuries against Bangladesh and in the final during Australia's brief chase against Pakistan, he eked out only 107 runs at 13.4.

Gilchrist took this check on his progress in good part. 'Obviously I didn't get the runs and the results I'd've liked in the World Cup,' he says. 'But I think I learned a great deal from it. It was a real good challenge, frustrating at times, but I think I learned a lot about myself, about applying myself, and about mental and physical preparation.' Gilchrist ascribes his difficulties in England to over-eagerness, both to free his arms for the square cut and to penetrate leg-side gaps. A conversation with David Hookes before the recent tour of Sri Lanka – where the former Australian left-hander recommended he mentally cordon off certain sectors of the field as run-scoring areas whenever bowlers began to angle their attack in – seemed to do the trick: in five one-dayers at Galle and Colombo in August, Gilchrist surged back to form with 231 runs at 46.

And if not quite a pageant of personal success, the World Cup furnished some indelible memories of collective achievement. Is he not bored by now with reliving Australia's helter-skelter Headingley tie with South Africa? Not at all, Gilchrist says: 'Just talking about that game sends a shiver up my spine.' Allan Donald's executioner relates a story bound to become a classic of its genre, with shades of the famous scenes in the home dressing-room during the unfading Tied Test of 1960: 'The adrenalin was really pumping afterwards in the dressing-room, everybody hugging and shouting and watching the replays. Then after five or ten minutes, I looked down and I saw that the ball was still in my glove. And I wasn't just holding it, I was gripping it tight. That was the point where Steve Waugh came up to me, pointed to it and said: "Do you want that?"' Gilchrist laughs: 'Bit of a double-edged question that, because there was basically not much doubt about where it was going the minute he said it.' Though the ball eluded him, Gilchrist scavenged one precious memento. Souveniring a stump, he lucked onto one with a faint trace of white near the top: a vestige of the kiss planted by the wicked Shane Warne leg-break that bowled Herschelle Gibbs and began South Africa's subsidence.

Many have advocated Gilchrist's Test succession over the past two years, but the feeling when it came in Brisbane was pure pleasure. 'I never took it for granted that I'd play Test cricket for Australia,' he says. 'And I never had a specific date in mind by which I wanted to.' Nor, though, did he ever feel typecast as a one-day specialist: 'The experts say that good players should be able to play both forms of the game.' Gilchrist suggested that the experts were right at the Gabba when he compiled an exhilarating 81 and kept wicket spotlessly. So perfectly had he filled the frame, in fact, that I almost finished our talk before the Second Test by jesting: 'Well, it can't get any better than Brisbane.' But I thought better of it. Lucky for me.

Wisden Cricket Monthly January 2000

ADAM GILCHRIST

The Exclamation Mark

In an atmosphere in which all cricket happenings somehow seem to point forward to the Ashes, Adam Gilchrist scrambles all calculations. Hilaire Belloc's couplet about the imperial peace comes to mind: 'Whatever happens, we have got/The Maxim gun, and they have not.' Whatever happens, Australia has Gilchrist, and advancing Geraint Jones as a counter is a dotty English conceit, like a perverse preference for Bognor over Bondi as a tourist destination. In his autobiography, Mike Atherton recalls sitting in England's dressing-room during the Oval Test of 2001 and looking across at Duncan Fletcher's clipboard with its tactical summaries of how to bowl to Australia's batsmen. Next to Gilchrist's name was a question mark. By now, it might well be an exclamation mark.

In between times, it went almost without notice, there was a brief ellipsis. After a regulation century in Perth against Zimbabwe in October 2003, largely submerged by the displacement of Matthew Hayden's 380, Gilchrist underwent an unprecedented spell of ten innings worth only 120 runs. His public professions that he wished to help out umpires may have been on his mind. By his own account, his team-mates had been 'flabbergasted' when he first 'walked' at Port Elizabeth six months earlier. And even if he felt he'd 'done it for the right reasons', staying in can be problematic when one becomes focused on the matter of getting out.

Whatever the case, Gilchrist's solution was to do what we're always enjoined not to: he chose to run, as it were, before he could walk. On a pair at Kandy last March, with Australia under the pump, he slotted in at number three. His team at their nadir were

65 in arrears on first innings with 8 second-innings wickets in reserve: Gilchrist made *his* wicket count with 144 from 185 deliveries, all but 50 runs of it in boundaries. It was the first of 20 outs for 1253 runs at 62.65, culminating in the recent series in New Zealand where Gilchrist seemed to invent a new cricket variant to rival Twenty20 in which, while everyone else carried on as usual, he thrashed about him with apparent impunity.

The temptation is sometimes to underestimate Gilchrist – perhaps to scale him down to mortal specifications – by describing him as the world's best batsman with the score at 5 for 500. This did not withstand scrutiny in New Zealand. At Christchurch's Jade Stadium, he joined Simon Katich at the hinge point in Australia's innings, 6 for 201 in pursuit of 443. Daniel Vettori was his probing self, James Franklin was extracting some worthwhile movement, and Stephen Fleming was hugging himself in disbelief that he had held the Australian juggernaut in check into the third day.

Gilchrist was next out three hours later at 413 after a fourteenth helter-skelter Test hundred, his 121 from 126 balls containing a dozen fours and a half-dozen sixes. The determined Katich, who made his Test debut under Gilchrist's captaincy and who has an ideally complementary game, cruised along in his partner's slipstream to a second Test hundred – it must be restful to bat with Gilchrist, given the minimal running involved. All that was missing, as for the whole series, was a crowd. The host broadcaster must have felt some embarrassment about repeatedly revealing empty stands as Gilchrist's blows were retrieved. Then it was the host team's turn: grudged a one-run lead, they had been wiped away by 9 wickets by late the following afternoon.

Australia were at another hinge point in Wellington, 5 for 247 on the first day, when Gilchrist joined Damien Martyn. They were separated after scoring 256 in 46 overs – most satisfactory one-day scoring – of which Gilchrist's share was 162 from 146 deliveries with 22 fours and 5 sixes. His breezy unbeaten 60 from 62 deliveries in Auckland was then little less valuable in a low-scoring contest. All of this was done, furthermore, without Gilchrist losing the beamish manner that leavens his irrepressibly aggressive approach, which recalls Charlie Macartney's sigh to Neville Cardus: 'By cripes I feel sorry for the poor cove who has to bowl at me today.'

Gilchrist made a point at press conferences of complimenting Vettori on his precision, saying that he had deliberately attacked the spinner because of the esteem in which he held him – praise indeed if the compliments could be indexed by the size of the sixes. England's bowlers can only hope he does not bestow his praise so liberally from July, for Gilchrist will have a say in whatever happens, whatever happens.

The Wisden Cricketer May 2005

DAMIEN MARTYN

The Step-Up

The steps that lead onto Premadasa Stadium in Colombo are both quite steep and very large. Let's make that clear immediately, because it's quite significant in the revival of Damien Martyn's international cricket career: it's why, on 31 August 1999, he fell down them.

Steve Waugh was out in the middle in the Aiwa Cup final on one of those muggy days when you seem to play in a permanent lather, and signalled for fresh gloves. Martyn, twelfth man, leapt to attention: the skipper wanted him and wanted him now. Momentarily, Martyn admits, he was 'in a bit of a panic'.

Gloves in hand, Martyn hared down those huge steps. 'Four at a time,' he sighs. 'Like an idiot.' The result was inevitable: he crooked an ankle and went arse over elbow. The embarrassment should have been acute: the crowd started laughing, and the Australian dressing-room cracked up. Funnily enough, though, Martyn was unconcerned. 'All I could think was: "Gee, if I don't get out there now, Tugga's going to absolutely nail me." I kept trying to get up, but my ankle was stuffed. I literally couldn't move.'

On the field, Waugh was more than a little irked. The captain is keen on prompt service: when Adam Dale crept on with replacements an over later, Waugh griped that it was 'bloody important for the reserves to watch the game and stay awake'. He was still fuming when he returned to the dressing-room, then entirely bemused by the sight of his rueful twelfth man on physiotherapist Errol Alcott's treatment table with ankle strapped and iced.

The story was retold, and Waugh finally saw its amusing side.

To him, though, it held greater significance. He recalled: 'I've only had the task of being twelfth man a few times in my career, but I've had the job enough to know that it can be an experience that brings you down to the earth with a thud. To be at the players' beck and call is a true test of just how good a "team" person you are, because the role forces you to make a full commitment without being able to reap the personal rewards on the field.'

The thud in this case had been literal, and the test had been capably, if rather painfully, passed: on the big steps of Colombo, Martyn took one of many small ones back into the Australian Test team. Waugh observed dryly that, in his experience, it was 'the first time a twelfth man has ever been injured while performing his duties during a match.'

*

Two years later, Damien Martyn is doing more becking and calling than fetching and carrying. After an Ashes series where he was by common consent the most attractive batsman on either side, scoring hundreds at Edgbaston and Headingley as inevitable as they were elegant, the thirty-year-old West Australian is finally turning possibilities into actualities: his average since returning to the Test side is 78.4.

Martyn is one of those cricketers who renders the game so simple that you want to pluck up your bat with the cratered edges and start your career all over again. 'So that's how it's done,' you're tempted to think: come forward when it's up, go back when it's short. His footwork is precise, his balance balletic. To call him a textbook batsman is not to flatter him; it is to flatter the textbook.

Martyn's signature is the back-foot cover drive, nowadays a relatively uncommon sight, most batsmen either pushing forward to hit on the up or waiting to slash square. At Headingley in particular, he provided a master class in the stroke, meeting the ball at the top of the bounce and repeatedly perforating point and cover. It was like watching a batsman rehearse his strokes in a mirror, the bat and every point of his anatomy in the perfect place.

The talent, of course, has seldom been in dispute; the enigma has been the temperament harnessing it. Martyn's reputation was well summed-up by his own Australian coach John Buchanan, who when issuing Queensland players their battle plans before the Sheffield Shield final of March 1997 recommended simply: 'Test his ego.' But by the alacrity with which he executed his errand in Colombo two years ago, perhaps we shall know him now. To a brash prodigy, sporting adulthood has come not a moment soon, amid feelings of pleasure, relief and gratitude. 'I know that even if my career finished tomorrow with me having played sixteen Tests,' he says, 'that's nine more than I was expecting to play a few years back.'

*

Those initial Tests seem a long time and another person ago. Martyn was then, he says freely, 'very young', in all the senses of that phrase. The game had come very easily to him, the breaks even more so. Even Cyclone Tracy, which hit his birthplace of Darwin at Christmas 1974, had worked in his favour: it blew three-year-old Martyn and his family back to his father's hometown of Perth, where he enjoyed a prolific junior cricket career.

Martyn's big moment at the age of fifteen was a week-long Christmas 'live-in' at Guildford Grammar where Sir Garfield Sobers was the chief coaching attraction. It was there he came to the attention of Kevin Gartrell, a former Sheffield Shield cricketer instrumental in bringing the careers of Tom Moody, Simon Katich and Brendon Julian to fruition, and who became an early mentor. That season, Martyn made 1007 runs for Wanneroo under-fifteens at 201.4, and filled in during afternoons with its fourth-grade team: on one January day in 1987, he made 129 not out for the juniors in the morning and 124 for the seniors in the afternoon. Gartrell took Martyn on as a pupil in the indoor nets behind his sports store, loaded him up with gear, and secured him a bat contract with Gunn and Moore. Martyn then made his first trip to England in April 1989, representing North Durham in the Durham Senior League where Sheffield Shield batsman Darrin Ramshaw was pro, and a year later was enrolled at the new AIS Cricket Academy in Adelaide. So far so good.

At the Academy, Martyn was a contemporary and comrade of Shane Warne's: something as chaotic and entertaining as it sounds. All the same, Martyn reflects on the famous story of Warne's first encounter with his spin guru Terry Jenner. Jenner asked Warne the humbling question: 'What have you ever sacrificed for cricket?' Says Martyn: 'That's such a great question. Frankly, when you're young, you don't sacrifice anything, do you? You're looked after. You can do everything you want to do, because people want to help you. It's funny, but if someone had asked me that a bit earlier, then I think my career might have been different. I hadn't sacrificed anything.'

Martyn made his first tour with Allan Border's Australians to Sri Lanka in August 1992, hitting the first ball of his baggy green career for four on the way to 61 off 108 balls against Southern Province. But having enjoyed such a gilded upbringing, Martyn viewed his first setbacks as more like roadblocks. On his first Ashes tour the following year, he quickly became disenchanted. Martyn had by that stage played nine Test innings, the most recent an accomplished 74 off 99 balls in a low-scoring Auckland Test during Mark Waugh's only appointment as Australian twelfth man. As such, he expected to feature in the starting Ashes XI, and smarted when he did not.

'It was just like being a kid again,' Martyn says. 'All I wanted to do was play. Looking back, the selectors probably made the right decision. Mark was experienced in English conditions and played really well, and he was a better bet than a kid with potential who probably wasn't the full package. At twenty-one I was raw to the whole thing, though, and I didn't have the maturity to see it.' Martyn had a bumper tour, making 838 first-class runs at almost 70, but did not fit easily into coach Bob Simpson's Stakhanovite set-up.

Then there was the Sydney Test of January 1994, which has tended, rather unfairly, to shadow Martyn ever since. From one for

51 chasing 117 late on the fourth day, Australia began to crumble. 'One minute we were doing it easy,' Martyn recalls, 'and the next minute I was in.' In fact Martyn was batting within an over of the last day's commencement – his captain having been bowled playing no stroke at Allan Donald – and lost Mark Waugh, Ian Healy and Shane Warne in the next hour. He grafted 106 minutes for 6, finally hazarding a drive when Australia was seven runs from victory and being caught in the covers.

It was a confusing situation, though Martyn denies that he himself was confused: 'Fanie de Villiers was bowling really well, across the seam, and we were losing wickets at the other end, so I just dug in. I was thinking: "As long as I'm here we're all right." Then Craig McDermott came in, slogged it round and made it look easy, which probably got me a bit worked up. I didn't want to be the hero or anything like that. It wasn't like I wanted to win the match with a couple of fours. It was just that I'd been out there a long time, and the risk seemed worth taking.' And the popular impression that Martyn cost Australia the match – an incubus for him ever since, and sometimes linked to his long Test exile – doesn't really stack up. In fact, he had made 59 in the first innings, the most fluent Australian batting of the match. He had, too, been only a late inclusion in the team for an injured Steve Waugh, and necessarily made way for him thereafter.

What did, however, prove significant was Martyn's response to a return to Sheffield Shield ranks. Far from gushing the runs expected, he managed only one half-century in his next seven innings: hardly an unassailable case for re-selection; more a convincing argument against it. Though missing a place in the Australian team to tour South Africa did not seem so costly at the time, Martyn might have fretted more had he known it would be more than six years before he'd play another Test.

*

Cyril Connolly warned that 'those whom the gods wish to destroy, they first call "promising."' It gives the gods a bum rap:

the 'promising' have a capacity for performing this task themselves. Martyn had ample opportunity in succeeding years to shake off the 'promising' tag, but seemed intent on adding to it the phrase 'and unfulfilled'.

Politics at the West Australian Cricket Association didn't help. In short order, the state lost a chief executive, a groundsman, two coaches and a captain. The last of these affected Martyn in particular: on Geoff Marsh's retirement in August 1994, he was approached to succeed him. Martyn felt ready. 'I always ask people: "What would you do in that situation?"' he says. 'If someone asks you to captain your state, it's pretty hard to say no.'

Martyn was, however, only twenty-three, and there was immediately apprehension. 'Damien's got awesome talent and can go a long way,' commented his predecessor. 'But when things aren't going right he has to bite his tongue a bit.' Like several senior players, Tim Zoehrer could not credit that Tom Moody had been overlooked for the job: 'To be a good captain you need the respect of every player in the team and unfortunately Martyn does not have that. He is respected for his ability as a player but is still seen as an inexperienced new kid on the block with a brash outlook on life.'

Brash outlook on life perhaps; brash outlook on batting certainly. The performance slump that followed seemed not so much a loss of form as a loss of interest, and Martyn admits that he tended to neglect his batting while leader: 'I got a hundred in my first game as captain, but I think after that I tended to get a bit overfocused on the captaincy. I stopped looking after my batting. With batting it's often as simple as something like you're just not watching the ball closely.' For twenty-one innings, Martyn didn't break 50, finally making amends with an unbeaten 203 from 207 balls against Tasmania. By that time, however, he'd surrendered the West Australian captaincy, after discussions with Moody and new coach Wayne Clark in December 1995. 'It will help Western Australia,' Clark told him. 'It'll also help Damien Martyn play for Australia again.' It seemed a fair deal. Martyn wanted to represent Australia again. The question was: how much?

The way Martyn describes it, there was no epiphany, no special awakening that stiffened his resolve. It was simply a question of philosophy: 'It was a pride thing. I just had to tell myself: "You're a good player. You've been all the way, but you're just not giving yourself a chance here." There's no magic formula in situations like that, and I knew it wouldn't take just one good year to get back, so I didn't set myself unrealistic goals.'

In his batting, Martyn went back to first principles. 'Everyone goes through it technically when they're not making runs and people are giving you advice all the time,' he recalls. 'I was thinking twenty things before the ball was getting to me. But I play best when I make everything simple, just keep still and play straight.' Then he got the whiff of an opportunity, when the Australian selectors foreshadowed their strategy of structuring different sides for Test and one-day cricket. The ill wind for Mark Taylor and Ian Healy blew Martyn and other members of the next cricket generation a lot of good. 'From the outside, the Australian side looked so settled that it was hard to think about how to get back in,' he says. 'Then the selectors started rotating guys and leaving senior players out of the one-day side, which offered heaps more chances.' Martyn set out to dominate the domestic limited-overs game, and on the basis of his 494 runs at 98.8 in the 1997–98 Mercantile Mutual Cup received an eleventh-hour call to join the Australian squad for the first World Series final at the MCG in January 1998.

In the end Martyn did not play – Darren Lehmann's hamstring mended in time for him to take his accustomed place – but it was a tonic. 'I was only ever on stand-by, but it was so important, that game,' he recalls. 'It was like my first time all over again. I remember I flew into Melbourne and went to the team meeting. I didn't say anything, just sat quietly in the corner. I think Stewy Law was twelfth man, and I helped him out a bit; nothing much, but I tried to do everything right. And it was fantastic. It was a game I didn't even play in, but it gave me the buzz again. It really fuelled the fires of wanting to get back.' When Martyn served again mostly as a reserve during the Pepsi Cup in Sharjah a few months later, he bore little resemblance to the impatient new boy of five years earlier. He did as he was told as a supernumerary, and even before he was asked. His average of 59 and strike rate of 82 in ten World Series matches in January 1999 then ratified his re-establishment.

Now he was back on the inside, Martyn was determined to block the exit behind him, setting himself something he'd previously eschewed: a fitness regime. 'I've never been a big trainer,' he admits. 'But I knew I had to make the effort.' He started attending a Claremont gym run by Steve Smith, following programs set by the Australian team's fitness instructor Dave Misson: mostly a daily routine of boxaerobics and sprints, though also involving merely walking on a treadmill. You must, after all, walk before you can run.

It was exciting to be back in the queue for a Test berth, a period in which Martyn could feel himself changing. He also moved house several times, and in one relocation surprisingly mislaid his original baggy green cap. 'It might turn up one day,' he says. 'It's probably packed away at the bottom of a box somewhere.' Given that there are a few regrets attached to that cap, would he wear it again? 'I don't know,' he says. 'Maybe, maybe not.'

*

Providentially, a new cap was round the corner, when an ankle injury kept Ricky Ponting from Australia's tour of New Zealand in February and March last year. 'I always buy Ricky a few beers for that,' says Martyn. He topped Australia's averages with 241 runs at 60.25 in his first Test matches for more than six years, and his unbeaten double of 46 and 34 against the West Indies at Adelaide last season helped Australia make light of the absence of Steve Waugh.

When his role as the baggy green puncture-kit ended in England a few months ago, Martyn was more than ready. Having Steve Waugh as a partner when he came in at Edgbaston ensured against both complacency and overanxiety. 'Before the tour, Steve told us that we'd need to get used to the conditions,' says Martyn. 'That it might be sunny one minute, overcast the next, that we'd probably play and miss a bit more than we were used to.' It proved wise counsel: Martyn waved a bit of air at first, then settled, and on the third day played scarcely a false stroke.

The first of many Test centuries? Martyn is genuinely loath to say. Returning home as a key component of a successful Australian team and giving well-wishers the 'Ashes spiel' is a pleasant sensation. But when talk turns to engagements further off – World Cups, future series – Martyn gets a little edgy. 'You can't count on anything,' he says. 'You never want to look too far ahead.' This is more than superstition talking; it's experience. After all – as Martyn found a couple of years ago in Colombo – big steps can be dangerous.

Inside Sport December 2001

DARREN LEHMANN

Afternoon Light

Cricket is sometimes thought of as a cruel and unforgiving game because batsmen are dismissed so peremptorily, without a second chance or leave to appeal. For Darren Lehmann, this aspect of the game is now especially meaningful: at thirty-four, he feels he is on the last opportunity of a career that can't be said to have abounded in them, and senses that the next time Australia's selectors decide to do without him it will be the last.

But, what the hell, eh? From another sportsman, the foregoing sentiment might seem grim, self-dramatising. Lehmann says it comfortably, even with a smile. When I tell him it might be otherwise, that he's gone and come before, he matter-of-factly demurs: 'At my age, you know that if you're dropped you're pretty well not coming back. As a selector, if you drop a Lehmann, you're saying: "That's enough". But, y'know, that's OK.'

Not that Lehmann feels any slackening of ability or motivation. In his new autobiography *Worth the Wait*, love of cricket burns almost incandescently. And despite a high regard for Simon Katich, he feels he warranted the selectors' preference for the First Test against New Zealand. It's just that his attitude to cricket has almost come full circle. 'I'm not someone who wants to play regardless,' he says. 'The money's irrelevant. I'm playing for enjoyment. I've kind of gone back to the way I felt when I first started playing cricket, and it's a good feeling.'

Lehmann lived this creed conspicuously in India when he startled onlookers by announcing that he would not be upset to have to stand aside for the irrepressible Michael Clarke. Even old friends like former Victorian keeper Darren Berry wondered if this wasn't taking selflessness a little far. Indeed, given Lehmann's view of his cricket expectancy, was this not tantamount to asking the selectors to end his career for him?

Lehmann doesn't answer directly, suggesting a choice felt rather than thought. He focuses on Clarke: 'I still believe he's gotta play. And my gut feeling was that he was always going to play. When a bloke comes on and plays so well, you don't send him back. You've got to encourage youth wherever you can. I just wanted to make clear that I wouldn't be angry if they picked Michael. I wouldn't *really* be disappointed.'

It isn't hard to detect some identification at work. The junior Lehmann, a 1980s prodigy, was not indulged. Chosen for the Sydney Test of February 1990 then cut from the XI, he somehow rejoined the queue of young batsmen at the wrong end, not making his Test debut for a further eight years – which still irks him, just a little: 'To pick a guy just to make him twelfth man just seems madness.' Is it that, having missed out on opportunities, Lehmann doesn't want to be part of their denial to Clarke? Would he feel the same if his own career had been more straightforward? 'Maybe not,' he says. 'Maybe not. Good point. That's not a bitter thing. But as you get older, you do look back on how different things could've been. No, I reckon you're about right.'

If you're sensing Lehmann as someone who's undergone a recent and thorough shift in priorities, you're right. The casual air and shambling gait remain, but he's philosophical. Unlike many athletes, he talks to you rather than at you, and unguardedly, as though thinking aloud. The reasons aren't far to seek. For one thing, he can feel more satisfied in his career, which bloomed in nine Tests in the year from April 2003 to encompass five hard-hit hundreds, culminating in his recent recognition as *Wisden Australia*'s International Cricketer of the Year. In the words of the almanack's editor, Chris Ryan, it was as if Homer Simpson had been reincarnated as Buzz Lightyear.

Then, almost two years ago, there was a trial by administrative and media fire when his fury at a careless dismissal in an Adelaide one-day game against Sri Lanka detonated in a shaming racial epithet – one that neither bears nor needs repeating but will forever be associated with him: 'Black cunts!' Though Lehmann still feels a cringing embarrassment about the episode, he doesn't back off from discussing it. 'It's the biggest regret I've ever had,' Lehmann says. 'But I can't take it back. I said it. I deserved to be punished.' He remains puzzled, nonetheless, by the quality of the International Cricket Council's justice. In view of his prompt and abject apologies to the Sri Lankan management who heard the words and even the team and captain who hadn't, ICC referee Clive Lloyd first merely reprimanded the Australian; his five-game suspension followed a second hearing demanded by ICC chief executive Malcolm Speed that still makes Lehmann's head spin. 'I don't have a problem with Malcolm stepping in,' says Lehmann. 'He's got the power to do it. I don't have a problem with the ICC going hard. At the end of the day, I fucked up; in fact, if I'd been making the decision, I might have made the suspension longer. But the process...

'I'm having a hearing. The ICC have got their lawyers there, but I have to get my own lawyer [Greg Griffin]. The [Australian Cricket] Board don't support me, despite my record: fifteen years of good time and no problem. Everyone's talking legal jargon, using words I just couldn't understand. And the bloke in charge [Clive Lloyd] isn't even a judge. He's already presided over the case and let me off with a reprimand, and all of a sudden he's saying: "Five games". I couldn't understand it.' Even though it didn't cross his mind at the time and he's glad he didn't, Lehmann says in hindsight that he might have been better off had he lied and denied everything – a frank admission that if it doesn't alarm the ICC, probably should.

Above all, Lehmann's attitudes have been recalibrated by the death of his friend and familiar David Hookes ten months ago. His personal journey reached another pass on 14 November, when he appeared as a witness in the manslaughter prosecution of the former Beaconsfield Hotel bouncer, Zdravko Micevic, who allegedly dealt Hookes his mortal blow.

The passages describing Hookes' death in *Worth the Wait*, which lift it above the ruck of cricket autobiographies, are vivid and deeply moving – and, Lehmann says, therapeutic. 'That chapter was easy,' he insists. 'The heart was writing. Not the head. I cried heaps. I still do. Today I was doing Bert Newton [an Australian television talk show]. And he asked me about David. Then he said: "This was you at the funeral." And I looked at the TV screen, and saw myself, and I was just gone. I had to say: "I'm sorry. I just don't feel comfortable." The book stuff has been really good. Not just because it's been kind of cleansing, but also because this week it's completely taken my mind off the case. I've had no time to think about it.'

Life since Hookes' death has, for Lehmann, been urgent – sometimes, one senses, almost frantic. 'I haven't been able to think about me at all,' he says. 'My energy's gone into thinking about other things, other people. My wife, Andrea – she worries about me 'cos I do too much. She says I'm always keeping everyone happy. She says: "Just wind it back a bit. Stop thinking about everyone else and give yourself some time."

'I think once I do wind down – well, I don't know. I don't know how I'll be. At the moment I need to be busy. Because I can't be thinking about what's coming up ... I don't know if that's a cowardly thing. I'm not sure. I won't know until I bloody go through it again. I can talk about it. It's funny, y'know. I can talk about Hookesy. Quite easily. I can, now. But I've blanked the incident out of my mind. I don't talk about it very much. All of a sudden having to go back there – I'm scared about how it's going to be, to be perfectly honest. I've got no idea.'

At least, the agonies of the first few months are now behind him. In *Worth the Wait* he describes reliving the incident every time he batted, recalls thoughts of Hookes flashing across his mind while he was batting, and recounts bad dreams and sleepless nights in sweat-soaked sheets. 'Yeah, they're gone,' he reports. 'Bad feelings aren't there so much. I'm remembering good times. The nightmares were bad. I'd wake up and I was sweating everywhere.

I'd be shitting myself. Same in Sri Lanka. Couldn't sleep. Couldn't go out. I love having a beer. I love it. A beer and a cigarette. And I couldn't do it. Well, I could, but not in relaxing. It took Adam [Gilchrist] and Ricky [Ponting] to take me out and get me absolutely rat-arsed before I felt comfortable with it again.'

Some changes, though, are almost chemical. Lehmann never used to drink coffee. He now drinks it in copious quantities – a habit he developed while killing time in the early hours of the morning. The sound of hospital doors swinging shut, which he heard after leaving Hookes' bedside for the last time, is engraved in his memory. Then there's this song: Robbie Williams' 'Angels'. 'Do you know it?' says Lehmann. 'They played it at Hookesy's funeral, just as he was leaving the ground. Our boys love it. The Aussie boys love it. It's bloody hard when they play it. Warney and I have to leave the room. They played it in India, in Chennai, in the Second Test, and I sat there and made myself listen to it. I had my glasses on, so it was fine. But I was crying. Warney knew.'

Lehmann isn't the only Australian cricketer whose behaviour has been altered by the Hookes calamity. The team, says Lehmann, is increasingly circumspect about social activities: 'We'll only go places the owners know us. And they can make sure we're looked after. It's also made us much more aware of our responsibilities to each other. We drink. Like everyone else. We have a good night, one or two of us'll go over the top at certain stages. It's an unwritten rule in our side now, though, that if someone's carrying on, one of the other blokes takes 'em home, the most soberest one. Whoever's soberest takes control. They cop the abuse – "No, I'm all right, fuck you" – and there haven't been any incidents where the bloke hasn't wanted to go home.'

Cricket mortality, when compared to the personal kind, also comes into clearer focus. Lehmann chuckled recently when alerted to the fact that he'd played first-class cricket for more than half his life; he laughs even more gustily when I tell him that he's the last Australian first-class player to have faced chairman of selectors Trevor Hohns in a match. 'Am I?' he says. 'Jeez, that's a good stat.

I've gotta ring him and tell him that. That's fuckin' hilarious. I heard another one the other day. This kid, Shannon Hurn, who's in our [South Australian Redbacks] squad. I've been playing longer than he's been alive! I played footy with his old man!'

When I say that cricket at lower levels has that pleasant tendency to blend generations, Lehmann cites an example even closer to home: his twelve-year-old son made his first hundred for East Torrens under-fourteens a fortnight ago. 'So,' he says, 'I might end up playing against him!' Don't you mean with him, Darren? 'Oh no,' says Lehmann. 'I'd play against him and sledge the shit out of him.' Whatever its drawbacks, age *does* have its prerogatives.

The Sunday Age November 2004

JO ANGEL

Look Homeward

Since the rise of Graham McKenzie then Dennis Lillee, Perth's pacey pitch and howling winds have been legendarily conducive to the nurturing of fast bowlers. In the 1990s, however, it was more often visitors who enjoyed the conditions. Surfaces varied in quality. Inexperience and injuries took a heavy toll. Only one bowler, Jo Angel, kept the lineage alive, becoming a kind of tradition of his own.

Western Australia's go-to guy for more than a decade did not share McKenzie's circus strongman physique and never imitated Lillee's histrionics. He was as lumbering as 203 centimetres and size-14 boots imply, and looked, as he was, an unselfconsciously amiable man; team-mate Brendon Julian thought him 'the most liked first-class cricketer in Australia'. Only in the presence of a ball, a batsman and a task did Angel's nature change: he jarred gloves, handles and splices perhaps as much as any Australian bowler of the period. He always looked a little weary – until you realised that he looked exactly the same after ten overs as after one, and was as committed in his third spell as in his first.

Angel came from a sporting family in the hills east of Perth: father Ken and brother Robert played Australian Rules football for Swan Districts. He stumbled into the Sheffield Shield in November 1991 when Bruce Reid and Peter Capes pulled out on the morning of a match against New South Wales, taking an unexpected call at work and 'shaking like a leaf' when he arrived, but did at once what came naturally and simply; his 31 wickets at 25 that season were instrumental in his state's Shield win. Rushed into the Test side on his home ground the following summer, he would have had a wicket in his first over had Craig McDermott caught a Desmond Haynes mis-hook.

Angel played only three more Tests, Glenn McGrath casting a long, narrow shadow over his career. He became almost a victim of his success at home – his 253 first-class wickets at the WACA cost less than 23 runs each; his 232 everywhere else cost almost 28 – for there was always some doubt about his effectiveness away. But he was never chagrined, and West Australians were happy to have him. Only Clarrie Grimmett has taken more wickets in domestic cricket, and he got around a bit. Angel was earthbound, and Perth-bound, with the greatest of pleasure.

Wisden Australia 2004–05

CRICKET BOOKS OF 2004

Our Heroes and Others

Just what *did* happen in Pretoria on the evening of 5 March 2003? One imagines, reading the *World Cup Diary* (Random House) of Glenn McGrath, that it was a pretty convivial evening. A few drinks, then dinner at a local steakhouse with Ricky Ponting, Andrew Symonds, fitness adviser Jock Campbell and former Australian Cricket Board media manager Brian Murgatroyd ('a top guy even for a Welshman'). It transpires that both McGrath and Ponting (with Murgatroyd's help) have publishing contracts. But hey, the more the merrier, eh? 'Even though two of us are writing tour diaries, they should make for interesting reading, with things seen from two different points of view.'

Quite so: 'different points of view' *do* make 'interesting reading'. For if we check the *World Cup Diary* (HarperSports) of Ricky Ponting, we find that Australia's captain was left rather unmoved by the festivities. In fact, as Ponting remembers it, he was alone in the hotel: 'I was happy to do very little this evening and just relax in my room. I haven't gone out very much in the evenings on this trip except with Rianna [his wife], and was in no mood to change that habit tonight. I think I will sleep well.'

Maybe we should attempt to triangulate. Let's check Adam Gilchrist's tour diary *Walking to Victory* (Pan Macmillan). But it turns out that Gilly's thoughts were elsewhere that evening, concerned instead with a newspaper article that had just appeared headlined 'Million Dollar Men': 'It was about how Pigeon [McGrath], Punter [Ponting] and I stood to crack a million dollars a year if we won the World Cup.' He was fretting: 'Whenever this sort of story appears it unnerves us all.'

So unnerved, perhaps, that either: a) McGrath failed to realise that he was dining with a Ponting clone; b) when McGrath started droning on about pig shooting, Ponting simply blotted out all memory of him and fantasised that he was back in his room; or c) Gilchrist, learning that he and his cobbers were on the brink of a seven-figure jackpot, decided that they should justify this by writing completely different tour diaries, and himself wrote a vivid first-hand account of a game of Russian roulette with Nelson Mandela – which his editor later took out to allow space for further stats.

Who knows? Who cares? Reading this year's crop of cricket autohagiographies, it occurred to me that the authors might as well start making things up. There's a story about the baseballer Dizzy Dean – how, whenever a journalist asked him his birthdate, he would tell them a different day. 'I always like to give 'em an exclusive', he explained. Almost anything would be preferable to the stupefying tedium of McGrath's apparently minute-by-minute account of Australia's progress.

To be fair, it is a work quite magisterial in its conscientiousness, starting daily with the alarm ('My alarm goes off at 6.30 a.m. for our 7 a.m. departure' ... 'My alarm goes off at 6.45 a.m.' ... 'My alarm goes off at 6.30 a.m.'), and exhibiting an almost fetishistic fascination with the author's luggage ('After waking up and getting ready, I take my bags downstairs at 8.45 a.m. to be checked in and identified' ... 'I wake and finish packing my bags' ... 'I finished packing my bags and put them outside my door' ... 'We're leaving for Port Elizabeth and our bags have to be in the foyer by 8 a.m.'). But that scarcely excuses it: on the contrary, McGrath knows how boring this is, and how repetitive is the nature of life on the modern cricket tour. 'You'll probably be able to work out by now why we call our days "Groundhog Day" ... we're either training, playing or travelling – or a combination of all three,' he says – then, helpfully, just in case we didn't get the reference:

'Each day is similar to the one before, as it is for Bill Murray in the movie *Groundhog Day*, where he relives the same day over and over again.' The funny thing about this allusion is that, if you remember, the plot of *Groundhog Day* is devoted to Murray's efforts to resist and ultimately overthrow this mind-numbing state of affairs. McGrath just goes with it. He's got a contract, dammit, and he's gonna deliver. The bowler whose *métier* is the dot ball has perfected the dot day, and produced a dot diary.

If not quite so formulaic, Ponting's diary has a similarly reductive tone; he would have prospered in the world of espionage, for he lets nothing slip, whether the subject is the World Cup banquet ('There were some speeches and in the end it all went on too long for my taste') or Austin Powers' *Goldmember* ('It was solid without being brilliant'). Would he, a reporter asked, shake hands with Robert Mugabe? 'My answer was that I couldn't answer that because I haven't been put in that position.' Makes John Howard look like the acme of candour. But Ponting is as used to the spin of politics as he is to the spin of cricket. He was alarmed not when Darren Lehmann racially vilified the Sri Lankans last year, but when baggygreen.com.au carried a report of Lehmann's words: 'Surely we had control over that.'

Control: it's a word pregnant with meanings these days. One unconsciously revealing section of Ponting's book concerns his team's preparation for playing New Zealand: Fleming? 'Bowl tight in the corridor just outside off-stump.' McMillan? 'Tight, short of a length bowling in the corridor outside the off-stump.' Astle? 'Good, tight, short of a length bowling in the corridor outside the off-stump, and spin.' Styris? 'Good corridor and length bowling.' Cairns? 'Tight corridor bowling.' Harris? Prepare to be amazed. 'Straight and tight in the corridor outside off stump.' Vettori? It can't be true, can it? Yes it can. 'Good tight line and length in the corridor.' Doesn't anyone bowl in the vestibule anymore? Those seeking an insight into the contrast between the new captain and the old will come away disappointed, although Ponting seems to have traded Waugh's 'mental disintegration' for what might be called the 'psychological squirrel grip'. Of England, he gloats: 'Mentally, we've got them by the balls.'

Perhaps the most telling passages in Ponting's book concern Zimbabwe – if mainly in what they do not say. While the impression conveyed by all those *in camera* discussions last year was that the issue provoked at least some debate in Australian ranks, Ponting insists otherwise. Documenting the meeting on 4 February 2003 with Australian Cricket Board CEO James Sutherland and Australian Cricketers' Association CEO Tim May, Ponting recalls:

> James is especially keen for the ACB and us, as players, to avoid going down the path of making moral pronouncements, especially as I reckon most of us would not really have much of an idea about what is going on in Zimbabwe. And while some of us might have misgivings about the regime, the safety issue seems to be the top of most people's agendas. The bottom line for me is that we are cricketers – our job is to play cricket, not get involved in politics ... When it all wrapped up, after a couple of hours, we opted not to say anything to the media, preferring instead to nominate James and Tim as our spokesmen. That may seem like a cop-out, but we really do want to focus on the cricket now and leave the decision of whether or not we play in Zimbabwe to the administrators. I hope people understand that.

Yes, skipper, it *does* seem like a cop-out – and I'm afraid I *do* find it difficult to understand. For decades, Australian cricketers complained about being treated like mugs, griped that they were never consulted by administrators, and moaned that they were always serfs to the board's barons. Now they have the power, they seem not to want it. Hey, don't expect us to think: we're sportsmen!

Or was it actually like that? While, for the most part, it lands in the same corridor of cliché as the books of McGrath and Ponting, Gilchrist's *Walking to Victory* contains some flashes of original thought. Of the same meeting over which Ponting draws a discreet veil, Gilchrist is more forthcoming: 'The meeting was very confusing. No one seemed sure which way they were thinking.' And the self-imposed silence irked him:

> We knew there would be a lot of press coverage about it, and so the players actually asked the ACB to put a blanket no-comment policy on the Zimbabwe issue. We were asking to be silenced. This really disappointed me. I voiced my disapproval, but I didn't hear or feel too much support around me ... Aside from the fact that I felt we shouldn't hide from the Mugabe issue, I find the contractual restrictions on our freedom of speech onerous enough without us trying to slap more bans on ourselves ... We're all grown-ups. Yet here we were giving up our independence and our ability to make decisions and to think.

In fact, as Gilchrist senses, this made a mockery of the courage of Andy Flower and Henry Olonga, striving to exercise their right to freedom of expression in the face of a regime that wished to deprive them of it. Gilchrist was ultimately content with playing in Zimbabwe, but not without misgivings, and he quotes from a post-match conversation in which Flower, looking like 'a man under great strain' but 'someone ... leaving his mark on the world', was asked why his whole team did not make a stand. 'It's not in our nature to stand up against things,' explained Flower. 'He [the average Zimbabwean] finds it hard to really speak out and protest against anything.' Rather like the average Australian, methinks. At least Gilchrist's candour kills the spin that the issue revolved around player security: 'There was a lot more to it, and everyone at some point was talking about the moral issues surrounding the regime. I wasn't alone in my desire not to go. Various players argued that it wasn't our safety, but that of spectators and protesters, that was at risk.' A pity that the same players were content for the same risk to be run if administrators took responsibility for it.

When I read *Walking to Victory*, I thought it would provoke a good deal of comment, presenting as it did a courageously different version of events from that peddled by the Australian board and captain. It certainly did stimulate a response: to the passages concerned with Gilchrist's decision to 'walk' when given not out by Rudi Koertzen during the Super Six game against Sri Lanka. These, it is true, are quite interesting, again quite open in their muddle-headedness. But it struck me as another instance of the media's inability to distinguish wood from trees that they devoted hectares of commentary to the ethics of 'walking' and overlooked the morality of playing against a country whose designated cricket authority has a criminal dictator as its patron. Funny old world, innit? I subsequently sat as co-host through an interview with Gilchrist in which a hard-hitting ABC radio morning host, known for taking it up to prime ministers and big businessmen alike, asked such questions as: 'So, is it hard being a wicketkeeper?' Perhaps *Walking to Victory* would have attracted more intelligent comment if it had borne a different title, like *Truckling to Tyrants*.

No player outpouring last season attracted more attention, of course, than that of the grandpappy of product, Steve Waugh. His twelfth book *Never Say Die* (HarperSports) focuses on his 'epic hundred' against England at the Sydney Cricket Ground in January 2003 which, in case the reader was marooned in the New Guinea Highlands or confined to a punishment cell at Villawood at the time, was completed with a boundary off the second day's final delivery.

Focus is a problem with *Never Say Die*: it is not tight enough. Two-thirds of the book are a blur of bumpf – about Tests against the West Indies and Bangladesh, the World Cup, the baggy green – bulking it out to sellable specifications. More, though, is less: it distracts attention from the third that does concern the innings in question, which is excellent. Apparently when he reached his hundred, Waugh's daughter Rosie told her mother: 'Mummy, my heart feels funny.' I know how she felt: in its way, that innings reduced us all to delighted children, and to read Waugh's retelling of it is to enjoy those sensations anew. Gilchrist's interpolations about the innings and its aftermath are, again, worth reading. 'It was quite an extraordinary feeling, just the energy and emotion in that room,' he recalls. 'It just felt like everyone couldn't really look each other right in the eye, maybe for fear of, I don't know, crying or screaming or whatever.' It's disappointing only that the publishers did not have the courage of their conviction: if they had cut this book in half, *Never Say Die* would have been a minor classic. But that, I guess, would have entailed selling it at half the price and making half the money – and we couldn't have that, could we?

Waugh's diligent amanuensis, Geoff Armstrong, also bided his time last year by producing a fair stocking-filler, *Top Tens of Australian Test Cricket* (ABC Books), with Ian Russell. Some of their lists are pretty good, even subtly reinforcing of cricket verities. Ten Umpiring Decisions that Went Australia's Way are balanced by Ten Umpiring Decisions that Went Against Australia, as if to verify that old saw about them all evening out. Mind you, The Top Ten Bizarre Decisions by Australian Selectors is not offset by Ten Strokes of Selection Genius – something, as chairman of selectors at the Yarras, I observed rather ruefully. On the whole there should have been more lists of this nature; the statistics get down to such a minute level as to become *de trop*. Do we really need to know the tenth-best bowling figures by an Australian at Bellerive Oval?

An alternative to all this authorised product is *Run Out* (Lothian), the highly unauthorised memoir of Graham Halbish, the CEO sacked by the Australian Cricket Board in February 1997. It qualifies as unique: our first book, I believe, by a senior cricket administrator about senior cricket administration (Syd Smith's two books were both historical works). As such, it deserves to be read, and Halbish's unrestrained apostasy lends it colour that it might not have had. There is the confession, for example, that in player contract negotiations of yore, the board deliberately understated its revenues: 'I suppose we cooked the pie. The books certainly weren't cooked, but the pie was from a recipe of the board's creation.' There are stories, too, that have not seen the light of day, such as the disclosure that board chairman Alan Crompton went to South Africa a decade ago with a legal letter for Bob Simpson's sacking as coach: Simmo's stridency in defending Shane Warne and Merv Hughes from the fines levied after the Johannesburg Test had turned the board against him. 'Their [the lawyers'] advice was that Simmo had clearly breached his contract with the ACB,' recalls Halbish, 'and the letter should be signed by the chairman and handed to him immediately.' A narrow squeak.

Those seeking a guide to the faultlines in Australian cricket administration over the last twenty years will also find *Run Out* required reading. It is very much the voice of the old guard: not just Halbish, but Crompton, Ian McDonald, Col Egar, Phil Ridings and even Darrell Hair. The villains are Denis Rogers, Bob Merriman, Malcolm Gray and Malcolm Speed (who, as an aside, we are told 'did not even know the players in the Test team when he arrived'). This is, of course, the book's weakness as well. For all the sympathy one might extend towards one whose dearest achievement was suddenly denied him, Halbish is simply too thoroughgoing in his self-justification and self-exculpation to be truly convincing.

Much of *Run Out*, for instance, is devoted to a *post hoc* rationalisation of the board's handling of match-fixing, especially the secret fining of Warne and Mark Waugh for their tarrying with John the Bookie. These are discussed independently of an account of the financial inducements for failure that Warne, Waugh and Tim May alleged they had been offered by Salim Malik. The connection between the two – the very real probability that John's approaches were to ascertain the players' venality – is thus unmade. And Halbish's attack on the ICC for letting the Pakistan Cricket Board deal with it as an internal affair – 'The matter should have become a vital, urgent issue for the game's governing body. Instead, the ICC allowed Pakistan to claim the allegation as an internal matter that it would sort out' – is at least ironic, seeing that he sought and received the same dispensation. Remember Justice Brandeis? 'Sunlight is the best disinfectant.' The fact is that the board's actions – however well-intentioned – eventually proved extremely damaging to the credit of

Warne and Waugh as witnesses to the Qayyum Inquiry, and to Australia's standing in this sorry affair. Halbish's beef is, essentially, that many on the board distanced themselves from the cover-up having earlier approved it – and here he might well have grounds for complaint. But this does not stop the cover-up and the lengths gone to in maintaining it from having been an unfortunate mistake.

Not being on the official payroll, too, Halbish is free to vent his spleen on issues confronting cricket, including what seems a rather tendentious analysis of the Muralitharan saga. 'We have an incredible situation now where a man is playing Test cricket and his action has never been cleared,' he asserts. But what's so incredible about this? For as long as the game contains Law 24, no bowler's action can be 'cleared'. And perhaps we should, at least momentarily, cease to wonder whether Murali's action is fair, and wonder about our own. The fact is that Murali has hidden nothing from his accusers and consented to every official test set him, in the face of some of the most despicable calumnies ever aimed at a cricketer. The Australian response has been to repeat for ten years: 'Well he looks like a chucker, so he must be a chucker.' This is not a simple question, and it serves no purpose pretending that it is. If you can be bothered following the findings of the biomechanists at the University of Western Australia – and Halbish clearly can't – then you will find a strong case for regarding Murali as a bowler *sui generis*. 'The problem is that he continues to win accolades despite an action which is unfair,' says Halbish, 'and the cost of this could be borne by those who fall victim to his bowling.' The same, of course, was said of the original round-arm and over-arm bowlers. The contrast of the treatment of Shoaib Akhtar, furthermore, is unfortunate to say the least: 'Shoaib was referred to the nine-man advisory panel on illegal deliveries. This system avoided all the drama, heartaches, sensationalism, embarrassment and torment which was forced upon Hair four years earlier.' Well yes he was. He was also allowed to arrive in Australia before being told he couldn't bowl, then unilaterally permitted to do so by ICC president Jagmohan Dalmiya, setting the process at nought. Another triumph.

Fortunately, not every book last season was a monument to self-regard. The outstanding publication of the season by far came out without hype or hoopla, entirely in keeping with both its subject and creator – and I'm not talking about *Wisden Australia.* In his marvellous book *The Fatal Englishman,* Sebastian Faulks stops to consider the ineluctable fascination exerted by the bright, brilliant, brief life. He conjectures that everything about such lives is naturally intensified and enriched by their brevity: 'The stories of young people who delight parents and friends with their talents have a concentrated significance in their beginnings, and in their premature ends there is a natural poignancy that brutally epitomises the disappointment that is also common but less evident in longer, duller lives.' No-one in cricket has struck this chord so effectively as David Frith, not only in his biographies of Archie Jackson and Drewy Stoddart, but in his survey of suicides among the game's great and obscure; retelling *The Ross Gregory Story* (Lothian Books), which he considers 'third in a trilogy of brilliant but ill-fated cricketers', comes naturally to him. For those who don't know, the diminutive Gregory represented Victoria while still at school, and represented his country twice, looking like a boy among men but averaging 51, only to die in aerial combat in May 1942. Though memory of Gregory has faded with the passage of time, Frith has produced a startlingly comprehensive book, longer and deeper than the biographies of cricketers with 100 Tests or more.

It might even be thought a little too long. Frith's recapitulation of Gregory's cricket career is exhaustively, perhaps exhaustingly, thorough. 'You will not mind if I do not say anything,' twenty-year-old Gregory told the press after he was chosen for his Test debut in January 1937 – which is rather charming, but little help to a biographer. Frith goes as far as he can on the sometimes cursory impressions of others, but has at one stage to confess: 'Ross Gregory was clearly one of those fellows about whom it would seem pointless to search for expressions of reservation or disapproval during that stage of his life.' The story obtains shade, as it were, from the penumbra of imminent tragedy. The scoreline at the end of his subject's highest Test score, Frith notes, has 'no parallel in Test history in terms of future tragedy': Gregory c Verity b Farnes encompasses three men destined to die in uniform.

The coup of Frith's book is the full text of the diary that Gregory kept as a Royal Australian Air Force navigator, which he started almost a year to the day of his death. Though it was this diary's purchase at auction some years ago that set Frith to writing the Gregory story, I was initially dubious of the wisdom of republishing it in its entirety. In fact, this bold choice comes off. Gregory was not a war hero. He was a cog in the military machine – the sense of which became increasingly oppressive to him. But while his diary was often pervaded by boredom, Gregory was anything but a boring writer. He was perceptive, droll, often caustic, especially where the British were concerned: 'A declining nation' who were 'too dumb and dogmatic', he thought, complaining of ineptitude that was 'just the pommies all over' and 'typical British organisation'. Frith writes that Gregory was 'coarsened' by war; he certainly grew up quickly. After a while, the *sang froid* is almost soothing – until you read an eyewitness account of a Wellington bomber exploding, or of Gregory's pilot causing a near-terminal tailspin by passing out. 'What a war!' he sighs in his last entry; and in recording the casual interplay of terror and tedium, Gregory not only reveals much about himself, but a good deal about combat.

Perhaps the most affecting remnant of Gregory's brief life, meanwhile, is the letter he wrote to his parents in November 1941 in case of his death: 'I am absolutely certain in my own mind that you both have the courage to face the facts as they are presented, and I would be keenly disappointed if you regretted my action in doing what I consider to be my duty.' And there's more, for, in a village in Bangladesh, Frith even found surviving eyewitnesses to the dogfight in which Gregory's last flight ended. The publishers have done Frith's book few favours with its unprepossessing cover and production; they obscure a small but multi-faceted gem. It even contains a line to appeal to lovers of Johnstoniana: 'There was a light interlude when Badcock was struck agonisingly in the groin.' On the perplexing question of what actually took place in Pretoria on the evening of 5 March 2003, alas, no light is cast. But, as Frith reveals, cricket is a game that abounds in extraordinary untold stories.

Wisden Australia 2004–05

THE WARNE AGE

SHANE WARNE

The Young Veteran

Shane Warne is currently having his Melbourne home renovated. And it's taking a bloody long time. 'It was meant to take five months,' Warne says. 'And it's taken eight-and-a-half, thank-you very much.' He's had to move his wife and infant daughter into a hotel for the duration, and spends a good deal of time on the road trying to oversee the process *in absentia.*

But things are generally taking longer for Warne these days. Like wickets. At the start of this cricket summer, Warne set himself a seasonal target: 36 scalps in six Tests, with the aim that by the end of the Third Test against South Africa at the Adelaide Oval he would have hauled in his 300th wicket at the top level.

While it's not unusual for athletes to set themselves statistical hurdles, Warne had done without them before. He'd rocked up, bowled, enjoyed the occasion, accepted the fates. And the fates had been uncommonly kind. But over the last few years, Warne has experienced more than enough intimations of sporting mortality to tell him that, if he hasn't reached the beginning of the end, he has at least seen the end of the beginning. First, there was the shoulder. Then there was the finger. More recently, there has been the groin. And pain at such pivotal points takes, in one's twenty-ninth year, longer to recover from than it did. With 22,000 international deliveries behind him, Warne is having to ponder just how many are ahead.

*

There is a powerful concept in higher mathematics called 'regression to the mean', evolved just over a century ago by a Briton called Francis Galton. After exhaustive surveys of the growth rate of sweet peas and the variance in the height of children, he remarked that, over time, observable phenomena converged toward an average figure. Basically, things happen to ensure that what goes up must come down. And, had Galton's data been bowling averages, he might have concluded that what goes down must come up.

Such is the case of Shane Warne. He is now deep in what might be regarded as the third stage of his international cricket lifespan. Initially, he was the bowler who might: though there was one memorable rout of the West Indies, 14 wickets in his first eight Tests cost him 50 runs each.

Then, amid disbelief and delirium, Warne became the bowler who did: in twenty-three Test matches to the end of 1994, Warne pilfered 140 wickets at a cost of less than 20 runs each, spinning past, round and through, with the climax that imperishable hat-trick at the MCG.

Since that time, Warne's become the bowler who has. The wickets have come all right, but they've been costlier: 123 in twenty-nine Tests have been extracted at almost 26 runs apiece. And another exogenous factor has entered the equation, one built like a flagpole, and who shoots pigs for fun: since 1995 dawned, Glenn McGrath has captured 143 wickets at 20 and an increasing proportion of the headlines.

The Shane Warne industry has maintained its strike rate: over the last three years, nine books have worn him on their cover, one of them Warne's own. But is Warne the bowler who will again? Or might his regression to the mean continue? Even for the bowler, that's hard to say.

*

In interview, Shane Warne is an easy man to like. He laughs a lot and talks straight. I liked him when I interviewed him for *Inside Sport* just over three years ago but, after the controversies of his

1993–94 South African tour, he was warier then. Now he's relaxed and talkative. At one point, he even sings.

So what's been driving Shane Warne's regression to the mean? Batsmen may be playing him better: ForeWarned, after all, is forearmed. Umpires, too, don't seem to be as accommodating nowadays. But the predominant reason is underfoot. When Warne first wandered into Test cricket five years ago, he feels, pitches were far drier: 'In '92 to '95 we had pretty flat wickets all over the world. And I got to bowl a fair bit on the last day, when there were footmarks everywhere, and wickets came my way. The last eighteen months all over the world in all these different places, it's been pretty hard work. You go to a country and they say: "Well, the Australians have got Shane Warne in the side, so let's prepare green wickets and hope our new ball bowlers knock over their top order."'

Pitches doctored to counteract Warne are a back-handed compliment, of course, but irritating nonetheless: 'It gets a bit frustrating. At least in Australia as you go round through Melbourne, Sydney, Perth, Brisbane, Adelaide, Hobart, you know basically what to expect. But overseas, you're out there bowling, ripping your fingers over the ball, seeing it turn one bloody millimetre, and you start thinking: "Gee, where's all the good old flat wickets gone?"'

The most egregious example of rivals stacking the deck came last July at Headingley, where England's chairman of selectors David Graveney detected a Warne-shaped shadow over the prepared pitch and sought a fresh surface. But David Graveney's intervention was simply the klutziest. Cast your mind back to Centurion Park just under a year ago, where Warne bowled for hour after hour on a surface as slow and blank as Forrest Gump. Warne can and does: 'I bowled 36 overs and I reckon it's one of the best spells I've ever bowled, but I got none for 89.' In fact, it's with some chagrin that Warne looks back on his most recent match-winning performance: 9 for 111 at Old Trafford six months ago on the first pitch for months that had turned more than a micron. 'He's back,' said the scribes. 'I was never away,' says Warne.

The other factor in Warne's lower profile, Glenn McGrath, is naturally borne more easily: 'Looking back, what I was better at doing was picking up the really big hauls. But when you've got a great bowler at the other end like Glenn, who loves bowling at the tail as much as I do, obviously your opportunities aren't going to be the same.'

*

Environmental factors, though, are only part of the story. Warne is an avid student of himself on video, and sees that the bowler of today is a different animal from the one of three years ago.

For one, he's a lot quicker through the air. For another, the prestidigitation is less pronounced. Time was when that big hissing leg-break was second nature, like John Daly's drives. Now it's seen less often, like John Daly's drinks (for the moment). Having submitted it to hours of masterful microsurgery by Greg Hoy, Warne admits that he is less inclined to stretch his spinning finger to the limit.

But while 22,000 deliveries at international level might have cost him dexterity, Warne thinks they have improved his discrimination. These days, he feels, he is more conscious of the 'when, what and why' of bowling: 'I'd love to bowl big leggies all the time, but these days I know I can't do it so often. At the same time, though, I've probably got a bit more streetwise. Experience is an amazing thing, really. A few years ago I wasn't really planning my bowling all that much, and I probably couldn't have explained why I was bowling what I did. I'd think: "Ah well, I s'pose it's time to bowl the toppie now." Now I'm thinking a lot more about how I bowl in a particular situation, which is a result of having been in that situation before. I'm setting people up more. If a guy's hitting me back over my head, I can say: "This is what I did last time, and this is what I should do now."' The monster leg-breaks are today saved for psychologically important moments, as at the start of a spell or when a new batsman arrives. Otherwise there are many more top-spinners, with commensurate emphasis on coaxing catches in front of the wicket, at short cover and mid-wicket (which Warne posts straight, provoking batsmen to turn the blade).

Off the field, Warne bowls less in the nets, submits to restorative massage from physio Errol Alcott at the end of a hard day's play, and visits therapist Lyn Watson every non-playing day in Melbourne to keep that golden shoulder turning. There was also, of course, his well-publicised decision to decline a £400,000 contract with English county club Sussex for the 1998 season: a solid indication he would like to see out the millennium in a green cap. As he puts it: 'I've never imagined myself hanging round just for the sake of hanging round, but I'm still enjoying it. I really love playing with this team, and I'll play for as long as that's the case.'

*

That Warne still enjoys the game is a general statement, for the first six weeks of the Australian summer were enjoyable for neither Warne nor his colleagues. As their Australian Cricketers' Association locked horns with the Australian Cricket Board over pay and conditions – amid threats of a cricket picket and the first Australian Scab XI since January 1885 – players did their best to keep their heads down. 'The players' association stuff has made it pretty hard to concentrate on the cricket,' Warne says. 'No disrespect to the New Zealanders, but I think it's lucky that we were playing them first rather than the South Africans.' For someone whose thatch is more conspicuous than Greg Matthews', keeping a sunken profile was easier said than done. And Warne didn't enhance the image of the downtrodden cricketers much by tootling to and fro in a brand new Ferrari.

What was missed at the time was that Warne was continuing a family tradition at least as much as indulging in conspicuous consumption. Warne's father Keith, a successful financial planner, had an automotive fetish that well and truly rubbed off on his son. When Warne was first selected for Australia in December 1991, indeed, he arrived at the ACB's portal in the passenger seat of the family Porsche. 'Dad had GTs and Monaros and Brock Commodores,' Warne recalls. 'And some of that must have rubbed off when I was shining the hubcaps at the weekend or something like that. Like the way I like Rod Stewart now, because when my parents had parties while I was growing up I could hear Rod Stewart and Slade playing through the bedroom wall, and I'd hear: (sings) "Wake up Maggie May, ah think ah've got something to say to youuuu ... "

'I bought the Ferrari three months ago, before any of the players' association stuff blew up. And I did it because it had always been a bit of a dream car for me, and because I thought I deserved it after working my arse off for seven or eight years. I mean, the bank owns it, not me. I walked in, said: "Can I have a loan for ... well ... (laughs) a bloody lot of money!" And the next thing I know is that the press is saying Shane Warne's bought a car worth $320,000.'

Like many of his colleagues, Warne was peeved when the board released figures concerning their existing contractual arrangements (figures revealing Warne's direct cricket earnings at between $440,000 and $480,000). But in his role as ACA secretary, he's philosophical about the industrial argy-bargy, and maintains that the body's priority has been to ameliorate the lot of first-class cricketers. 'Nothing like this has happened before,' he says. 'And I think both the ACA and the board have been on a bit of a learning curve, and both have made a few mistakes. What we want really is a better workplace for cricketers in general, because Shield cricketers these days can't hold down jobs, and employers won't give them time off. Once employers might have been happy to say: "Oh, we employ so-and-so who plays cricket for Victoria." But today, there's no benefit in it for employers. And what happens to a guy who's got a job is that it hampers him when it comes to selection, because he can't get to state practices or he arrives a couple of hours late. I mean, we've got a guy in the [Victorian] Shield squad at the moment who's in the position where his boss is saying: "You've gotta make a choice. It's either work or cricket." And when you're making $25,000 a summer out of playing Shield, well, it's a pretty easy choice.'

*

You might say also that, when you're making half a million a year out of playing cricket, it's a fairly straightforward decision to persist. But that overlooks some of the downside of a career of continuous cricket that Warne has come to comprehend. For a long time, cricket was Warne's home. Now, it's somewhere he leaves home for. Warne feels that becoming a father to Brooke on 27 June has changed him. 'I probably didn't realise how huge the impact was on your life. I think I'd always assumed that, you know, you fed them and changed them and then they went off to sleep. In fact when you're round Brooke, you're always having to look round for her. Is she swallowing the blanket? Is she dribbling on herself? It's a bit unbelievable really. I'm pretty ordinary on nappies. In fact, I have to admit I haven't actually changed one yet, although I've held the odd bottle. I'm looking at the trophy for the "most improved father".'

The birth demonstrated again to Warne that celebrity is a mixed blessing: it irked him that reporters and photographers trailed him throughout his week's paternity leave from the Ashes tour to see his newborn. Because he attracts it without trying, Warne seldom solicits publicity: he and his future wife Simone Callahan spoke to a women's magazine for $500 six years ago, but have not dabbled in that lucrative market since. And some of the media's excesses – like the newspaper that published his parents' street address because they would not grant an interview – are tattooed deep in his memory.

'When Brooke was born, we had people camping outside our house,' he recalls. 'And when we drove out of the hospital, we had to rig up these black sheets over the windows to protect her [from flash cameras]. I mean, we could have sold the baby photos to a magazine, just like I could have sold our wedding photos, but that's not something I want to do. And I think the media should respect people's privacy more. If you ask for some space, they should give you space.'

That said, the kick Warne obtains from cricket remains. Despite time away from home, he's strengthened ties with his close-knit family by employing brother Jason as a personal assistant. He professes to enjoy the Victorian captaincy, when he's available to take advantage of it, and is conscious of his status as a senior member of the Australian team. One of the most eye-catching passages in his recent autobiography, in fact, is an extended gripe about the attitude of modern junior players to their elders.

Asked about it, Warne replies: 'I'm not saying we should go back to the old days, the old guys telling the younger ones: "Shine my boots!" Or: "Get me a beer!" I mean, in the Australian side now we've got a really good atmosphere: everyone's even whether they've played one Test or one hundred. Ricky Ponting's not only a great kid, but he's got a good cricket brain; in fact, he's probably a future Australian captain. But I do think young players have gotta earn their stripes. Sometimes they lack respect for guys who've been round a while.' Which Shane Warne has, and hopefully will be for some time yet.

Inside Sport December 1998

SHANE WARNE

The Comeback Kid

Leg-spin bowling is all about spinning away, with the occasional variation of one coming dramatically back. Shane Warne, perhaps its greatest practitioner, has turned this into a way of life.

When he steps onto Melbourne's Junction Oval tomorrow to join the second day of the Victorian Second XI's game against Queensland's Academy of Sport, he will again be starring in a drama of his own creation. Australian cricket careers used to be like American lives: seldom if ever did they feature second acts. Among many things, Warne has changed this utterly: if, as is widely expected, he is chosen for Australia's forthcoming tour of Sri Lanka, it will represent his sixth significant return to the colours.

Where sporting comebacks usually involve the appearance of some portly travesty of the former great, moreover, thirty-four-year-old Warne returns perhaps as strong and streamlined as he has ever been. Over the last six weeks, he has been undertaking three 50-ball bowling sessions a week, plus a program of bike rides, swimming sessions, sprint work, weight programs and skipping, boxing and karate routines. With his earring, photogenic smile and hair grown fashionably shaggy, he looks fit to star in a reality television show – which over the next few weeks, he essentially will.

Nonetheless, this is a comeback of a kind Warne has not attempted. Previously, he has been rising nobly above incapacitating injury; here he is returning from the self-inflicted wound of an embarrassing drug offence. It is a year since, on the eve of a World Cup he had expected to crown his career in one-day cricket, he was suspended by Cricket Australia for using a 'prohibited method':

specifically a diuretic with the 'potential' to mask performance-enhancing drugs.

Whether smoking or sledging, texting or testifying, Warne's has been a life relentlessly exposed. But his ruin by urine was a moment to test the loyalty of even hardened fans, and more followed, 2003 becoming something of an *annus horribilis.* Cricket Australia enforced the ban strictly, and Warne found himself unable even to play charity matches until he challenged the extent of the prohibition. He was on the side of the angels in a bizarre attempted blackmail of Cricket Australia by a Gold Coast man, which also involved Brett Lee. But he looked less innocent when accused last August of harassment by a South African model and of infidelity by an Australian stripper – accusations which pushed his sorely-tried wife Simone to the brink of abandoning their marriage.

In a recent interview with *Australian Women's Weekly,* part of the Consolidated Press empire of Kerry Packer to which Warne is contractually bound, he admits to feeling fortunate it survived: 'I think this is my last chance at everything. My last chance here [with Simone]. My last chance with my life. This is it.'

Will he be given that chance? Getting on the field considerably improves his odds. A couple of years ago during a Melbourne Test match, I was in the Melbourne Cricket Club library shortly before play recommenced when the subject turned to Shane Warne. The conversationalists, traditionalists to a man, chorused their disapproval: he was a lair, a larrikin, a rogue, a ratbag. He'd brought the game into disrepute so often that it was a wonder there was any repute left over.

When play began and Warne was thrown the ball, however, the disputants gathered at once round the library's television. A worshipful silence fell, punctuated by the odd 'oh' and 'ah' at the vehemence of Warne's spin and the voluptuousness of his loop. 'You know,' said one watcher finally, 'when he's not bowling, I simply can't stand him. But when he's bowling, I could watch him all day.'

Where Warne is concerned, fans are what it's all about: both the legions round the world whom he transfixes with every delivery, and the ones that the shit hits with uncanny regularity. And when the former have something to cheer about, they tend to drown out the latter.

Australian cricket fans will welcome his cricket abilities: Warne's stand-in, Stuart MacGill, with 14 wickets at 50 against India, scarcely made an unassailable case for continued selection. They will like, too, the restoration of a sense of continuity. Waugh says goodbye, Warne says hello: it will be like a cast change in a long-running soap, where a retiring star is replaced by a former favourite.

It is unlikely, furthermore, that Warne's skills will have atrophied significantly during his exile. It may be a year since he has bowled in an official match, but it is only two since he seemed to have returned to peak efficiency against South Africa. Between 1998 and 2001, the Warne Index looked to be in slight but steady decline. His 135 wickets cost 32.24 – handy, but hardly Warnesque. Injury hampered him, as did a preoccupation with bowling round the wicket into the rough, as though he needed reassurance that he was still the big spinning dick.

For all his outward ebullience, in fact, Warne is a superstitious, even sensitive character; he looks for reasons to be confident, and usually finds them, rather than generating confidence internally. His leg-spin paterfamilias Terry Jenner tells a story about Warne's first tentative deliveries after major finger surgery in 1996. Everything seemed right at once – the rip, the curve, the deviation – but Warne regarded Jenner's praise with suspicion. 'If it was good,' he asked, 'why didn't it *feel* good?'

It is because he is an intuitive cricketer that he is so irrepressible when he senses that the fates are with him. And so he appeared in 2002, when his purchase and penetration improved markedly after an impressive recommitment to personal fitness, and his 67 wickets cost 19.55. The next episode in his career looked like being his passing Courtney Walsh's Test record 519 wickets in the Caribbean – until he shredded his own script.

That record remains Warne's great statistical challenge: he has 491. But there remains one other imponderable: in some senses, Warne belongs to a subtly different era, and is a cricketer of a type no longer being minted. Of the Australian first-class players around when Warne first represented Victoria in February 1991, only half-a-dozen remain. He was only briefly, and none too happily, a scholar at Australia's Cricket Academy. His bowling has been a personal development, abetted by the likes of Jenner, Ian Healy, Ian Chappell and Richie Benaud, rather than incubated within the Australian team.

His immediate task is straightforward. After the Second XI match, he will have five days of senior cricket to make his mark: a limited-overs ING Cup fixture against Tasmania at the Melbourne Cricket Ground on Saturday, and a four-day Pura Cup match against the same opponents beginning two days later. A wicket or two will whisk him back into international ranks for Australia's first Test in Sri Lanka on 8 March.

Yet at stake now may be not so much Warne's place in the Australia team as his role in Australian cricket. In the lean, mean John Buchanan machine, with its statistical benchmarking and video gizmos, a cricketer so spontaneous and a character so mercurial might seem incongruous. Warne is close to Waugh's successor as skipper, Ricky Ponting, who has already warmed to the prospect of his return: 'I would love to have him back.' Ponting's vice-captain Adam Gilchrist has been more circumspect, stating that Warne will have to 'work out how he is going', and that he is 'going to be learning'.

Warne himself is at best ambivalent about the coach's analytical tools: in his autobiography he referred to a preference for using 'the old brain'. For all his experience at returning, Warne will this time be treading a somewhat different route, where the test will be less the comeback than the staying-back.

The Guardian February 2004

WARNE'S RETURN

He's Back

Shane Warne's return to official cricket in Melbourne yesterday, after a year in purdah for popping a banned slimming tablet, proved an anticlimax as complete as it was unsurprising. Complete because he batted only twenty minutes and did not bowl before rain set in over the picturesque Junction Oval where he was representing Victoria's Second XI against the Queensland Academy of Sport; unsurprising because, to live up to the air of expectation in advance of the game, he'd have needed to bowl Bradman with a ball that drifted like the *Mary Celeste*, dropped like the US dollar, and spun like Alistair Campbell.

'I Am Still the Best', screamed the headline in the tabloid *Herald Sun*, reporting Warne's conviction that he remained the country's premier leg-spinner – not that controversial a call, considering that he was classed by *Wisden* as the greatest bowler of the twentieth century. Reporters, camera crews and the burly ex-footballers and skinny bottle-blondes who front television sport in Melbourne began congregating not long after dawn in order to catch a glimpse of Warne arriving for his team's 7.30 a.m. yoga warm-up.

Cricketers dropping down a level or two are often a little hazy about their colleagues. A story is told of Edgar Mayne, the Aussie Test batsman of the 1920s, who one day opened for the Victorian Second XI and enquired ingenuously of his partner, a colt called Cosgrove: 'You bat left-handed, dontcha son?' Cosgrove replied: 'No sir, but I can try.' Warne wasn't so gauche. According to Victoria's assistant coach Mick O'Sullivan, Warne politely introduced himself to those members of the Junior XI he had not previously met; he then participated eagerly in the morning training session, calling everyone by name, taking a lengthy series of throwdowns, then bowling for as long as there were batsmen.

'I think Shane's very excited,' said O'Sullivan. 'He loves playing cricket. He's a real cricket nut. He can't wait to get out, have a bat, have a bowl, and more than anything be part of the team. As we know, one of Shane's great qualities is his team-manship.' Warne brushed up on his dressingroommanship and paddingupmanship until 11.30 a.m. when, ending a 273-run fourth-wicket partnership with Brendan Joseland, Nick Jewell was stumped for 137. The great man was accompanied to the gate by a Chubb security man, perhaps not so much to protect Warne as to shield onlookers from his charisma.

It was – almost – the moment we'd all been waiting for. As they parted for him, even the television cameramen couldn't resist urging him on: 'Good luck Shane'; 'Go Warnie'. At least, one presumes it was the cameramen, given that there have been previous misidentifications.

Not surprisingly, Warne looked a little rusty in the middle, eventually squeezing out an off-drive to open his account, middling a few, missing a few more, then nicking twenty-four-year-old Academy medium-pacer Steve Magoffin to twenty-one-year-old keeper Chris Hartley. That said, thirty-four-year-old Shane Warne looked as firm and fit as perhaps he has ever been, sleeveless sweater hanging loosely from his shoulders, slimming tablet entirely unnecessary. A cheeky lone banner agreed: 'It's Been Worth the Weight!'

Warne gave little sign of feeling the fuss, beyond a slightly self-conscious smile when he ran another video gauntlet as Queensland's reply commenced, Victoria having declared at noon with the fall of their sixth wicket at 379. Standing at first slip, he chatted animatedly with others in the cordon, conspicuously applauded good deliveries, and obediently ferried the close-catching helmet from one end to the other. Any more visibly obliging and he would have ordered a round of ice-creams from the Mr Whippy van.

Spectators kept drifting in as word spread that Warne's first spell was in the offing, until about 400 people were congregated in the rambling Blackie–Ironmonger Stand and draped over the oval's benches and grassy embankments. Warne gave them something to salute by leaning nonchalantly to his right and pouching a casual catch to dismiss Ryan Broad. But just when the moment seemed ripe, rain began falling at 1.40 p.m. Within a quarter of an hour it justified an adjournment, then continued with sufficient intensity to prevent a resumption and steadily disperse the crowd. Few were still around when play was abandoned just before 5 p.m. One imagined, nonetheless, that they would be back.

The Guardian February 2004

WARNE AND MURALI

Long Playing Records

When Fred Trueman was asked who he thought would break the Test wicket record he set in the 1960s, he famously said he could not be sure but whoever it was would be 'bloody tired'. One of the most enticing aspects of bowling's joint blue-riband holders Shane Warne and Muttiah Muralitharan is that they are not.

No sooner had Warne equalled the record with his 527th Test wicket on Tuesday – amid a typically persevering spell into a stiff breeze on a pitch in tropical Cairns that did him few favours – than he was wending his way back to his county Hampshire. Whatever his appetites in other areas, he has always been a glutton for cricket.

Yet his record's joint venture status will probably last only three weeks at best. Muralitharan, conspicuously absent from this series, has just rejoined Sri Lankan comrades in the Asia Cup, will probably resume Test cricket against South Africa at Galle on 4 August, and predicts he has six more years in the game.

Warne is thirty-four, Muralitharan thirty-two, and the International Cricket Council's Future Tours Program guarantees them a lot of games in times to come. Both have spoken of the probability that the record will change hands between them at intervals over that period; third place on the list will soon be filled by increasing quantities of daylight.

With their statistics symmetrical, and their careers of similar duration, it is tempting to parallel the pair. They first met at Colombo in August 1992: Warne's second series was Muralitharan's first. The callow Warne endured a fearful beating in the first innings of the First Test, giving up 107 from 22 wicket-less overs. But when Allan Border gambled on him in the second innings, Warne took 3 wickets without conceding a run in an improbable Australian win. Border subsequently faced the first Test delivery of a spindly twenty-year-old Tamil, interpreting the whirl of arms and wrist as a leg-break; he was startled when it turned massively the other way.

The encounter proved a harbinger of their subsequent careers. Warne's bowling has often involved striking back from the brink of despair – the adversity sometimes a result of his personal peccadilloes. Muralitharan's methods continue to baffle – not just batsmen but also the biomechanists appointed by the ICC to determine its legality.

For their countrymen, both have had symbolic qualities. The only Tamil in a largely Sinhalese side, Muralitharan has been a uniting figure in a country wracked by civil war. His torments under the supervision of Australian umpires have made him a regional martyr: he inspired the character in the Bollywood blockbuster *Lagaan* whose whirlygig bowling from a standing start outrages the English cricketers but is deemed not to transgress the laws.

Warne the man divides his countrymen, most of whom continue to prefer the old Australian sporting archetype who wins without fuss; Warne the bowler melts difference away. Twelve years ago, the search for a great leg-spinner was Australian cricket's version of Lewis Carroll's hunting of the snark. Wise old heads scoffed at the selection favour Warne enjoyed; his own Victorian captain sniffed: 'I think if you bowl leg spin in this country they go a bit honky-tonk.' These circumspect initial reviews now remind one of the famous notes written after Fred Astaire's first audition: 'Can't sing. Can't act. Can dance a little.'

The question of who is the greater bowler looks likely to tax us for years to come. The numbers superficially favour Muralitharan, who has harvested his wickets 2.5 runs more cheaply and in twenty-five fewer Tests. But his record includes 107 cheap scalps against Zimbabwe and Bangladesh, while Warne has enjoyed only one Test against the former. Muralitharan, too, as Warne pointed out rather tersely last week, has the advantage of bowling on home pitches tailored to favour him. Warne away from Australia (292 wickets at 24.85) is a more formidable figure than Muralitharan away from Sri Lanka (190 wickets at 26.9).

Statistics obscure as much as they reveal, however, for one is not comparing two static mechanisms with all other variables suspended. Muralitharan is clearly the outstanding bowler in a mediocre attack. He bowls an extraordinarily high proportion of Sri Lanka's overs, which maximises his opportunities to take wickets but also reduces him to a stock bowler. He enjoys most of his success at the start of series; with ample opportunity for study, batsmen can get used to him. Playing for Sri Lanka, Muralitharan must also defend smaller totals, strive more often in losing causes, and be supported by less adept fieldsmen. How would he have fared with a keeper like Ian Healy, or catchers like Mark Waugh and Mark Taylor, making wickets out of half-chances?

Warne, a great bowler in an omnicompetent team, faces considerable competition for his wickets from the likes of Glenn McGrath, Jason Gillespie and Brett Lee. But he can also be used when the circumstances are most conducive, bowling as he pleases to attacking fields backed up by many runs.

It is hard to divorce Muralitharan and Warne from the controversies that have dogged them, the former over his action, the latter over his actions. Muralitharan is now unlikely to persuade detractors that he ever bowled fairly, particularly those in Australia, who include, it was recently revealed, the prime minister: thus his decision, disappointing but not unexpected, to skip Sri Lanka's recent tour of Australia's top end. Operating at the edge of a fuzzy law, he has sometimes looked a lonely figure, hiding delights and disappointments behind an inscrutable smile. Cricketers have been saner in their treatment of him than others. 'It's a great achievement to get the world record,' said Steve Waugh at the end of May. 'He should be celebrated for the fact that he's taken so many wickets. He makes Sri Lanka a very competitive side, he gets people through the gate to watch the game, and he's also a nice guy.'

Warne, meanwhile, is the captive of forces of celebrity that he once said had made his career resemble a soap opera – although a television series based on Warne's life would never get off the ground thanks to its sheer implausibility. 'I am a cricketer,' he has commented in his autobiography, 'and a human being.' As good as he is as the former, his skills as the latter have sometimes been found wanting.

Here, then, a rivalry rich in meaning and without precedent. Records usually hold obligingly still while pursuers give chase. Rarely are they antes raised by turns. And it is part of the joy of cricket that it can encompass two talents so heterogenous.

Scotland on Sunday July 2004

SHANE WARNE

Bad Boy, Bad Book

The American baseball legend Casey Stengel was once asked if sex interfered with athletic performance. No, sex was not the problem, Stengel replied: 'What *is* a problem is the staying up all night looking for it.'

Stengel, however, never met Shane Warne. If Paul Barry's unauthorised, unexpurgated and unadulterated biography is to be believed, cricket's greatest slow bowler, with 978 international scalps on his belt, also has 1000 notches on his bedpost. And the later he's stayed up, it would seem, the better he's become.

On the other hand, this isn't the kind of statistic *Wisden* would recognise. The source is 'one of Shane's mates at Channel 9'. Barry admits to a certain early scepticism – then to that scepticism giving massively way. 'I thought at the time this was a crazy exaggeration,' he writes. 'But now I'm not so sure. I personally know two other women who have been propositioned (or more) by him, and my limited knowledge of statistics makes me think there must be a host of others with similar stories.'

Say what? *Two* other women? Which leads to *a host*, and then to *a thousand*? This makes Kitty Kelley look like Martin Gilbert. But wait, there's more: 'Most of these would have been made public if Australian cricket writers had regarded it as their job to report on such infidelities. But they did not. Nor did they rat on the team official who saw it as his duty to carry a plentiful supply of condoms for the players or on journalists who occasionally took advantage of the service.' It's Our Shane Shame!

Review of *Spun Out* by Paul Barry (Random House, 2006)

It was hereabouts in *Spun Out* that I felt my own scepticism hardening. Not about Warne, incorrigible and foolish as he is, but about Barry, a journalist held in high professional esteem and author of several serious business biographies. Because in two paragraphs, he had perpetrated two of the give-aways of lazy reporting: giving credence to a wild, unsourced innuendo on no evidence other than guess-work, then alleging a conspiracy of silence which he, righteous man, nobly scorned.

The implication is that it is a cricket-writer's job to report a cricketer's personal indiscretions; never mind, of course, that it's far from clear whether the responsibilities of a political journalist include documenting politicians' extramarital exploits. And what's the big deal about the condoms? Sounds pretty responsible to me. Indeed, it was Artie James, physiotherapist on nine Ashes tours from 1930 to 1968, who inaugurated distributing condoms to Australian players, sexual intercourse being one of the few activities not tightly circumscribed by Australian Cricket Board tour contracts.

Barry sets up his straw Warne early in *Spun Out*: 'He is a walking paradox, they say. He is supremely confident, yet profoundly insecure. He is brilliant, but also a buffoon. He is generous and thoughtful, but utterly self-obsessed. This book is the search for why.' It is, bollocks. The conjectures are cod psychology where they are not complete inventions. 'There must have been something in those early years that made Shane the person he is today,' insists Barry of Warne's upbringing, 'because for all his talent and fame and self-confidence on the field, he is said to still be chronically insecure.' So ... what? Was he abused? Was he bullied? Did he find out that Darth Vader was his father? Barry hasn't a clue; nor am I sure he really cares. He simply has 540 pages to fill, and it may seem a more worthwhile expenditure of his energies if he uses banalities like 'walking paradox' and, worse still, 'a genius locked in the body of a fool'.

If you're to write about Warne with authority, you must be able to understand his cricket. Barry at least has a go, and the early chapters of *Spun Out* are by far the most thorough. But he doesn't *really* get it. He obsesses over Warne's sliders and flippers to the exclusion of the essence of his whole art: his stock ball, the leg break, which the merest fraction of cricketers can bowl even passably, but which to him is second nature. What we're left with is pseudo-technical mumbo-jumbo like: 'Warne gets this drift because he tweaks the ball so hard. If you watch on the super slo-mo you can see how much the ball spins in the air – far more than English spinner Ashley Giles achieves, for example.' That Warne is a wrist spinner and Giles a finger spinner seems a point not worth elaborating.

When he writes about Warne the cricketer, it is clear that Barry is idling until he can return to Warne the philanderer and philistine. Yet this palls quickly. The book's last third, frankly, perfectly reflects the title, replete with pointless digressions about the Barmy Army and Merlyn the spin-bowling machine, and bovine ruminations like 'sport at the top level is ninety per cent about self-belief and mental toughness' and 'what made the Australians so hard to beat was that they always put their opponents under so much pressure.' Recounting Warne's jejune sexual misadventures, Barry himself becomes a 'walking paradox', loftily superior to the tabloids' tawdriness, yet blithely turning their work into grist for his mill.

Stengel also observed that the trick was growing up without growing old. Warne has not perfected it, but he's hardly on his own there. *Spun Out,* in fact, proves a rare hatchet job where the biographer comes off worse than his subject. At least Warne hasn't squandered his talent so utterly as Barry does in writing about him.

Sydney Morning Herald October 2006

SHANE WARNE

Genius?

In Robert Musil's *The Man Without Qualities,* the anti-hero Ulrich famously abandons his ambitions of becoming a great man upon reading a newspaper article referring to 'A Racehorse of Genius'. Why, he reasons, strive to achieve genius, in a world where even a horse can attain it?

Ulrich would surely be baffled to find the word 'genius' routinely bandied about in the context of Shane Warne, for not even the cricketer would lay claim to 'inborn exalted intellectual power'. Simon Wilde at least qualifies it here with 'flawed', although I'm not sure why. Genius has nothing to do with character: Mozart and Einstein weren't 'flawed geniuses' because of their personal indiscretions. Warne is better fitted by an acknowledgment of his 'talent', which the OED defines as 'a particular faculty, regarded as something divinely entrusted to him or her for use and improvement'.

As talents go, of course, Warne's is mighty big, and Wilde, hard-working cricket correspondent for London's *Sunday Times,* here does a solid job of appreciating and describing it. Some lazy and inept books have been published about Warne in recent years – Louis Nowra's clippings job, Paul Barry's hatchet job – but Wilde guides the reader through the intricacies of his craft perhaps better than any previous writer: Terry Jenner describes his unconventional loose grip, Jack Potter his unorthodox finger configuration, Ian Healy how he kept to him, Nasser Hussain how he batted against him.

Review of *Shane Warne: Portrait of a Flawed Genius* by Simon Wilde (John Murray, 2007)

Wilde, as befits a journalist whose pressbox nickname is 'Oscar', turns a nice phrase himself. Where his spin bowling predecessor Peter Taylor 'wore his shirts buttoned to the wrist and looked as though life in a bank would be far too racy for him', Warne 'seemed to love the warm glow of celebrity like a cat asleep in front of a fire'. Wilde conjectures thoughtfully that 'orchestrated sledging' has increased since 'the physical threat from hostile fast bowling subsided', and speculates that 1970s audiences might not have been as spellbound by Warne as those of the 1990s because television coverage was then too primitive to act as a kind of secondary elucidation of his abilities.

On the matter of Warne's psychology, Wilde seems to me less convincing. He hypothesises in chapter one that Warne's propensity for getting caught *in flagrante* became a 'creative spur', and that 'the more trouble he got into, the more he seemed to want to make amends'. Yet by chapter six he is convinced that Warne 'compartmentalised very well', maintaining a sharp separation between his private and professional lines. It can't really be both. My own feeling is that the bordered, controlled, unpredictable but not especially risky environment of cricket provided Warne with a refuge from the chaos beyond the boundary. That explains why he has continued to ply his trade for Hampshire when his body must be crying out for relief: cricket brings an order to Warne's life, absolving him of the need for complete self-mastery.

Portrait of a Flawed Genius might have benefited from an Australian proof reading. Warne's ex-wife is the former Simone Callahan, not 'Callaghan'; the Australian philosopher is David Stove, not 'David Stone'; Ian Chappell in retirement didn't become 'a vociferous supporter of better treatment of Australia's immigrant communities', but a critic of Australian policies of mandatory detention for refugees. The account of Warne's final Test summer also reads as if composed in haste ('He put absolutely everything into his bowling. Some of the England players had never seen anything like it'), and the conclusion is just a little limp. 'Warne will be OK in the sporting afterlife', Wilde believes. Maybe; maybe not. For all his personal charm and bonhomie, Warne still puts me in mind of Sid 'Mad Mick' Emery, the Australian leg-spinner a hundred years ago who was once counselled: 'If you could control your googly, you would be a great bowler.' Emery replied: 'If I could control myself, I would be a great man.'

The Bulletin July 2007

A CLUTCH OF CHARACTERS

BELINDA CLARK

The Little Mistress

If you were teaching a child to bat, to whom would you turn for a technical template? Tendulkar? Lara? The Waughs? Perhaps a little of each. Alternatively, you could just watch Belinda Clark.

John Harmer would. 'Technically,' he says, 'Belinda is the best player in the world, man or woman.' He may be a little biased: he is coach and Clark captain of Australia's all-conquering women's cricket team, currently defending their World Cup in New Zealand. But fifty-eight-year-old Harmer, a biomechanics expert who coached several district clubs and state junior teams before commencing his present job six years ago, brooks no argument: 'For the size of her body, Belinda gets more power into her strokes than anyone else around. She maximises every ball. She'll be batting for a while, and you think she's 20 or so, but you check and she's 60.'

Harmer can claim some credit for this, of course, but wouldn't want much. A famous cricket yarn involves the young Leonard Hutton's first bat in the nets at Yorkshire, how the county's great coach George Hirst told him: 'There's nowt I can teach thee, lad.' Harmer sometimes feels similarly. 'Belinda's my greatest challenge. If I can keep her challenged, then I know the other players will be.' Fortunately, Clark hungers for challenges. If your image of women's cricketers is as charming amateurs, happy enough to be playing let alone improving, think again. Harmer puts it succinctly: 'Belinda wants to be better every time she bats.'

*

The avidity of Clark's pursuit of excellence can be partly deduced from her record. In Clark's first Test series ten years ago, she averaged 80. She still does. Her 2959 one-day runs, meanwhile, have come at 58. She has been dismissed in single figures once. Yet it's the fastidious perfectionism Harmer describes that clearly marks her out. When Clark takes guard, it must be just so. Always centre. And it must be a neat line. It's annoying when she starts a season with new footwear: if she's unfamiliar with the pattern of the spikes, she might have to scratch away for a while until it's located correctly. The bat, too, must feel right. Any heavier than 2 pounds 4 ounces and her bat speed on the cut and pull might be compromised. It should have a thin cylindrical handle and a single grip: thicker, shaped handles, she believes, subtly alter one's stroke patterns.

Thirty-year-old Clark is a tiny figure, even among a group of women's cricketers, a wiry, angular 162.7 centimetres displacing 54.8 kilograms. But even in a net session and a few minutes of throwdowns, she is manifestly leagues ahead: neat, composed, her timing crisp, her placement freakishly precise. A ball on the hip is clipped square; one a foot shorter a couple of degrees finer; one two feet shorter a little finer still: the way it should be, but usually isn't. You get the impression – as often when watching an outstanding technician – of someone who didn't so much learn cricket as work it out. For batting is Clark's subject as well as her object. Even with her record, she's found room for improvement in the last couple of years. She felt she was cutting in the air: she slightly altered her grip to ensure that her bottom hand didn't grow too influential. She decided to begin manufacturing shots, developing her sweep and lofted slog-sweep. Not that, as she explains, she always needs them: 'I can play most shots, but I won't use them all in a game, which is the bit about batting people forget: you don't need to play thirty shots to be a cricketer; you need to play five or six really well, know when to play them and have the guts to play them.' Simple, really. 'Batting,' wrote Sir Donald Bradman in *The Art of Cricket*, 'is a fascinating art and worth all the study you can give it.' Clark is a disciple of the creed.

*

Invocation of the Don isn't idle: Clark's upbringing actually has a vaguely Bradmanesque quality. When she was growing up with her brother Colin and sisters Helen and Sally, Newcastle High School teachers worried about her. She was always at school at 7.30 a.m., long before the bell, hitting a tennis ball against the wall: was everything all right at home, they wondered? Everything was fine, Belinda explained, except that the garage door and driveway were too small for a full rehearsal of ground strokes.

Walls were handy, too, when her interest in cricket was aroused by watching Colin play first-grade for City in the early eighties. She marked a brick on the side of the family home with an 'x', above an impression of a set of stumps, which she pelted so incessantly from 15 metres that it detached from the mortar. Shades of the Bowral tankstand, and the world's most famous stump-and-golf-ball set.

Yet Clark had to go her own way for a reason: there was no local girls' competition. She had eventually to join City's under-sixteen boys' team, where she felt 'pretty hopeless'. In fact, quite how cricket captivated Clark, eventually eclipsing in appeal the tennis and hockey she played at state junior level, still puzzles her. It was, she suspects, as elemental as its physical sensations: 'It's not the chance of going overseas with it, or playing at Lord's – it's the idea of someone bowling a ball at you. Simple as that: the actual sensation of facing a ball and hitting it is what grabs you. With most sports, the ball is stationary or coming to you on the full. And although there's a bouncing ball in tennis, you're not protecting anything behind you. I actually think that cricket itself is the cornerstone of its own appeal.'

Clark finally found her feet in the micro-environment of indoor cricket at the Howzat Sports Centre; the women's team which included Sally Griffiths, a quick bowler destined to play seven

Tests, was coached by Martin Soper, also coach of Raymond Terrace in the Maitland Cricket Association. Soper was stunned: here was a fourteen-year-old girl who, apparently merely through watching, had already assimilated a technique to die for. 'Belinda was a very good indoor cricketer, but obviously had talents way beyond that,' he recalls. 'Actually, she didn't really know how good she was, although it was pretty obvious to everyone else.' He was already coaching Griffiths privately, and it seemed natural to take the kid along as well.

Recollecting Clark today, the softly spoken Soper still finds her hard to believe. 'She was embarrassing, really,' he says. 'She had a much better technique than anyone I'd ever coached before. I'd coached a lot of first-grade male players, and she had more talent than all of them put together.' When Clark began badgering him for extra sessions, Soper noticed another characteristic: Clark was so relentlessly keen to improve that she was inclined to beat herself up if she failed to fulfil her own expectations. 'She was a perfectionist to her bootlaces,' he recalls. 'If she played a shot that was only ninety per cent correct, say a perfectly placed cover drive that was six inches off the ground, she'd be very disappointed. If anything, in fact, she was too critical of herself, which is something I tried to work on. It's all very well to have high standards, but sometimes if you're too self-critical, you can get down on yourself.'

This is something Clark still wrestles with. Two years ago, Australia's women toured England, and she still sounds dejected about her performances. 'I didn't have a good tour at all,' she says. 'I had fun and the team was very successful, but individually I didn't feel comfortable. I just wasn't as on top of my game as I should have been.' For the record, Clark made 223 one-day runs at 55.8 and 277 Test runs at 69.3. Very disappointing.

*

Soper's coaching was basic and incessant. Clark loved it. 'Martin had a very simple approach,' she recalls. 'Footwork was the most important thing: coming down to the spinners, hitting through the ball, playing correctly. Basically hitting a lot of cricket balls. To me, it was just "play". We weren't necessarily working on something. But later I realised that what he was doing was consolidating a base for me.' She transited through women's junior cricket smoothly, and was capped by the state senior side for January 1991's National Championships in Melbourne.

In a high-visibility sport like men's cricket, rituals of graduation to higher standards are thoroughly evolved. Reputations count. For female cricketers, the process is different. Some of Clark's state team-mates were only names to her, others not even that: 'When I was batting for New South Wales, there were three Australian players in the team, and I didn't know who they were. I batted with one of them at one point and didn't know it, came off and asked who she was. They said: "That's so-and-so, she's an Australian player."' Strangely, though, it helped: 'I didn't stop and think, and because I hadn't thought about it, I wasn't overawed by it.'

Topping the championship averages, Clark found herself in the national team, again a slightly unreal experience. 'One minute I was going to a National Championship for which I thought I was lucky to be selected, next minute I was playing for Australia at Bellerive Oval. I thought: "This is all right. I get to go away and play cricket." Got the tracksuit and the uniform and that was great. Played for Australia, went back to club cricket and thought: "Gee, that was a bit weird wasn't it?"' This weirdness encompassed a century on her Test debut against India from 170 deliveries, and sharing a dressing-room with some legends of the women's game: captain Lyn Larsen, keeper Christina Matthews, quick bowler Debbie Wilson and record-breaking batsman Denise Annetts formed the core of a team that, as Clark puts it, 'never doubted for a moment it would win'.

Men's and women's cricket are similar, however, in another respect: they run in cycles. And a lacklustre 1993 World Cup implied that Australia's top players were ageing. Embodiment of the next generation, Clark succeeded Larsen after the National Championships in Perth in December 1993. But her appointment was overshadowed by the omission of Annetts, who vented her frustrations by alleging that she'd been victimised for being heterosexual and married. As media outlets barely aware that women even played cricket latched onto the whiff of scandal, twenty-three-year-old Clark led Australia to a deflating defeat in the annual Rose Bowl against New Zealand.

'I'm convinced we wouldn't have lost that series but for the Annetts controversy,' says team manager Christina Brierley. 'It was very hard for Belinda. She was the new captain but didn't even get a mention.' Clark is more guarded: 'It had an effect insofar as someone was saying that they'd been left out for reasons other than performance, with the implication that others were being selected for reasons other than performance. People were wondering: "Should I be here, or shouldn't I? Am I here because I can play or not?" I think that, if it had been investigated properly, it would have been seen as untrue, but it put pressure on us, and wasn't enjoyable.'

Media coverage of women's cricket remains problematical. Australia might be world champions but you'd hardly know; hackneyed comparisons with men's cricket continue to abound, exasperating Clark: 'People don't expect Venus Williams to beat Pete Sampras or Cathy Freeman to beat Michael Johnson. It just won't happen. But people always seem to want to know how fast the girls bowl, and whether they'd fit into a men's team. I think it happens more with cricket than other sports, perhaps because people don't see us playing; unlike Venus Williams, who they can see and make judgments about, all they know about us is through newspapers or radio.'

More exposure, though, isn't always better. Five years ago at North Melbourne Cricket Ground, Australia and New Zealand met in a women's Test ruined by rain. A commercial television crew – there for the obligatory 'hey-guys-here's-the-girls-playing-cricket, aren't-they-cute?' stories – had a brainstorm. Footballer Wayne Schwass was on hand; perhaps he could toss the coin so that the winning captain could say they'd bat or bowl? Good for a few seconds' footage anyway. The result of the toss would have to be binding, but that'd be okay, wouldn't it?

Ridiculous, said Clark. Play was impossible, and conditions might change before it commenced. Would they have asked a men's team to make such a stupid gesture? See you later. Clark recalls: 'It was like: "Oh come on, the cameras are here. Surely you're going to bow and scrape." That doesn't make sense to me. You're not doing your sport any favours.'

*

Batting or talking, Clark doesn't mess around. She believes in women's cricket, and in September moved to Melbourne to become Women's Cricket Australia's executive officer. But that was a rational not an emotional decision: 'With most amateur sports, you're required to do more than just play. And although it sounds all warm and wonderful, part of it's selfish. The cold hard facts are that the sport won't exist if you don't put something back into it.' Nor does she want sympathy for women's cricketers who invest so much time for so little reward: 'We're not a group of martyrs. There's actually a helluva lot of reward; it's simply not financial reward.'

What's more, there are benefits to playing as amateurs. No-one hangs around because they've nothing better to do. Everyone on tour is there to enjoy themselves. They're ready, moreover, to make the best of everything, as during the last World Cup three years ago. When Australia arrived in India, it wouldn't stop raining. Confined to a Chennai hotel with no prospect of outdoor training, they transformed it into their own indoor cricket school. They played in the corridors, ran up and down stairs, took aerobics classes, and annexed a conference room for fielding drills: the mirrors down one wall and dangling chandelier had to be avoided. They even did their own laundry, drying clothes by hanging them over lamps: Clark's began smouldering and had to be extinguished.

Australia had the hardest draw – traversing more than 3000 kilometres between eight venues – but took it in their stride. 'It was an advantage in India to be on the move,' says Clark. 'There was no time to get bored or frustrated.' On the field, they were ruthless: English veteran Jan Brittin described them as 'possibly the best women's team ever'. Hapless Denmark were routed by 363 runs: Clark made an unbeaten 229 out of Australia's 3 for 412 in three hours from 155 balls: a women's record. Cup holders England, hosts India and experienced New Zealand were overwhelmed in succession: Clark aggregated 445 runs at 148.

Not everyone was rapt. In Peter Davies' wry tour book, *Mad Dogs and Englishwomen*, England's Clare Connor complains of the Australians: 'They're gobby, they're annoying, they've got shrill voices, they stare you out.' A broad smile creases Clark's face at its mention. 'We found that most amusing,' she says. 'We wanted to know who was shrill, who was gobby, and most importantly who was most annoying.' She composes herself for the formal reply. 'I think that was a clashing of two different ways of playing the game. The Australian game has different traditions to the English game. We certainly don't go out of our way to putting anyone off by attacking them personally, but there's a level of gamesmanship in any international sport because it is international competition and should be pretty fierce.' Then she smiles again: 'If there wasn't that psychological battle going on, it wouldn't be fun to play, would it?' Which is good to know: after all, man cannot live by technique alone, nor woman either.

Inside Sport December 2000

DANIEL VETTORI

Sebastian Flight

On a surface not so much underprepared as orphaned from birth, the Test match at Eden Park should have been a Shane Warne spectacular. It might still turn out that he has something to celebrate if the depression over Auckland, and the one over his head, lift in time.

So far, however, the greatest beneficiary of conditions has been New Zealand's twenty-one-year-old slow-bowling prodigy Daniel Vettori. And his 12–149, establishing him as the youngest man to capture 100 Test wickets, has been an unusually welcome development for a branch of the game that had seemed in steady decline.

The rapture attending the resurgence of wrist spin during the 1990s overshadowed what a grim decade it was for finger spin. Besides the double-jointed Muttiah Muralitharan and the double-dealing Saqlain Mushtaq, few finger spinners prospered anywhere; even India – cradle of Bedi, Prasanna, Venkat and Doshi – ceased producing bowlers of note.

Several factors played their part in this eclipse: covered pitches, a general improvement in defensive techniques (particularly among tail-enders), even the mechanisation of ball manufacture and the obsession with its polishing which produced a shinier sphere far more difficult for a spinner to grip than twenty years earlier.

Wrist spin came back to popularity because it was regarded as an attacking option, but captains increasingly cast orthodox slow bowlers in a containing role. Bowlers like West Indian offie Roger Harper and English left-armer Phil Tufnell, each of whom began their careers with a generous loop, were steadily turned into automata: Harper bowling round-arm at a pace verging on medium, Tufnell looking for footmarks to pitch into from over the wicket. And who wanted to bowl like that?

Vettori, indeed, did not embark on his cricket as a slow bowler; at St Paul's Collegiate School he was a batsman who bowled medium-pacers. The flirtation with spin began after he cracked two vertebrae in a road accident in August 1994 and renounced his seamers so as not to jeopardise his convalesence. It became an infatuation when he toured England with a New Zealand Youth team a couple of years later. Recognition then came with breath-taking swiftness; he was capped by his country just three weeks after his first-class debut.

With a name like Vettori, he should probably be singing arias or fighting bulls. Instead, with his unruly hair and willowy physique, he has the air of a 1920s Oxford aesthete; perhaps he should be nicknamed Sebastian Flight. The spectacles, meanwhile, suggest Bill Gates' kid brother.

Vettori's virtues as a bowler are his height, his attacking line, and his artful use of the crease's full width. He experimented last season with the over-the-wicket style, pecking away at leg stump, but has not repeated it since; indeed, he probably bowls as slowly as anyone for the last decade. He can be patient, as on Monday morning when the roller briefly stifled some of the pitch's fire, and stoical under fire, as he displayed during Justin Langer's attempts to belt him out of the attack. The Eden Park Test will end today, one way or other, but we might still be watching this delightful bowler in 2020.

Wisden Online February 2000

MATTHEW MAYNARD
Lost and Found

Visiting London briefly a short while ago, I decided to make a pilgrimage to Lord's for a day of county cricket. Arriving just before lunch, I paid my nine quid, ran foul of a surly jobsworth for sitting in the wrong precinct of the ground, retreated to the Grand Stand with twenty other forbearing souls, and watched rain fall intermittently for the rest of the day. Not a ball was bowled. The public address was, of course, quiet as the tomb. I bought some food: it was inedible. I tried to call a friend: the payphone disobligingly ate my coins. I guess the counties would like people to continue patronising first-class cricket – but they *do* have a funny way of showing it.

It's Matthew Maynard's misfortune that his career has been confined almost completely to such cheerless environs, and it stands to his credit that he has batted throughout those sixteen years with such unfailing brio. Not that Maynard views his paltry four Test caps with regret: his autobiography – an understated and undemanding read that rather belies its title – resolutely repeats that he is content with his lot. In that sense, it may be that *On the Attack* is unconsciously self-revelatory. If Maynard truly feels that he 'achieved far more than I ever thought possible when I started my career' and that 'my lease was always going to be a short one', then it may explain why his appearances at the top level were so few. You wouldn't catch an Aussie writing a book like this. But then, perhaps an Aussie with Maynard's gifts wouldn't have had to.

Review of *On the Attack: The Batsman's Story* by Matthew Maynard (Mainstream, 2001)

On the Attack commences by revisiting Maynard's thwarted international career, with special attention on his last tour, to the West Indies seven years ago. After a promising beginning to that trip, Maynard fell by the wayside, scorned by a coach in Keith Fletcher prone to 'kicking us when he should have been looking to pick us up'. He is critical, too, of 'a selection system which gave too many players too few chances' and of 'a selfishness within the dressing-room'. There is a hint here of disappointment, but just as quickly we're assured that 'I do not regard my career as a failure' and 'when I look back on my career in retirement there will be no regrets'. And we're assured of it again and again. It does seem at least paradoxical that an autobiography should contain such sentiments as 'there is nothing to be gained from looking back', and 'all that matters is the future' – if so, where is the point of the book?

Maynard does get steamed in discussing his relations with Glamorgan's committee, which he candidly admits precipitated his resignation as captain last year. This is all mildly interesting, though it is hard to conceive of anyone east of Abergavenny caring much about such localised disturbances. More illuminating are Maynard's reminiscences of three formative influences: Javed Miandad, Viv Richards and Duncan Fletcher. Remember the days when English cricket was purportedly being worm-eaten from within by imported internationals? Maynard remembers them rather differently.

Paul Rees is not an interventionist ghost, although he has Maynard using words like 'vituperative' and speaking of 'the dark recesses of the committee labyrinth'. The collaborators should also have consulted their copy of the Laws, because Maynard perpetuates the common misconception that 'the LBW law states that any benefit of the doubt has to be given to the batsman.' Oh no it doesn't.

Nonetheless, Rees has a good ear for stories, and there are some nice lines threaded throughout the book. Glamorgan's president Gerard Elias once asked Tony Cottey why he was so inconsistent. Cottey's reply was the only one possible: 'If I knew that, I wouldn't be.' Also worth committing to memory is the response of Glamorgan's young keeper Mark Wallace to a verbal going-over by Nottinghamshire's Paul Franks: 'There are ten blokes in our dressing-room who cannot stand you. Stop being a prat or you will make it eleven.' It may be a shame for Maynard that he was not possessed of quite the same stuff.

Wisden Cricket Monthly August 2001

BRIAN LARA

First among Unequals

No talent is so efflorescent, no burden so exquisite, as that of a great player in a mediocre team. Yet batting's old and new blue-riband holders, Allan Border and Brian Lara, show how the same challenge is not always met equally. Border was the bravest batsman of his generation, a boulder-like presence in Australia's middle order set always to sell his wicket dearly; no captain has been as reluctant, then as respected. Lara, who overhauled Border's 11,174 runs at Adelaide Oval on 26 November 2005, is the boldest batsman of his era, a creature of impulse, pricing his wicket exorbitantly one day, cheaply the next, and a captain who coveted the office then cast it aside.

Lara seized the commanding heights during an innings of 226 amid a total of 405. It was his eighth double hundred, and scarcely in doubt once he had passed 50. It also followed ten international innings worth 148 runs, and came amid the 58th Test defeat Lara has experienced. The West Indies are a unique phenomenon in international cricket: a region competing among nations, a remnant of hopes for a union that never happened. Its star batsman reflects its modern reality: he is a source of hope *and* disunity, a lonely island of excellence in a bedraggled archipelago.

Lara the cricketer came into a rich inheritance: the team into which he first slotted fifteen years ago was as heavy with talent and honours as any in history. From his nickname, the Prince, can be inferred the expectations held for him; from the fact that he has kept the nickname can be inferred his failure to mature. In 1994, Lara scaled the twin peaks of the highest Test and first-class scores;

yet by 1995, he had decided that cricket was 'ruining my life'. His attitude to playing under others was such that it became difficult to appoint anyone else as the West Indies' leader, yet it turned out that he could not do it all on his own: the world's most successful batsman will go down as one of its least successful captains, ten victories in which he averaged more than 80 being offset by the twenty-three defeats in which he averaged less than 40.

Lara's batting has changed little, at least in intent. When Sachin Tendulkar's innings in recent years have been epics of self-mastery, Lara remains a slave to his passions. 'Nascitur non fit' is the title of the chapter in C. L. R. James' *Beyond a Boundary* that concerns the first great West Indian batsman George Headley: 'Born not made'. The same applies to Lara, both in the sense of innate talent and impulsive prodigality.

It is possible to forget while watching Lara how much West Indian cricket has changed in his watch – but never, ultimately, for all that long. And therein lies perhaps the chief difference between Lara and the batsman whose mantle he has inherited. Border set himself second throughout his career, and still does; on the eve of losing the record, he described Lara as 'so much better than I could have hoped to be'. Lara is a born egotist. Border set an example Australian team-mates could emulate; West Indian team-mates emulate Lara at their peril. Border brought his country's cricket with him, creating an environment in which others could succeed him; that Lara will be irreplaceable is a mark of his strengths *and* his shortcomings.

Wisden Cricketer January 2006

BILLY BOWDEN

Billy the Kidder

'The umpire at cricket is like the geyser in the bathroom; we cannot do without it, yet we notice it only when it is out of order.'

When Sir Neville Cardus penned these words many years ago, he clearly never foresaw an umpire like New Zealand's all-action Billy Bowden. In an age where technology seems to be reducing umpires to ball counters and cap racks, he enlivened the last two Tests of Australia's absorbing series with India with a pageant of ebullient gestures and idiosyncratic signals.

To give batsmen out, forty-year-old Bowden flourishes a right forefinger that is cocked, as if round a revolver's trigger. When fours and sixes are scored, he seems to have difficulty keeping both feet on the ground, adopting poses associated more often with ballet dancers and flamingos. Bowden was even in the thick of celebrations when Steve Waugh played his last day of Test cricket on Tuesday, laying a heartfelt hug on the valedictee, giving him one of the stumps he'd souvenired, and prowling round the presentation ceremony snapping off photos like a paparazzo.

From the son of a Baptist minister from Auckland who is himself a practising Christian, one might have expected officiation with a more ecclesiastical air. But the sense of play is partly an expression of gratitude that he is involved in cricket at all. Like the greatest of English umpires Frank Chester, who turned to umpiring after doctors amputated a wounded arm at Salonika during the First World War, Bowden is making up for the playing career he never had. He was a promising slow bowler when struck down at twenty-one by a virus that left him with rheumatoid arthritis too excruciating to play with; he still finds it uncomfortable to cradle sweaters.

Bowden, of course, is hardly the first umpire with a distinctive manner; he is not even the only one on the International Cricket Council panel. David Shepherd signals leg byes with a distinctive chorus-line kick; Srinivasaraghavan Venkataraghavan's manner of giving batsmen out has been likened to flushing an old-fashioned toilet. Steve Bucknor, meanwhile, has attracted attention for the very opposite reasons to Bowden, maintaining a manner as inscrutable as a cigar-store Indian.

The difference is that Bowden's act is self-aware. He is there, he says, 'to enjoy it and entertain the crowd'. In doing so, he has courted criticism, both in his home country and in England, where *Test Match Special* commentator Graeme Fowler remarked severely: 'The umpire's job is to control the game. It is not a stepping stone to make himself famous.' Bowden's saving grace is that he does control the game. In Sydney, his eleventh Test since a first appointment at Auckland in February 2000, he had about as good a game as an umpire could have. Captains Waugh and Sourav Ganguly saluted his performance, while Sachin Tendulkar presented him with a signed shirt – quite a gesture to the umpire who gave him out first ball caught down the leg side in Melbourne.

The challenge for Bowden, however, will be maintaining that standard, for his manner invites the aspersion often cast on charismatic politicians, that he is all personality and no policy. The glut of international cricket and the slow-motion surveillance of their decisions has placed officials under unprecedented strain. The tendency seems to be for umpires on the ICC Panel to have a couple of good years then go off the boil somewhat, worn down by long days and long journeys – Bowden was back on duty yesterday in Christchurch in a one-day international between New Zealand and Pakistan. And while Cardus's dictum that umpires are noticed only when wrong might now be obsolete, in the era of the replay the umpire can now be wrong over and over again.

The Sunday Age January 2004

DARRELL HAIR

The Lightning Rod

Jack Fingleton once jested that Test cricket umpires were the world's most powerful individuals, able with the motion of a finger to send one nation into ecstasy, and pitch another into mourning. It is a job for nerves of steel and a heart of flint – and, whatever else may be said about him, Darrell Hair has both.

The shambling, ursine Hair, from Orange, rose faster through umpiring than through playing ranks. He plateaued as a pace bowler at grade level, but was given the first of seventy-six Test appointments at Test level in Adelaide in January 1992 three years after his initial appearance in the Sheffield Shield. Hair struck observers at once with his no-nonsense demeanour and cast-iron certainties – in an era, moreover, where the cumulative effects of television, the introduction of the third umpire and the ICC referee were making umpiring calls look like mere bases for negotiation.

Hair's physique these days has a touch of Warwick Armstrong; so, increasingly, does his insouciance. Just as well: at one time or other, he has aroused the indignation of almost every cricket nation. South Africans sang a song exhorting him to 'put your finger elsewhere' after his decisions in the Adelaide Test of January 1994. Englishmen were dumbfounded by his refusal to involve the third umpire in a run-out involving Mark Taylor at Sydney a year later that replays showed was out. Indians took such exception to his decision-making when they played New South Wales in Sydney in December 1999 that Sourav Ganguly stood mid-pitch ostentatiously watching replays on the big screen; he, Venkat Prasad and Javagal Srinath were reported for dissent to team management, who declined to act. Hair even tackled West Indian supporters who stormed onto the ground at Antigua when Brian Lara passed the Test record score. 'Darrell Hair was flapping because the crowd were running all over the pitch,' recalls Mike Atherton in *Opening Up* (2002). 'He grabbed the spectator nearest to him by the scruff of the neck and gave him a roasting.'

Hair's rigid, perhaps puritan, stance on Law 24, and his public proscription of Muttiah Muralitharan in the Boxing Day Test of 1995, have also alienated Sri Lankans; Zimbabweans, puzzled by his calling Grant Flower in September 2000; and Pakistanis, aggrieved even before the Oval Test by his querying the actions of Shoaib Akhtar in November 1999 and Shabbir Ahmed in January 2004. 'You're messing with my career, Darrell,' complained Mark Ramprakash after Hair had given him out caught at the wicket at Lord's eight years ago: the burden of potentially doing so, however, does not look to worry him. He has become, in fact, rather more an umpire's umpire than a player's umpire, supported by his brethren, if not by administrators. 'Darrell's opportunities for umpiring on the international circuit have been severely restricted – and his earning capacity reduced,' wrote David Shepherd in his autobiography *Shep* (2001). 'To me, he's a strong, courageous and very good international umpire.'

As evinced by his own autobiography *Decision Maker* (1999), Hair is not just strong on the field; he also knows no inhibition where his public accusations are concerned. Not only did he criticise Muralitharan for having a 'diabolical action', but the Sri Lankan team for being 'determined to isolate and intimidate me', and the ICC and the Australian Cricket Board for not standing four-square behind him. He was then behind a confrontation with members of the Pakistan management team before the CUB Series in January 2000, when he challenged them to stand behind imputations of racism made against Australian officials, further irking his employers. Squeezed from the inaugural elite umpiring panel in 2002, he was nonetheless squeezed back in when the panel was expanded the following year. In the wake of incidents at the Oval, Hair signified a new approach by offering to resign in return for a severance payment. Its outcome was no more satisfactory, and in some respects less: the ICC piously released the contents of his emails. In fact, they revealed nothing except that Hair does feel the public odium, and that the modern umpire is a man under pressures unimaginable a generation ago.

One of the most memorable episodes in Hair's career was umpiring with Dickie Bird in his final Test, at Lord's in July 1996, with its lavish displays of public and professional affection. In the age of umpiring 'entertainers' like Bird and Bowden, his officiating fashion can look old-fashioned. He isn't pally with players. He has no endearing mannerisms, like Venkat's chain-flush out or Bucknor's nod. But he has taken Fingleton's jest a little further, with a gesture of his hands proving able to plunge the cricket world into dismay.

Cricinfo Magazine September 2006

A PACKET OF MATCHES

PERTH 1997

Nasty, Brutish and Short

Want to believe? It would have taken a brave West Indian fan to trust anyone after the fiasco at Adelaide Oval. Nonetheless, on a Perth pitch no-one liked the look of and in an atmosphere no-one liked the sound of, Brian Lara's team took only three days to mangle Mark Taylor's Australians by 10 wickets, closing their hosts' margin of series victory to 3–2. The co-conspirators, as ever, were Curtly Ambrose and Courtney Walsh, who ignored groin and hamstring strains to bowl at speeds that bordered on the supernatural.

The game's biggest mystery was how its pitch, once as hard and flat as marble, ended up like crazy paving. Portentous cracks on the first morning had by the third day, in airless, forty-degree heat, come to resemble ugly surgical scars. But the association was saved further scrutiny by the brevity of the match, and the elongated inquests into ill feeling between the sides, touched off by Lara's claims that the Australians picked-on opener Robert Samuels, and Taylor's counterclaims that Lara was 'an antagonist'. This tit-for-tat tittle-tattle culminated when Lara, a provocative choice as runner to Walsh on the last morning, collided with close fielder Matt Hayden and went down like Diego Maradona looking for a penalty: which perhaps he was, although referee Peter van der Merwe levied no fines. The umpires Willey and Hair then did something that umpires might profitably do more often: called both captains into conclave, and asked them to calm their teams. The game proceeded after a perfunctory but meaningful handshake.

Ambrose bowled wonderfully from the first on a pitch tailored for his talents. Hayden's loose defensive shot to the match's third ball arced to slip, and Taylor's ruinous run continued courtesy of Chanderpaul, who leapt left to arrest a screaming square drive at point then hit the stumps from his supine position: a superstitious man might by now have begun to imagine conspiracy theories. Mark Waugh and Michael Bevan added 110 between lunch and tea with panache and pluck, but a rehydrated Ambrose expunged Waugh, Healy and Reiffel in twenty minutes after the interval, and Bishop quelled the rest. Both bowlers looked all the better for some thoughtful captaincy: Ambrose bowled his 18 overs in seven spells, Bishop his 18 in nine.

A troubled start to the West Indies' reply seemed to ease when Warne initiated a ball change, and Lara finally endowed summer with a Test century – his eighth, and first in seventeen months. Making up for in mettle what he lacked in method, the reinstated Samuels lasted five-and-a-half hours, although three minutes of this was consumed by the third umpire in deliberating on a direct hit run-out that no racing steward could have separated. Tempers frayed in the enervating heat, McGrath becoming fractious with Samuels and Warne with Hooper, though the only censure they incurred was Lara's, who accused the Worrell Trophy custodians of 'rubbing it in' – something which used to be a West Indian prerogative. Otherwise, Lara kept his cool by hitting 90 in boundaries, and at one stage 26 in 14 Warne deliveries; the second new ball did not put down the insurrection until the visitors' lead was 141 on a pitch now playing at wildly varying altitudes. Ambrose sounded the Australian retreat, blowing the captain away with a lifter, and tunnelling beneath Blewett with a shooter. Walsh then rose from the treatment table to dismiss the Waughs in consecutive overs after lunch, and only a few tail-end strokes followed Hayden's failure to offer, the West Indies' final chase needing no more than three-quarters of an hour.

Despite the compression of play, the Test produced enough paranormal phenomena to merit investigation by Agents Scully and Mulder. Walsh batted with a runner, then bowled 20 overs for 5 wickets – shades of Kapil Dev, 1981. Shane Warne bowled a bouncer to Lara – shades of Phil Edmonds, 1983. Australia's Adelaide match-winner Bevan barely bowled – shades of Allan Border, 1989. Ambrose was run out on the third morning by Healy's back-handed flick, his bat having lodged in one of the pitch's crevices; his valedictory over then took 15 deliveries – two more than Gubby Allen's infamous Old Trafford over in 1934. In all, in fact, the series was swollen by 43 overs of illegitimate deliveries: West Indies 147 no balls and 20 wides; Australia 88 no balls and 3 wides. It was the West Indies' fifth consecutive WACA win, and the fourth in the last ten Worrell Trophy matches to finish inside three days: a comment on the quality of their pace bowling and the inadequacy of pitch preparation, or perhaps defensive frailties revealed and attention spans shortened by one-day cricket. Take your pick. The truth is out there.

Test Match Year 1996–97

THE 1997 ASHES

The View from Couch Central

Winter 1997 in Australia offered two enticing competitions: one traditional, in the form of the Ashes, the other newer but growing more familiar, of Cricket versus the Rest of the World of Sport. Arriving at Heathrow in May, Mark Taylor's men could be confident they had England's measure. But could they prevail in the battle for column inches and screen time against Australian Rules football, two loggerheaded Rugby League competitions, a Bledisloe Cup, World Youth Soccer, Wimbledon, sundry Grand Prix, three US golf majors and a British Open?

As it happened, they more than punched their weight – if in a fashion quite impossible to forecast. For not only did the Ashes campaign prove quite the most entertaining of the last decade, but dressing-room dramas and commercial argy-bargy exerted a critical influence on the way events were seen – and on the way they weren't.

The preliminaries were inauspicious. After cut-throat series against West Indies and South Africa, few journalists were enthused by the prospect of watching Australia mete out six of the best to an English side incapable of matching Zimbabwe six months before. Writers at the *Australian*, in particular, left little doubt of their voting intentions at a future plebiscite on an Australian republic. 'It is difficult to understand why England is still so widely-regarded as a champagne series,' griped its correspondent, Malcolm Conn. 'Playing the beleaguered Poms is cheap and unfulfilling.' Columnist Mike Coward was even more damning: 'Apart from sentiment and tradition, England has nothing to do with cricket's real world at the end of the twentieth century.' Sentiment and tradition, of course, being things cricket should have no truck with. But perhaps they were merely echoing some of their own players. In a pre-tour interview with the *ABC Cricket Magazine,* Mark Waugh likewise prophesied a walkover: 'They [England] just haven't got the toughness you need to win Test cricket consistently. Man-for-man they are not that far behind us, but they lack hunger.'

One dissonant note as the tourists arrived was the captain's protracted spell in the batting dumps, which caused Ron Reed of the *Herald Sun* to liken the team to a Formula One racing car with a loose steering wheel. Among those urging Taylor to fall on his Stuart Surridge were an unlikely coalition of former coach Bob Simpson and the brothers Chappell. Greg of that ilk even turned amateur psychologist in the *Sunday Herald Sun,* contending that Taylor was 'in no fit state to carry on' and a 'classic case of denial' – the curly thing about denial being that it is supremely awkward to deny.

Taylor's redemptive 129 at Edgbaston a week later, consequently, became the greatest cricketing comeback since Graham Gooch's hair. 'Edge of abyss to the highest peak' shrieked the front page of Melbourne's *Herald Sun,* while beneath ran reams from a breathless Reed: 'Of all the many thousands of runs that have been scored in 120 years and 287 games of Test cricket between Australia and England, no more emotional shot has been played than the gentle push for a single that took Mark Taylor to his century at Edgbaston.' More inside singing Taylor's praises demonstrated that, while a week may be a long time in politics, 397 minutes with 13 fours and a six is a veritable cricketing eternity. The story of virtue triumphant came complete with several juicy subplots: it emerged that another Australian sporting icon, Olympic swimmer Kieren Perkins, had spurred Taylor with an inspirational fax; and that Taylor's wife Judy had cleaned up by standing by her man at the betting tent. Even more lavish praise flowed on the broadsheet editorial pages of the *Australian,* where its venerable columnist Frank Devine explored parallels between Taylor's innings and

Gary Cooper in *High Noon*, with its 'eerily topical' theme tune: 'If I'm a man I must be brave/And I must face the deadly killer/ Or lie a coward, a craven coward/Or lie a coward in my grave.'

Taylor's new lease on life – and, indeed, England's – was by now competing for space with a brewing local controversy over the maltreatment of Test match telecasts by the owner of free-to-air rights: Kerry Packer's mighty Nine Network. Rather than disrupt its primetime schedules, Nine had elected to take up broadcasts after lunch, leaving full service in the hands of pay-TV carrier Optus Vision and ABC Radio. Those turning on their televisions to verify Australia's 8 for 54 on the first day would instead have seen the celebrity panellists of the *Footy Show* interviewing a touring troupe of sumo wrestlers.

Nine defended itself on ratings grounds, CEO David Leckie telling the *Herald Sun*: 'You cannot disregard the viewers who choose to watch your regular programming week-in, week-out and who would be appalled.' But an Australian's television is his castle, and commercial considerations carried no weight when the *Age* published a vox pop from prominent Australians. 'No wonder Michael Jordan is number-one hero to our schoolchildren,' blustered Victorian Sports Minister Tom Reynolds.

Nine could claim victory at the box office, where its evening ratings remained consistently strong. But as a piece of public relations, it ranked with Union Carbide at Bhopal. McGrath's opening salvoes at Lord's and Jason Gillespie's lethal 7–37 at Leeds, for instance, were supplanted by such telefodder as *Butterbox Babies, All-American Murder* and *Television: The Way We Were.* And of Steve Waugh's Manchester majesty, Nine's viewers saw nothing at all: the Test had been dumped on an unwilling ABC to make way for the broadcast of rain from Wimbledon. But the *pièce de résistance* was Nine's approach to the last day of the Fourth Test: it featured live coverage of one delivery, an apparent sign-off from anchorman Greg Ritchie, a ten-minute ad break and, unannounced, a replay of the first session. As 'You've Lost Us' of Barooga commented in the *Herald Sun*: 'Great work with the cricket, Channel Nine. Now can we look forward to seeing the last ten minutes of a movie before you show the beginning?'

Australia's eventual retention of the Ashes restored the cheery mood, Devine of the *Australian* again leading the salaams for Taylor after seeing him *en famille* amid his Trent Bridge triumph: 'It is hard to think of a more resplendent demonstration of masculinity.' No motorcades this time, but Prime Minister John Howard and Kerry Packer lent support at a 12 September Taylor tribute luncheon.

In all the on- and off-field theatre, however, probably winter's most significant story was overlooked. As the First Test unfolded, the respected *Sunday Age* correspondent Mark Ray reported that Australian Test cricketers had, under the auspices of their new Australian Cricketers' Association, recently contemplated strike action 'as part of a fight for better pay and conditions with the Australian Cricket Board'. Rather remarkably, no member of the travelling troupe in England elected to pursue the story. But, as the 1997–98 season dawned, the alert was sounded again by the *Australian*'s well-informed Coward, who warned on 4 October that 'a perceived militancy among Australia's leading cricketers is creating a sense of uncertainty and confusion among the directors and management of the ACB.' Another new-fashioned contest may be brewing to take our minds off the old.

Wisden Cricketers' Almanack 1998

WORLD CUP 1999

One-Day Best

In the aftermath of Australia's transfixing tie with South Africa in the World Cup semi-final, a stray remark of Steve Waugh's caught the ear: the captain described the game as 'the best I've ever played in'.

The comment wasn't inappropriate in the context of a match that finished amid as much confusion as an expressway pile-up, and was of a type to which sportsmen are prone in the aftermath of drama: Waugh described the Third Test of the recent series in the Caribbean in exactly the same terms.

Nonetheless, Steve Waugh is cricket's young fogey, the man with the baggy green scalp – and here he was valuing above all other games in a fourteen-year career a contest involving cricket's limited-overs variant: a form of the game deplored by connoisseurs as, to quote Frank Devine in the *Australian* four months ago, 'so perverse, boring and grisly that it might have been designed by George Orwell's Big Brother to turn people into mindless zombies.' To traditionalists, it was like hearing Jack Nicklaus nominate as his favourite sporting memory a round on a mini-golf course, his favourite shot a particularly cheeky chip through the little windmill.

From its inception thirty-six years ago, in response to flagging support for the English first-class game, one-day cricket has been a financial success. 'A triumphant sporting experiment', said Peter Wilson of the inaugural Gillette Cup final. Others resented cricket's *nouveau riche* upstart, such as Sir Neville Cardus, who dismissed it as 'slogget' and 'snicket'. Cricketers were often equally dismissive.

Players with some counties took perverse pleasure in early elimination from one-day competitions so they could devote themselves to the serious longer forms.

They had a point, too. Compressed cricket can be, and often is, dreary to play. Bowlers can bowl only a fixed number of overs; they must channel their attack to avoid proscription of wides; they must watch snicks fly through depopulated slip field; they must see their figures distorted when they are delegated the closing overs. Batsmen, while at liberty to bat for the duration of an innings, are often forced to sacrifice themselves for the sake of the run rate. As Peter Roebuck puts it: 'In Tests, the players dictate the course of the game; in one-day cricket, the game is the boss.'

Thus the ambivalent embrace of the format by the Test-playing nations when they convened for the first World Cup twenty-four years ago. As great a batsman as Sunil Gavaskar signified his contempt for the format by batting through a 60-over innings for 36 not out, while even compliments had a back-handed quality. 'I think one-day cricket has its place,' said Ian Chappell, 'and we all quite enjoy it.'

Once released from the bottle, however, the one-day genie could not be contained, and two years later placed itself at the service of a market-savvy master. Kerry Packer's World Series Cricket obtained its centrifugal energy from a circuit of constant one-day games, increasingly played at night, in coloured garb and using a white ball. Administrators belatedly grasped one-day cricket's potential, and the form's unchecked spread is reflected in the statistic that, on the first Saturday of this Cup, the number of one-day internationals played exceeded the number of Tests. International teams have now met 1484 times over the short course in fewer than thirty years, 1454 in the long format over more than 120 years.

Such a statistic would not so long ago have produced widespread lamentation about cricket catering to the plebeian palate, like a poll revealing that more people can quote readily from *Seinfeld* than from Shakespeare. But this Cup has disarmed critics for the reason it excited Steve Waugh, tackling habitual complaints head-on with cricket of a wild, woolly, sharp-edged, shape-changing kind.

One-day cricket's weakness has been its regimentation: batsmen attack, bowlers contain, audiences cheer, commentators fake it. John Arlott once registered his detestation of his country's Sunday League by feigning sleep at the microphone during one match, finally rousing himself to grumble: 'The last four overs were non-descript and did not deserve comment.' Conventional wisdom has been that the ideal team is composed of a few outstanding attacking batsmen, a spring-heeled fielding side and a bunch of medium-pace automata who can slog effectually in the closing overs.

This World Cup, however, was anything but predictable: Bangladesh beat Pakistan; Zimbabwe routed South Africa; teams recovered regularly from seemingly impossible positions. Captaincy, which in one-day cricket often appears as if it could be delegated to a lower primate, was an intellectual challenge – so much so that when South Africa's Hansie Cronje appeared to be talking to an imaginary friend, he was, in fact, in cahoots with his coach Bob Woolmer via an earpiece.

Above all, on English pitches and with a white Duke ball that deviated sharply off the seam, bowlers became more than harmless drudges, trying to get batsmen out, stretching for the maximum effort, willing to barter wickets for runs. Almost 1000 runs and extra deliveries were given up in wides and no-balls, although they were worth straining for: 375 of them were donated by the finalists Australia and Pakistan. There was no use just hanging on hoping for the best: the most economical team in runs per over, the West Indies, didn't make the Super Six stage of the tournament. Spinners, once considered *de trop* in one-day cricket, were here *de rigueur.* Only one spinner took more than 8 wickets in the 1992 Cup; in the 1999 Cup, Shane Warne and Saqlain Mushtaq took 37 wickets between them. England, without a spinner, joined the West Indies on the sidelines in the Super Sixes.

In the unexpected position of having to earn their runs, some outsized batting reputations were scaled down. South Africa's Gary

Kirsten, who averaged 79 on the pebbledash pitches of India during the 1996 Cup, averaged 25 in England – probably a truer reflection of his talents. Alert fielding, meanwhile, was a prerequisite of this tournament rather than an advantage. After 63 run-outs in thirty-seven matches, there were only 49 in forty-two games in 1999: a function of bowlers' increased penetration, and less ambitious running between wickets. The most influential fielding effort was error not excellence: Herschelle Gibbs' bid for immortality at Headingley, when he dropped Steve Waugh, and perhaps also the Cup.

Above all, we savoured the exotic and incongruous sensation of one-day cricket that resembled the genuine article – subtly balanced, overflowing with skills, ebbing and flowing, rushing and decelerating. Incongruous because this contradicts another wisdom, latterly conventional among administrators, that the short and long forms of the game should be as distinct as soccer and Subbuteo. 'We're in the entertainment business,' said the Australian Cricket Board's CEO Graham Halbish four years ago. 'We believe that one-day cricket is a form of pure entertainment provided for the enjoyment of the public.' None of the Cup's best games – Australia's tie, its first meeting with Pakistan, South Africa's courageous comebacks, the boil-overs of Bangladesh and Zimbabwe – looked anything like 'pure entertainment' provided for something as vague as 'enjoyment'. Such spectacle as they contained was mixed with the dour and the dogged, the grim and the chaotic: in this way, they were as nuanced and textured as the best Tests.

A television audience of two billion tuned in for the final, which regrettably disintegrated into a walkover: always a risk in a game without Test cricket's opportunity for second innings redemption. The point, however, had already been made: the phrase 'memorable one-day match' is no longer an oxymoron. Just ask Steve Waugh.

The Age June 1999

DAY 5 THE OVAL 2001

As Good as It Gets

While England's cricketers pondered the enticements of India yesterday morning, Steve Waugh was being interviewed by Channel Four as though he was a visitor from the planet Krypton. How did Australia's captain explain his staggering return to the colours in this Test, from what his interlocutor made sound like the brink of death, though was actually a calf injury? Waugh made it sound compellingly simple. 'I'm a professional cricketer and I love playing for Australia,' he said. 'What else was I going to do?'

What indeed? Yesterday provided another reason why he loves it too: a performance of aggressive bowling and out-cricket at concert pitch. When Adam Gilchrist preached the doctrine of attacking cricket after defeat at Headingley, it seemed a little guileless. When Steve Waugh practised it at the Oval, it appeared altogether intimidating.

Although the English batsmen looked peeved to have been called out on a Bank Holiday, it was another day at the office for Waugh, inhibitingly close to silly point throughout. Hussain drove his first ball off the back foot into his rival's ankle – Waugh did not move, let alone flinch. Ramprakash did the same – Waugh this time barely blinked. Both batsmen fell with the surrounding convention of fielders very much in mind, Hussain playing pad first, Ramprakash trying to steer a leg break to safety.

Stewart later repeated the error, holding his bat from harm but neglecting his stumps. With others, there was justification for Homer Simpson's dictum: 'Trying is just the first step to failure.' Afzaal lit on the vaguest evidence of a half-volley and skewered it to slip. Occasionally, between overs, as he swapped from helmet to cap, Australia's captain was seen bare-headed. It looked odd, like a clean-shaven Groucho Marx or Buddy Holly wearing contacts. But then the headgear, and the pressure, came back on.

So the Australians made a little more history. The Oval was English cricket's final fastness – Australia had not won here since 1972 – yet it fell like all the citadels before it. Rather like the Perth Test of February 1995, where the euphoria of an English win in the previous match lingered no longer than the next Australian innings, the conclusion was sadly anti-climactic. Never mind that Stewart and Gough are suddenly shy of going to India; a few others in this Test have made cases for a winter free of cricket employment.

Where there's history, there has all summer been Warne (31 wickets for the series) and McGrath (32 wickets). They find it difficult to do anything these days without setting a record of some sort, especially with whole websites now devoted to instances of five-wickets-or-more-by-bowlers-favouring-floppy-hats and rejected-LBW-appeals-by-cricketers-with-surnames-containing-two-or-more-vowels.

Yesterday's landmarks, though, were not insignificant. By dismissing Ramprakash, Warne passed Curtly Ambrose's wicket total, moving to fifth on the Test list. By dismissing Afzaal, McGrath left Dennis Lillee behind, moving to second on the Australian list. It is strange that we think of bowling partnerships only in terms of new-ball attacks: Hall and Griffith, Lindwall and Miller et al. In fact, with both Warne and McGrath in his charge, Steve Waugh has had perhaps the ideal coupling, covering all possible conditions and contingencies.

Warne and McGrath have performed their prodigies, moreover, with little support. Brett Lee has been a failure and, after bowling skilfully for the first three Tests, Jason Gillespie has looked in need of the shade of a coolabah tree. More prolonged resistance from England's batsmen might have tested the robustness of the four-bowler formula, but it never arose.

The talent in this Australian side runs deep. It may be stronger than the impressive ensemble that Mark Taylor led here four years ago. Yet the difference between the contestants in this rubber, rather than being a question of man-for-man talent, seems rather to condense to Waugh's pre-play comment. He and his players are, paradoxically if you like, professionals who love what they do. For them, missing a Test is painful, missing a tour an ordeal.

This is their captain's creed, though he himself inherited it from his first skipper Allan Border, who in fifteen years as a Test cricketer did not miss a single trip abroad, and who played more consecutive Tests than any player in history. This spirit is now part of the team's DNA, and destined accordingly to pass to the next generation.

Throughout this series, by contrast, England have projected an image of confusion about their objectives: in their faulty fielding, their plague of injuries, their coyness about responsibility, and now their misgivings about touring. The Australians, who draw strength from the psychological frailty they perceive in others, have found them almost willing victims. In eighteen months, England and Australia meet again. Some of the faces will be different, but it is difficult to see England uncovering a supply of kryptonite in the meantime.

The Guardian September 2001

MELBOURNE 2001

Luck's a Fortune

Bad luck leaves us rueful, but can also be a consolation. South Africans regrouping from today's defeat at the MCG will be tempted to mitigate it by reference to some unkind rubs of the green, not least from umpire Eddie Nicholls. But luck isn't always blindly apportioned. Consider the 'unluckiest' player on either side in this series: in three of his four innings, Boeta Dippenaar has been victimised by the sorts of catches that whip Bill Lawry into frenzy, and are replayed from every angle except beneath the batsman's feet.

In the first innings at Adelaide, it was Ricky Ponting who levitated at gully; in the first innings of this Test, Matt Hayden hurling himself right from the same position and telescoping his arm like Inspector Gadget. Today, it was Hayden again, this time encamped at short leg, who was the stumbling block when Dippenaar tried to punch a Warne loosener through mid-wicket. On each occasion, Dippenaar has looked stupefied, as though discovering that what had begun as a game of draughts had surreptitiously been changed into a game of chess. In fact, in each case he's been more like the dupe of a hustler with three cups and a ball.

Neither stroke in the first two instances was necessary; on the contrary, both were foolhardy. Dippenaar is a firm straight driver, but plays with an open blade when the ball is wider, to the extent that he is unable to place or control strokes square of the wicket. In both first-innings cases, too, he had been forewarned, earlier wild slashes having sailed just beyond reach. But he proceeded to mistake a slice of luck for a whole cake. Today, Dippenaar had the whole of the on-side in which to place the ball, and could profitably have turned the ball finer; instead, he struck it straight at the helmeted Hayden. The fielder's reflexes were as quick as the batsman's thinking was slow.

The point is that Steve Waugh's Australians are not only accomplished in their own terms; they also punish error in others more reliably than any other team on the ICC block. Dippenaar might also profit from heeding Hayden's alacrity at short leg. When Dippenaar himself was under the lid during Australia's innings, he stood a metre too deep throughout, and was observably on his heels: twice he was too tardy in advancing on chances that Steve Waugh offered early in his innings. That's another aspect of luck. Sometimes you make your own.

Wisden.com December 2001

MELBOURNE 2004

Boxing Day Massacre

Pakistan and the institution of the five-day Test took another drubbing from Australia in Melbourne, despite inclement weather and an unusual local hankering for a Test worthy of the name. The visitors' capitulation was no less thorough for coming a little later than in Perth, for the surface was blameless; indeed, the hard, abrasive pitch might have reminded them of home.

Inzamam-ul-Haq was absent, nursing a bad back; the ICC's chuckocracy had rendered Shoaib Malik ineligible to bowl; Abdur Razzaq was incapacitated by mysterious dizzy spells and nausea that were as close as he came to a stroke in two limp innings. Otherwise, there were no mitigating factors: Australia's 300th Test victory, securing them the three-Test series, was as inevitable from day one as any preceding it.

This was despite an admirable partnership on the first day between stand-in skipper Yousuf Youhana and Younis Khan. Youhana mixed lissom strokes with hearty slogs, four times depositing Shane Warne in the crowd; with the well-organised Younis, he added 192 in even time from 278 deliveries, Pakistan's best for the fourth wicket against Australia. The left-handed Salman Butt also impressed with a game 70 from 99 balls until Clarke's chase and throw punished a failure to ground his bat when returning for a second to third man. But 3 wickets in the first 33 deliveries of the second new ball cost Pakistan the initiative, and the tail was overthrown all too easily. Kamran Akmal even took a leaf from his opposite number's etiquette book by fessing up to a nick without reference to the umpire. Perhaps he'd noticed the bold Johnnie

Walker slogan on the hoardings in front of the MCG's on-going building works: 'Keep walking'.

Nor was there karmic payback: Kamran immediately dropped a straightforward edge from Hayden, and was pushed back to the sponsor's symbol 25 metres behind the stumps by Shoaib Akhtar's pace, where the ball still hit the gloves with an audible whack. Peeved by pre-match comment on the length of his run and hell-bent on justifying it, Akhtar took 5–108; Langer, despite a bulging disc in his back, pluckily bore the brunt of his bowling while Martyn established himself: further testimony to his value to this Australian team beyond his runs.

After a tenth Test hundred in Perth beneath cloudless skies, Martyn's eleventh took a most discontinuous 245 deliveries and 370 minutes, thanks to rain breaks and delays; typically for Melbourne, the best light in this Test match was to be enjoyed at about 6.45 p.m. on day two, after play had been abandoned for the afternoon and the ground was all but empty. He finished a year in which he has recovered all his old certainty with 12 fours in 142, relaxing his ironclad discipline only when challenging Akhtar and Sami with the second new ball. Gillespie, whose bat used to be as deadpan as his demeanour, then straight drove Sami for an impudent six, and consolidated Australia's lead with a chanceless, unbeaten 50 in two-and-a-half hours.

There were no more surprises, Pakistan seemingly intent on shrugging off their reputation as the world's most unpredictable side by folding up as meekly as everyone else against Australia. Their top order had been swept away by stumps, McGrath and Warne tidying up on the fourth morning before Hayden and Ponting did the needful against an attack that quickly lost interest: as ever. It was a poor show to set before Melburnians who'd done their best to invest in the game, building crowds of 130,000. So too was a cringeworthy comic footrace at lunch on the first day involving a former footballer turned TV personality, a comedian whose shtick is that he is stupid, and a comedienne who trades on being fat – a new benchmark for crass stupidity justified rather too airily as benefiting Shane Warne's new charitable trust. It seems that one can't be left unamused for a second at Australian Test matches these days; eating competitions and celebrity mooning – in aid, of course, of sick kiddies – cannot be far away. They are closer, at any rate, than Australian defeat.

The Wisden Cricketer January 2005

SUPER SERIES GAME 1

Super Snooze

The first match of the International Cricket Council's much-heralded Super Series with a capital S turned out to be an Anti-climax with a capital A, a determined Australia beating an underprepared and rather casual World XI by 93 runs at Melbourne's Telstra Dome.

No-one can say they weren't warned. A one-day international is what the ICC had declared this game to be; a one-day international is what we saw, and a boringly one-sided one at that. Whatever it felt like, it certainly wasn't a competition of galacticos playing übercricket. Against the backdrop of sparsely populated stands in a ground with all the atmosphere of a giant aircraft hangar, it felt as fake as the Hitler Diaries.

If the official crowd figure of 18,535 is to be believed, the corporate boxes must have been as crowded as steerage on the *Titanic.* Mexican waves became Mexican stand-offs; even those richly humorous cries of 'no ball' as Muralitharan bowled steadily faded. At one point, the crowd struck up a chant of 'Warnie, Warnie': the man himself was a spectator, and would have been an admirable candidate for the world's first Super Duper Sub.

Some blamed the poor attendance on the live television coverage of the game in Melbourne on Channel Nine; some lamented the time of year, more commonly associated with horseflesh than howzats. Whatever the case, it was drab fare. Australia played some solid, consistent cricket, recovering some of its old zip in the field; the World XI seemed to have spent too long reading the match program vaunting their talents to bother showcasing them.

The experimental aspects of the game, meanwhile, added little of interest and improved nothing, two episodes in Simon Katich's innings seeming to encapsulate umpiring past, present and possibly future. At 24 Katich top-edged a pull shot from Flintoff to deep backward square leg, where it was safely taken by Virender Sehwag. It was then seen that umpire Simon Taufel's arm was extended, and replays confirmed that Flintoff had cribbed a nanometre on the front line: good, firm, instantaneous adjudication which nobody questioned.

In Flintoff's next over, Katich whirled into another pull shot at a faster delivery and missed. Flintoff enquired, almost as an afterthought, and Taufel acquiesced to off-field arbitration – as he is now permitted, at least for this series. Two-and-a-half minutes elapsed before another ball was bowled. The batsmen had a drink, the fielders had a chat, third umpire Rudi Koertzen peered at a murky replay in his video eyrie, and a frisson of tension became a shudder of boredom. Why the ICC thinks that cricket should feature more of this is hard to tell. Perhaps it will allow for more commercial breaks.

The new one-day playing conditions also obtained another perfunctory airing. Neither of the Super Subs made any impact, the World's Shahid Afridi lasting 4 deliveries, Australia's Cameron White barely touching a ball. The three Power Plays were disposed of, as has become the pattern, by the 20th over of each innings. It may be time for the ICC to allow the Power Play to be neutralised by the Super Off-Switch, except on those occasions where it is run off the Mega Double-Adaptor when the Ultra Fuse-Box isn't overloaded.

After a positive beginning led by Gilchrist's 45 in 48 balls, Australia lost 3 wickets for 30 between overs 20 and 30: a kind of Power Cut. Clarke then closed the face early on Vettori and Australia was in danger of having the gas and the water disconnected as well. But although Vettori made good use of the conditions, varying his pace and arc intelligently, Symonds and Hussey added 52 cautious runs in 59 balls, and Lee gave the innings a final surge. His unbeaten

26 in 17 balls included the shot of the match: an improbable six, baseball-batted to left field from his old rival Shoaib Akhtar.

Australian captain Ricky Ponting said that his team was always confident of defending their 8 for 255: the slow outfield, still scarred by the deeds of the Australian Rules footballers for whom this ground is usually the preserve, made the score worth 280. In fact, it might as well have been worth 2800, as the Australians made short work of international cricket's longest batting line-up. Only Kumar Sangakkara took the time and care necessary to get in on a pitch that retained its early moisture, his 64 in 94 deliveries including seven boundaries.

Brian Lara was victim of a casual check drive to cover, while Jacques Kallis, Kevin Pietersen and Shahid Afridi missed straight deliveries as they wandered across their stumps. Rahul Dravid got into the strangest position of all, hopelessly chest-on as he played a hook, as though disturbed in mid thought. McGrath provided an opening spell to his usual specifications of 7–1–13–2; Watson relieved him with 8–0–30–2, regularly breaking through 140 kilometres per hour, and also threw out Pollock with a direct hit from backward square leg.

It might have been more embarrassing still. When he was five, Flintoff ladled a ball from Watson down Lee's throat at long leg which would have left the World XI 6 for 90. Like Warne with his comradely reprieve of Pietersen at the Oval, however, Lee dropped his old mucker, and allowed him to narrow the eventual margin of defeat with 38 from 52 deliveries. When Flintoff finally holed out in Watson's final over, the match was lost, as was its point – if indeed it had ever had one.

The Guardian September 2005

SUPER SERIES

Back to the Future

The International Cricket Council is promoting its Super Series as the game's brave new world. In fact, there's lots for nostalgists to savour. A contrived and artificial game of cricket stuffed with hype, staked with cash and staged for television on a drop-in pitch at a big Melbourne football stadium with lights pitting an Australian team against a bunch of foreign stars – and the crowd stays away in droves. Sound familiar?

Aficionados will recognise the reference to the inaugural day of the World Series Cricket extravaganza on 2 December 1977. History records that only a few hundred were scattered round the concrete bowl of VFL Park in Waverley as Kerry Packer's professional cricket troupe first came to town.

The same fate has now befallen the first game of the ICC's official brainchild, with the crowd at Telstra Dome alleged to be about 18,000, perhaps with the inclusion of people in the general vicinity. The only difference is that the Australian XI's opponents twenty-eight years ago were West Indians, and that they were involved in a so-called Super Test; the Super Test of *this* Super Series begins at the Sydney Cricket Ground next week.

It wasn't just the stands that yawned on Wednesday; so did the spectators. In advertising, the phrase 'switch-selling' describes the act of promoting one product but selling the punter an inferior substitute. Something similar has been in evidence this week. Tuesday's tournament launch was full of talk about the magnificent teams about to play for a magnificent trophy in this magnificent city's magnificent stadium with its magnificent roof. The car park went shamefully unrecognised.

The odds on magnificent cricket, however, were always long: most of the World XI are out of match practice, and those not, like Andrew Flintoff and Kevin Pietersen, have come from gruelling northern summers. The game itself duly managed to look daft as well as dull, right down to the speakers blaring Survivor's 'Eye of the Tiger' and Toto's 'Africa' every time Andy Flintoff and Shaun Pollock respectively went near the ball. Were Bradman still playing, he would probably be taking guard to the tune of '99.94 Luftballoons'.

The indoor cricket experience, meanwhile, is unearthly. As in a modern hotel, one feels sequestered from the outside world; as in a modern casino, there is no sense of the passage of time. Telstra Dome's eerie coldness is just about bearable for the two hours of a football game; over the eight hours of a one-day international, it begins to feel like a morgue.

No secret surrounds the auspices of the Super Series. The ICC wishes to establish some commercial properties of its own to go with the World Cup and the Champions Trophy – rather than risk a private promoter plundering the game's best talent for a DIY cricket circuit – and has settled official status on the Super Series to demonstrate its competitive edge over *arriviste* entrepreneurs.

If you bring together the best players in one place, furthermore, maybe people will overlook that the other end of Test cricket is about county Second XI standard. As for the so-called 'innovations', they are an attempt to rev up the flagging 50-over franchise, so lucrative for television, before Twenty20 renders it obsolete: Jagmohan Dalmiya is, of course, no stranger to the occasional Power Play himself.

None of which, of course, means that Super Mega Boffo attractions will not find an audience. Many vulgar, pointless and wasteful sporting spectacles succeed – otherwise, there would be no Formula One. Bear in mind that within a year of that first debacle at VFL Park, World Series Cricket was hosting crowds in excess of

50,000 at the Sydney Cricket Ground. This may be an omen: the first three days of Super Test at the SCG are already sell-outs.

In one sense, too, the Super Series has already found its public: Indian television viewers. Indian sponsors' symbols festoon the billboards at Telstra Dome; Indian accents fill the press box. But Packer's eventual success was because he realised that spectacle alone was insufficient. One needed also to touch the patriotic nerve. Fans in Australia and England have just been thrilled by an Ashes series to die for; fans in India and Pakistan expect something similar of their teams in January. If the Super Series represents a newie but an oldie, traditional Test cricket is currently an oldie but a goodie.

The Guardian September 2005

SUPER TEST

Defeat without Honour

Sydney's Fox Studios are currently hosting the shoot of *Superman Returns,* latest and biggest reincarnation of the man of steel. Just down the road at the Sydney Cricket Ground yesterday, however, the odds on a blockbuster version of *Super Series Returns* were lengthening.

No sooner had what was planned to be a six-day Test ended in fewer than half the allotted overs with Australia the victor by 210 runs than the ICC's man of steel, chief executive Malcolm Speed, was revealing that the idea of holding the Super Series every four years had only ever been 'one option': the ICC had viewed the series as 'an opportunity' and never committed to repeating it.

Looking back, one can see that there was always considerable flexibility about plans for the Super Series. After all, the ICC website says vaguely that 'every four years starting on 1 April 2005 the top team in the ICC Test Championship will qualify to play the Team of Champions in the ICC Super Series Test', and ambiguously that 'every four years starting on 1 April 2005 the top team in the ICC ODI Championship will qualify to play the Team of Champions in the ICC Super Series ODI matches.' No commitment there. And cricket *is* a funny game.

Sometimes it is, anyway. Yesterday was actually pretty grim. Seldom can the SCG have seemed so deserted at a scheduled start time. With rain falling at 10 a.m., the ground staff outnumbered patrons. There was a quorum present by the time play began after a three-quarter-hour delay, but the temptation would have been to lock the gates just in case anyone left. According to the official figures, there were somehow 8259 in the ground, somewhere, bringing the match total to just over 80,000. One can only assume the players' families were counted.

As for the play, it never threatened to be any more than an Australian shut-out. After Rahul Dravid and Brian Lara had safely negotiated the first hour, Hayden, either wearing two baggy greens on top of one another or modelling the new Super Baggy Green, showed that he deserved the honour with a smart slip catch off Warne in the very next over.

Thereafter, it became a procession. The sleeve of the World XI uniform features the famous symbol of its sponsor Johnnie Walker, the striding man with top hat and cane. As their last 5 wickets fell for 22 runs in 88 deliveries, it might easily have been replaced by the figure of a retreating cricketer with helmet and bat.

The last 3 wickets were collected by Stuart MacGill in 5 deliveries, to give him 5–43 in the innings and 9–82 in the match, which if it was not MacGill's best Test performance was certainly his best paid. The Australians received a US$25,000 match fee and US$56,923 each as prize money. Added to his one-day booty, Ricky Ponting's fortnight earned him US$132,708.

The World's players had to scrape by on their match fee, also US$25,000. At least they managed for the first time in five innings the landmark of batting 50 overs: in fact, as if to fulfil a contractual obligation, that is exactly what they faced. But the ending was so tame that one half-expected the match to continue into Super Innings, where Power Substitutes would bowl with their other arms and be voted out by home viewers with their remote controls.

The day would not have been complete without yet more umpiring travails, the additional recourse to technology having completely disrupted the game's traditional balance. When Taufel gave Dravid not out without consulting third umpire Hair early in the day, McGrath gave a slightly querulous look, as though to say: 'Get with the program, mate.' In McGrath's next over when a ball passed between Lara's bat and pad, Taufel duly made use of cricket's new equivalent of 'phoning a friend' by making the movie symbol from charades. A minute's forensic examination was needed to confirm the impression of the naked eye that the ball had simply missed everything.

Such caution, however, is forgivable. Another effect of the availability of technology is to add pressure to the instances when it is not used. The LBW verdict that Rudi Koertzen inflicted on Inzamam-ul-Haq yesterday was a misjudgment: the ball was jagging back and all three stumps were visible. To uphold the appeal without consultation, however, looked like a schoolboy howler to outdo anything perpetrated by the Senate subcommittee in the presence of George Galloway. At US$5000 per ball survived in this match, of course, Inzamam probably doesn't have too much to complain about. But perhaps the most damning judgment was from World XI captain Graeme Smith when he was asked if the technology had improved the accuracy of the decision-making. 'No', said Smith simply.

The accuracy of the decision-making at the ICC looks as though it might bear some scrutiny too. Malcolm Speed was apt to remind everyone yesterday that the Super Series had been 'profitable' for member nations, and that he was 'very happy with the things under our control', even though he 'shared the disappointment' of the World XI players. Disappointment, however, will not do: *Super Series Returns* will need to leap a big credibility gap in a single bound.

The Guardian September 2005

SOUTH AFRICA IN AUSTRALIA 2005–06

Payback Time

Graeme Smith's South Africans are flying their team psychologist to Australia to help them cope with the challenges of playing three Tests here over the next month. Shane Warne thinks they will need him; and, if the last fortnight of talk is anything to go by, he may well be right.

Not for some time have the airwaves round a touring team in Australia crackled with so much propaganda. The punchy Smith has publicly targeted the Australian top three; Herschelle Gibbs and Andre Nel have professed relish for the four-letter game; their erstwhile comrade Pat Symcox has prophesied 'payback time' for South Africans at Warne's expense. For the press conference during the First Test beginning in Perth tomorrow, however, Smith may have to consider wearing a helmet, so utterly has his team already been written off after suffering an innings defeat at the hands of Western Australia.

The International Cricket Council's chief executive Malcolm Speed has taken the quaint step of urging players to desist from their 'war of words', perhaps foreshadowing an official ICC code of cliché. If Muhammad Ali was reincarnated as a cricketer, he'd scarcely get out the gate; 'This might shock and amaze ya/But I'm going to re-tire Joe Frazier' alone would be worth a six-match suspension at least.

Something is certainly needed to spice up summer, after three abjectly dull Tests against the West Indies in which Cricket Australia scarcely had to think about dusting the Frank Worrell Trophy let alone removing it from its glass case. Already, in fact, there is a lot about this summer to remind one of previous seasons under the southern sun. Ricky Ponting's team has extended Australia's record on home soil since its last series defeat here to fifty-three Tests interspersed by only eight defeats, and ensured against a possible future shortage of tacky and meaningless metal objects vaguely resembling stumps by retaining the Chappell–Hadlee Trophy in New Zealand last week.

All of which has made the part of their trophy cabinet occupied until September by the Ashes crystalware the more puzzling, even embarrassing. Since traipsing off at Trent Bridge to the sound of his own feet, for instance, Matthew Hayden has bludgeoned 771 runs at 96.37. It is like a sequel to 'Jack and the Beanstalk' in which the giant picks himself up, dusts himself off and says: 'Lucky I landed on this voluminous goose-down quilt draped over a mountain of mattresses. Now, where's that sodding treasure?'

England's unexpected confiscation of the trophy has truncated a few careers, notably those of Michael Clarke and Simon Katich, and kicked along a few others, like Brad Hodge, Andrew Symonds and Michael Hussey. The thirty-year-old Hussey, whose reputation in England was probably greater than here until recently after three county triple centuries, has been the revelation of summer. First as stand-in opener, then as middle-order counterpuncher, he has accumulated an average of 120.33 in his first half-dozen Test innings.

The depth of Australian feeling about the Ashes and omens for the rematch in 2006-07 has also, however, been this summer's back-story; a back-story more interesting for most of the time, in fact, than what has been out front. Next Christmas in Melbourne, for example, far-sighted English tourists thinking ahead to the Boxing Day Test seem to have booked out even the mangers.

Last week in Canberra, on a less congenial note, the Australian Institute of Sport announced that it would be withdrawing the welcome mat traditionally laid out for foreign athletes and officials wishing to avail themselves of its facilities and technology. It was an awkward moment in the annals of the AIS after twenty years in which the spirit of sport has transcended nationalism, but director Peter Fricker pinned the blame somewhere countrymen could understand it: on those pesky foreign countries now rudely disinclined to simply roll over and be beaten. 'We have lost the Ashes in England, we have been beaten by New Zealand in rugby and rowing and netball,' he complained. 'The rest of the world is now doing really well what we have been doing for the last twenty-five years. In the 1990s, countries started to take an interest in what we were doing and came to see us and we gave everything away. We gave them in twenty minutes what we had spent twenty years developing.' If they must do all this hoisting, was the message, let it not be by Australian taxpayer-funded petards.

Australians are a conspicuously hospitable lot where sport is concerned. A famous cricket story concerns the whimsical legspinner Arthur Mailey, who it emerged during the Ashes of 1930 was passing tricks of his trade to an English protégé Ian Peebles. The Australian team manager, a man called Kelly, took Mailey to task: loose lips, he complained, could cause chances in slips. Mailey's retort has gone down in history: 'Spin bowling, Mr Kelly, is an art. And the art is international.' Harold Larwood, of course, went from the most hated man in Australia during the Bodyline series to a dear old pommy bastard when he settled in Sydney fifty-five years ago. But if raising the drawbridge and lowering the portcullis on our facilities is what it takes to regain the Ashes and renew national sporting prestige, then so be it.

There's little, of course, that Cricket Australia can do about the country's global coaching diaspora: Rod Marsh (ICC), Tom Moody (Sri Lanka), Greg Chappell (India), Dav Whatmore (Bangladesh) and Bennett King (West Indies), to name but the best known. But another sidelight story in the same vein last week was news of the imminent repatriation of Troy Cooley, the Tasmanian who put the punch into England's pace attack last summer. He joins John Buchanan's coaching staff in May, now also augmented by a performance analyst, former academy coach Richard McInnes. More changes can be expected in the Australian set-up as time ticks away to the Ashes of 2006–07. And while a lot of talk surrounds Australia's confrontation with South Africa, murmurs about next summer are already well and truly audible.

The Guardian December 2005

WINNING AND LOSING

THE WEST INDIES 2000

Decline and Fall

On the last day of the Fifth Test at the Oval between the West Indies and England two months ago, two acts of cricket chivalry marked the end of an era. As they marched to the victory which obtained them their first series win against the West Indies in thirty-one years, England's Test team formed guards of honour marking the appearances at the crease first of Curtly Ambrose, then of Courtney Walsh.

Ambrose and Walsh. Walsh and Ambrose. 888 wickets in 220 Tests between them. To some, it seemed like organising a whip-around for a couple of Luftwaffe pilots in appreciation of all that high explosive during the Battle of Britain. To others, though, it looked more appropriate; every funeral needs mourners, even when the deceased is West Indian cricket.

The West Indies: they used to be baaaad; now they're just bad. For some years, at least, Ambrose and Walsh have formed a figleaf covering the embarrassment of a team rather modestly endowed. Without their great pace pair, however, they're now looking more exposed than a centrespread in *Hustler*. It seems like only yesterday that the Frank Worrell Trophy was being hyped as the unofficial championship of the Test world. But on the basis of current form, including an infamous rout in two days at Leeds, the West Indies' meeting with Australia appears one of the gravest sporting mismatches since the Christian Invitation XI tackled the Lion All-Stars at the Colosseum.

Brian Lara is coming, although his recent batting form suggests someone intent on a good time not a long time. So is the lissom left-hander Shivnarine Chanderpaul, despite seeming in England to be in need of a good psychiatrist. Of the rest, what can one say? Gifted twenty-year-old batsman Ramnaresh Sarwan looks like a diamond in a very deep mine shaft. Ambrose has definitely retired. Walsh may yet come to Australia; they're hoping to persuade him, although his inclusion would be akin to glueing a Rolls-Royce hood ornament on a Holden Camira.

The West Indies rank on the current Wisden World Championship table at number three. That's a defiance of gravity, if ever there was, underpinned by the achievements of yesteryear, which are discounting by the day. It's also symbolic, for this is an XI living off an inheritance that they are fast frittering away, and seem to have lost all feeling for. No cricket team in the last hundred years made the advances of the West Indies. No cricket team has reverted to mediocrity quite so swiftly or abjectly.

That the series starts in Brisbane on 23 November 2000 is a cruel twist. Where better to be reminded of how far the mighty are fallen? Seventy years ago in Brisbane, the mighty George Headley made the first West Indian Test century against Australia. Forty years ago in Brisbane, Frank Worrell and Garry Sobers, later both knighted, illuminated what became Test cricket's first tie.

Sixteen years ago, in culmination of this tradition, Clive Lloyd's West Indians slaughtered Australia at the Gabba to extend a run of consecutive Test victories to ten; which they made into an unprecedented eleven in Adelaide. Defeat at the Gabba this year would allow Australia a share of that record; defeat in Perth would see its surrender. How vexing to be surrounded by evidence that your cricket team is not a patch on its precursors. How galling to know that it's true.

For the Australian observer, there's a feeling of déjà vu at hearing West Indian administrators and commentators lament the demise of cricket in local schools, talk of the need for an academy, and plead for patience during a period of long-term rebuilding. What was Australia's plight in the eighties and England's in the nineties has become the West Indies' in the noughties. Yet

Nasser Hussain's Englishmen showed no pity, and nor will Steve Waugh's Australians; they are building their own dynasty as surely as Lloyd's West Indians built theirs and, by way of a perverse compliment, in much the same unrelenting and unapologetic manner.

*

Normally, it would smack of overhastiness to damn a side like the West Indies. They didn't lose a series, after all, for fifteen years, until Mark Taylor's Australians bearded them in their den in April 1995. They have also proved capable, even in recent years, of springing surprises. Eighteen months ago, they startled Australia by sharing a four-match series as Brian Lara ran hot. In March and May this year, without Lara, they clawed their way back into Test matches at Port-of-Spain and St John's to claim remarkable victories. In the former, Zimbabwe needed 99 to win in the fourth innings and lost by 35. In the latter, Pakistan allowed the West Indies' last pair to make 19 and conjure a one-wicket win.

Zimbabwe, however, is Zimbabwe, while the Pakistanis at the time of their defeat were receiving a simultaneous drubbing in the Qayyum Report, hardly conducive to buoyant morale. And even if one were to accentuate the positive, there's no way to eliminate the negative, because there is no Mr In-Between. The West Indies have lost thirteen of their last fifteen away Tests, while their only win in that time at Edgbaston was so completely the handiwork of Walsh and Ambrose that the remaining nine positions could have been filled by holograms.

Some of those losses, too, have been not so much defeats as wanton capitulations. After the first day of a Test at Port Elizabeth in December 1998, South Africa was 7 for 142; the West Indies then allowed Pat Symcox and Allan Donald to put on 70, and disintegrated twice for 260. After the first day of a Test at Hamilton in December 1999, the West Indies were 0 for 276; they proceeded to lose all 20 wickets for 166 runs in less than 100 overs and gave up the match by 9 wickets.

Nor could the collective genius of Ambrose, Walsh and Lara avert the first two-day Test defeat in fifty-four years at Headingley three months ago. English conditions do, on occasion, expose defensive frailties, but usually among English batsmen. Never has Test match batting looked more like eleven men falling down a flight of stairs. The number three Test nation? That's number three with the bullet – straight down.

In what was once the West Indian specialty of one-day cricket, meanwhile, their record is even poorer. The winners of the first two World Cups were bundled out of the last in the preliminary rounds when Australia skewered them for 110 at Manchester, and they proved still more feeble in the recent Natwest Triangular Series in England, going down thrice to Zimbabwe and failing to make the final.

The West Indians reached the end of their tour of England complaining of tiredness. Although it couldn't have been from running between wickets, they had a point. In twenty-five weeks of non-stop cricket, they had crammed in ten Tests, twelve one-day internationals, and seven first-class matches. Players also participated in their domestic tournaments: the three-day Busta Cup before England and one-day Red Stripe Bowl afterwards. Immediately they're finished in Australia, too, they host a five-Test series against South Africa. Yet this treadmill is, at least partly, of their own manufacture.

Not quite two-and-a-half years ago, after financial assistance from their board, West Indian cricketers founded their own Players' Association, based in Barbados, with Walsh as president and Jimmy Adams as secretary. Their express ambition was to improve the lot of their membership, and they chose their moment to strike with care. In November 1998, on the eve of the West Indies' first tour of South Africa, a cricket trip rich with symbolism for that country's emancipated coloured population, the team led by Brian Lara decided to stage a sit-in for the purpose of wangling a better financial deal. Senior players could expect about $100,000 for the trip, but refused to budge from London's Excelsior Hotel until they had received better pay and conditions; they even retained event marketers CSS International to help with the nineteen hours of negotiating that eventually unfolded. Legitimate it may have been, crass it certainly was, embarrassing it proved. Improvements were promised, incentive deals organised, and Lara then led the West Indies to the worst trouncing in their history: 5–0 in the Tests, 6–1 in the one-dayers.

'If this is the best we have,' said manager Clive Lloyd after that tour, 'then we are in deep trouble.' And there's the rub. The West Indies now receive more money, but as a mediocre team must play almost incessantly to earn it – to the point where listless, surfeited players must wonder whether the game is worth the candle. Carl Hooper has gone. Chanderpaul seems undecided: he abandoned the England tour early after a tendonitis injury that would not have disconcerted a hungry cricketer. Others like the pacemen Vasbert Drakes and Ottis Gibson prefer to play first-class cricket in South Africa. But the strangest equivocations of all have been Lara's.

After the West Indies' wretched tour of New Zealand last December, where both Tests and all five one-day internationals were lost, he not only resigned the captaincy but declined to attend a two-week training camp and then to play in the home series against Zimbabwe and Pakistan. He was tired, and told friends he had lost interest in cricket. Lloyd also resigned, while coach Viv Richards was jettisoned in favour of Roger Harper and Jeff Dujon.

For three months, the West Indian cricket public was locked in a 'will-he-won't-he' guessing game about Lara's intentions. For three months, the West Indian board was in the pillory, Lara's withdrawal being construed as reflecting loss of faith in his administrators. For a time, all seemed lost: selectors actually drafted a Lara-less team for England, of which a leaked copy was published in Trinidad's *Daily Express* beneath the headline 'Goodbye Forever'.

Talk about today's newspaper being tomorrow's goat-curry wrapper. The next day's headline read 'Hello Again'; for, yes, Lara was back, at the expense of his Trinidadian colleague Daren Ganga. The hidden persuader was Lara's friend Dwight Yorke, the Manchester United striker, and shareholder with Lara and Trinidadian soccer international Russell Latapy in sports marketing firm LLAY. But it might have served Lara's interests, and would certainly have served his batting record, had he remained at his palatial residence in the hills of Port-of-Spain; one spectacular hundred aside, he scraped together only 127 in eight innings. Lara's average, in fact, almost 61 five years ago, has now dipped below 50: a leading indicator of West Indian decline.

*

Lara remains, nonetheless, the West Indies' last and best hope of making an impression on Australia this summer. Arrowing in from round the wicket in Australia four years ago, Glenn McGrath managed to cut him down to size, but there was no stopping him in the Caribbean last year. Treading the fine line between genius and recklessness, Lara will never be a red-hot certainty: the lofted hook with two men out looks magnificent when it succeeds, culpably irresponsible when it fails. But his presence will matter.

Lara's example and influence, nonetheless, may be one of the reasons why the West Indies now abounds in batsmen of brittle brilliance. West Indian top orders of the eighties were not only bold and exciting, but advertisements for the first principles of batsmanship. Now they stage displays that parents should keep from impressionable children. Tall left-hander Wavell Hinds slapped 165 against Pakistan in Barbados, but his static front foot was exposed in England. Having struck a whirlwind 124 off 93 balls in the Singapore Challenge two years ago, Ricardo Powell came to grief on slower pitches in New Zealand. Opener Sherwin Campbell has a ton of pluck, but tends to remain rooted to the back foot. Partner Adrian Griffith had a reputation for leaving the ball expertly, but in England seemed to lose all track of his stumps. Captain Adams, meanwhile, has seldom prospered in Australia, where he averages a modest 28.

The closest thing to emerging talent in the visiting side is Ram Sarwan, a slender, boyish right-hander with a repertoire of attractive strokes and the discretion to use them. When Guyana picked him at the age of fifteen, he was the youngest first-class player in the history of the islands. After twin hundreds against Zimbabwe in a President's XI match seven months ago, he made a collected 84 not out on his Test debut against Pakistan, and topped the West Indies' averages in England comfortably.

Also from Guyana is the team's spinner; for a change one with the sniff of a regular berth, which would be a first in Australia for a West Indian in a quarter of a century. Mahendra Nagamootoo, a nephew of Alvin Kallicharran, bowls flat leggies accurately enough to curb scoring, if without the zip that upends Test batsmen. But he could be left with some work to do given the poverty of a pace attack in which only the persevering Nixon McLean seems cut from the same cloth as Ambrose and Walsh. The death of Malcolm Marshall a year ago was widely mourned by former comrades; the loss of his expertise and kindred spirit may in time be felt even more keenly by the next generation of West Indian speedsters.

Here, again, lack of patience and maturity has been a weakness. The likes of McLean, Reon King, Franklyn Rose, Merv Dillon, Pedro Collins and Corey Collymore have had their days at international level, but all have been inconsistent and often expensive. Bouncers bring baying Caribbean crowds to life; in Test cricket, when bowled in profusion, they waste energy and play batsmen into form. Michael Slater may eventually receive an unplayable delivery from King or Rose, but by that stage will be 150, so it will scarcely matter. Against Ambrose and Walsh, a batsman seldom knew where his next run would come from. Now it's more a case of wondering where the next one will go.

*

Defeat in Australia need not be a disaster for the West Indies. Australia has seldom been stronger, and any resistance the visitors can mount will be admired and appreciated; not least by the Australian Cricket Board who, in scheduling a five-Test series, have an attraction equivalent to a troupe of buskers in the Royal Albert

Hall. A 5–1 licking in Australia twenty-five years ago, in fact, proved the West Indies' darkest hour before the dawn. 'Without doubt, it was the hardest, meanest cricket tour that I have ever been involved in,' Viv Richards has written, 'and it changed my whole concept of Test cricket … but, although we were bumped all over the place and lost the series 5–1, I still enjoyed it, mainly because we all learned so much.' Those lessons eventually provided the philosophical foundation for the West Indies' domination of international cricket.

Yet, in all likelihood, defeat this time will be no more than a defeat, another in what is becoming a ruinous succession. After watching a Test against India at Port-of-Spain three-and-a-half years ago, Caribbean Football Union president Jack Warner commented that cricket in the West Indies was 'dying a slow death'. He scoffed: 'Imagine. You have both Lara and Tendulkar in the Oval and the crowd ... I have more people in my office!' At the time, this seemed beyond comprehension. Yet there is now a palpable malaise in administrative circles and in schools cricket, which contrasts acutely to the vibrancy of soccer, athletics and basketball.

Old centres of excellence have shrivelled and not been replaced. An example is Wolmer's, a secondary school in Kingston. It has a tradition of wicketkeepers that no school in the world could match; a product of Wolmer's has been behind the stumps in more than half of the West Indies' Test matches, up to and including Jeff Dujon. Yet when the English writer Scyld Berry visited there a couple of years ago, he found the pitches in poor repair and school numbers too great for proper games, which were in any case under the supervision of phys. ed. teachers rather than cricket coaches.

Domestic cricket, too, is in crisis. As in Australia, because players must travel by air, it's always been expensive to stage. But in the palmy days, England provided an informal subsidy; every April, dozens of leading and not-so-leading-but-they-*were*-West-Indian players hopped the Atlantic to join counties and league clubs, following the path charted by Andy Roberts and Viv Richards in 1973. During the eighties, every county had at least one big black man who bowled fast; some had two or three. Hampshire v Somerset was Marshall v Garner; Derbyshire v Middlesex was Holding v Daniel.

The counties, though, steadily got choosier, because of the increasing amounts of dross among the diamonds. They now look primarily to Australians, with a sprinkling of South Africans, Pakistanis, Indians and Sri Lankans. Member islands of the WICB used to complain that their players spent too long in England. In fact, it was a blessing. Now that players are freely available for, and usually dependent on, domestic cricket, there's the problem of paying them a living wage.

Time will tell whether this spiral of decline is stoppable. Australia reversed theirs, and England seem momentarily to have arrested theirs. But that in both cases required investment and, while Australia and England are wealthy members of the First World, the West Indies are rooted in the Third. To some, cricket remains the sport of the Caribbean. 'It is the representation of who we are on the world stage,' says Prime Minister Lester Bird of Antigua–Barbuda. 'It is a manifestation of our self-esteem.' But what counts for his generation does not for others. Cricket is, to the region's young, one sport among many, and one in which recollections of greatness are steadily receding. And this summer in Australia won't be jogging many memories.

Inside Sport November 2000

THE RETURN OF THE ALL-ROUNDER

Queue Jumpers

Sitting round waiting to bat. Sitting round contemplating your duck. Squatting behind the stumps for the edge that may never come. Standing at fine leg wondering whether you locked the back door. Best not to think about it, but no game involves more wasted time than cricket. Perhaps it could only have been invented in England, spiritual home of the unmoving queue. Perhaps, too, that is why cricket developed its equivalent of the queue-jumper: the all-rounder.

The all-rounder not merely masters a range of the game's disciplines, he seeks to master the game. Ian Botham explained it succinctly: 'When I am batting, the bowler is not good enough, and when I am bowling the batsman isn't good enough.' It's not simply an issue of versatility, like rubbing your stomach and patting your head at the same time; it's also a function of personality, one that craves action and involvement every moment. No wonder all-rounders are so celebrated, from Keith Miller to Imran Khan, from Sir Garry Sobers to Sir Richard Hadlee. And no wonder there have been so few really outstanding ones.

During the 1990s, in fact, it was hard to see where the next of these blue touchpaper men would come from. Cricket was embarked on two interleaving trends. One, inspired partly by the proliferation of one-day games and partly by the trend to choosing four strike bowlers, was the drift away from specialisation: the pure batter and pure bowler of the past were succeeded by the batter who could step in for some relieving overs, and the bowler who could hold up an end or slog effectively. Almost every team now has one or two batsmen who can roll his arm over respectably: Sourav Ganguly, Sachin Tendulkar, Marlon Samuels, Carl Hooper, Ricky Ponting, Nathan Astle and the English Marks Butcher and Ramprakash. A host of bowlers who started at nine, ten, jack also began to take pride in sticking around: Jason Gillespie is a classic example, while other duffers-made-good include Allan Donald, Saqlain Mushtaq and even Glenn McGrath.

Yet the ranks of true all-rounders – capable of turning a match with bat and ball – thinned drastically in the early 1990s. The retirements of Sir Richard Hadlee, Imran Khan, Ian Botham and Kapil Dev left a vacuum that no-one stepped forward to fill immediately. Pakistan's Wasim Akram was the cricketer closest to their spirit, but even with his blue-chip status as a bowler was seldom more than a spec stock with the bat, as even he admitted. On one glorious day at Sheikhupura in October 1996, he blasted an unbeaten 257 against Zimbabwe, enough to try on the all-rounder's hat, but an experience that told him it didn't quite fit: 'The mental and physical demands are great ... if you want to be an opening bowler who bats in the middle order. After that double hundred, I could barely put one foot in front of the other for a couple of days. My hamstrings and back ached because I'd been using different muscles for hour after hour. I don't know how Imran and Ian Botham did it for so many years.'

Cricket runs in cycles, though, and may again be changing before our eyes. This summer in Australia, four cricketers will be on show with pretensions to all-round greatness: Kiwi Chris Cairns, Proteas Shaun Pollock and Jacques Kallis, and hometown hero Adam Gilchrist. All are experienced enough to have earned their stripes, yet young enough to add to them: they hold the power in their hands to shape both this season's Tests and a new cricket era.

*

If Chris Cairns' career was a tune, it would be the Enigma Variations. He had played forty-nine Tests before the start of this summer and missed thirty-eight, collecting injuries like a VW collects dents. And, worse than a Beetle, there's always been a suspicion that it takes the merest bump to render him unroadworthy.

To be fair, Cairns has always looked the part when on the park: a fierce hitter with a sound technique, and a seamer who hits the deck hard. At intervals, however, there's been a hint of valetudinarianism. During the prelude to the Second Test at Bellerive Oval in December 1993, for instance, he complained of a mysterious leg injury, but bowled without apparent discomfort at practice, and assured captain Ken Rutherford and coach Geoff Howarth of his availability. 'I was therefore dumbfounded when he told me prior to breakfast on the morning of the first day – twelve hours later – that he wasn't 100 per cent and was withdrawing,' complained Rutherford. 'The only way he could have done anything to re-injure himself was in his sleep.' Howarth recalled: 'I took Cairns at his word that he could not play. But I put a question mark beside his character from that time on.' The Aussies were waiting for Cairns during the Third Test at the Gabba. Shortly after he came out to bat, Shane Warne abruptly stopped in his run and reached down with a cry of: 'Ah, my ankle.' Ian Healy delivered the punchline: 'You'd better watch out mate. If you do that you'll be out for a couple of weeks.'

Cairns missed almost a year's cricket after surgery, conveying the impression that he was in no great hurry to rejoin his Test colleagues. Having just returned from a tough tour of South Africa, Rutherford heard Cairns being interviewed on radio about a domestic one-day hundred he'd made the day before in which he airily deprecated his fitness. No, he still wasn't well enough for Tests: 'I just wanted to see Canterbury through the final so they can win the cup again.' Rutherford was ropeable.

Cairns' response to regaining fitness raised hackles further: he jetted off to become a dominating performer for Nottinghamshire in England's County Championship. Rutherford griped: 'There's a somewhat cynical school of thought around that Cairns is keener on the pickings in county cricket than the hard graft of international play. Certainly, he's unproven at Test level. Sure, he's bullied attacks like Sri Lanka in one-day cricket on the odd occasion but he's often looked wanting against better-quality opponents.'

It wasn't until New Zealand's last Australian tour four years ago that Cairns began putting flesh on eight years' worth of bones, with 172 runs at 34 and 13 wickets at 25. The talent always evident then began to ooze out. After man-of-the-match performances against India a year later in a Hamilton Test (126 and 6–137) and a Christchurch one-dayer (115 and 1–48), Cairns masterminded New Zealand's 1999 series win in England, averaging 30 with the bat and 21 with the ball.

Steve Waugh's Australians went to New Zealand last year respectful of Cairns, but still feeling they had the edge on him. Coach John Buchanan's now celebrated Wellington memo profiling the Kiwis described their key all-rounder as: 'Fragile. A good front runner, but lacks confidence if you get on top of him.' Such is the Australians' own self-belief that this didn't mean that much; Buchanan's case note on King Kong is probably along the lines of: 'Secretly afraid of heights. Biplanes worry him.' And in the event, Cairns' bravura batting and bowling had Steve Waugh describing him as 'another Ian Botham'. The more noteworthy for contributing to a losing cause, his 341 runs and 10 wickets included a 109 and 69 at Basin Reserve from a total of 220 balls, one of his 6 second-innings sixes ending in a rose garden outside the ground.

Unfortunately, having proved that he no longer bent the knee before quality opposition, Cairns discovered during last year's ICC knockout in Nairobi that he could no longer bend the knee at all. He stuck it out for long enough to pilot New Zealand to victory in the final with a bold 102 and, after surgery on a patella tendon in February entailing a six-month lay-off, rejoined the colours with a four-hour 124 against Zimbabwe in September. Cairns has left his run at all-round distinction late – he turned thirty-one in June – but some of the greatest sporting triumphs have been pulled off at the last possible moment.

*

The sporting isolation that swallowed up thirty years of South African cricket history didn't interrupt one continuity: that country's conveyor belt of all-rounders. The submerged Springboks of the 1960s featured the likes of Mike Procter, Eddie Barlow and Trevor Goddard; the emergent Proteas of the 1990s rely heavily on the likes of Shaun Pollock, Jacques Kallis and Lance Klusener. Indeed, of all the tails in international cricket, South Africa's is the most articulated: Mark Boucher, Nicky Boje and Pat Symcox also have Test centuries to their credit.

For all his World Cup heroics, it would be a stretch to depict Klusener as a Test-quality all-rounder: in the last two years, his Test batting average has gone from touching 40 to a more mortal 34, while he hasn't bagged five international wickets in an innings since his Test debut five years ago. Yet this has hardly been noticed, because Kallis and Pollock have developed twice as quickly. Six years ago, both were junior members of South Africa's under-24 team touring Sri Lanka. Since then, in the immortal words of Fred Dagg, 'strength and strength is pretty much a summary of where they've been going from and to.'

Kallis was a frail beginner, eking out only 57 runs and 5 wickets in his first five Tests, before the first of 8 hundreds in the Boxing Day Test of 1997 established his credentials. Like Cairns, he recently cracked the current World XI as selected by Shane Warne in *My Autobiography*: 'a solid, dependable batsman who will continue to improve' and 'a genuinely hostile bowler with a fast outswinger'. Seventh to the double of 3000 runs and 100 wickets in Tests, and sixth to 4000 runs and 100 wickets in one-day internationals, Kallis is that rarest of commodities, a top three batsman good enough to take the new ball, and capable of dominating in either role. In the Cape Town Test against the West Indies in January 1999, he bracketed twelve hours' batting for 110 and 88 not out with 43 overs bowling worth 7–124.

Pollock is likewise a late-blooming all-rounder. His impact on Test cricket with the new ball was immediate, his chances with the bat fewer and further between: despite a gene pool including an uncle with a Test average of 60, Pollock seldom batted higher than number ten for his native Natal. Three handy half-centuries in his first twenty-one Tests also seemed flimsy evidence for coach Bob Woolmer's assertion three years ago that he was 'one of the finest all-rounders since Garry Sobers', and Pollock was minded to agree: 'Ach! The coach is always blowing his mouth off.' In the wake of Cronjegate, however, Pollock has put his money where Woolmer's mouth was; in his first seven Tests this year against Sri Lanka and the West Indies, South Africa's twenty-eight-year-old skipper aggregated not only 28 wickets at 20.7 but 413 runs at 82.6. In 125 years of Test cricket, there have only been 10 centuries scored from the number nine notch: Pollock now has two of them, both at better than a run a ball.

The only obstacles to continued achievement for Kallis and Pollock seem to be fitness and fortune. Kallis suffered stress fractures of the back as early as 1996 and a knee injury two years ago, and the Waughs and Martin Crowe can attest to the difficulty of combining middle-order demands with medium-pace duties. In continuing to lead from the rear, meanwhile, Pollock will always run the risk of the innings expiring at the other end: already, he has been not out in more than a fifth of his Test innings.

They may, in fact, be best off meeting somewhere in the middle: Kallis at number six and Pollock at number seven would be a formidable duo. In Greek mythology, Castor and Pollux were half-brothers, transformed by Zeus into the brightest stars in the constellation of Gemini. In South African mythology, Kallis and Pollock are blood brothers who could become the brightest stars in the constellation of cricket.

*

Great XIs don't necessarily need all-rounders to substantiate their greatness. The mighty West Indian ensembles of the 1980s got by without. Though all had their days in the sun, none of Andy Roberts, Malcolm Marshall, Roger Harper or Eldine Baptiste strictly fitted all-round billing, while the effectiveness of wicket-keeper Jeffrey Dujon's batting also declined in the second half of his career. Likewise, Australia's rise in the 1990s was without a significant all-round underwriting, Ian Healy's punchy strokes at number seven excepted.

That, though, was then: Adam Gilchrist is now. In only two years, he has raced to 100 Test dismissals, and positively bolted to 1334 Test runs, at the fat average of 51.3 and at a strike rate in excess of 80 per 100 balls. It is not as though opponents haven't developed plans to counteract him. His most recent rivals, England, had many, though none lasted much longer than a handful of overs. At Trent Bridge, for instance, Darren Gough decided to tackle Gilchrist from round the wicket. When two of the three deliveries were riveted through cover for four, Mike Atherton cast his paceman a long-suffering glance, rather like Blackadder dismissing one of Baldrick's cunning plans.

Is there a weakness here? To answer apprehensions about his burden as stumper cum thumper, Gilchrist has responded that he bats best while doing double duty as keeper. If those skills are so closely coupled, though, sustained pressure on his batting form may also show up in his keeping. This seemed to be the case in India seven months ago when Gilchrist underwent a brief but macabre run with the bat of 2 runs in four innings, which seemed to make him tentative behind the stumps, and showed up as an nervous echo when he started the Ashes series by dropping two catches in the first session.

Gilchrist's 152 from 143 balls with 110 runs in boundaries two days later, by the same token, suggests that his best form is never more than an innings away. And Gilchrist's career has unfolded at the same breakneck pace as one of his innings: he has fourteen man-of-the-match awards in Test and one-day cricket already, and has twice led his country in Steve Waugh's stead. Clearly a glutton for responsibility, he would if he took on the captaincy full-time probably also commentate on his own performances.

In the meantime, Gilchrist has ample responsibility: interestingly – at least for the pointy heads – number seven in the Aussie order has become something of a barometer of the team's fortunes. Australia's last ten Test defeats have had the common factor of failure at that mezzanine twixt top order and tail: the number seven batsman has averaged 12.73. Quell any possible regrouping by the tail, it seems, and you can keep the world's best Test team to a beatable score. All the more reason for Gilchist not to get ahead of himself, and for us not to get ahead of Gilchrist.

*

All-rounders are both born and made, though the born ones still need nurturing and the made ones will amount to little if the raw material is second rate. Pakistan had an example of the former five years ago in Kenya during the Sameer Four Nations Cup, when their selectors sent sixteen-year-old leggie Shahid Afridi out to replace the injured Mushtaq Ahmed. Thinking him a bowler, captain Wasim Akram asked if he'd like to have a bat in the nets as well. Afridi said he'd quite like to, smashed all the practice pills to kingdom come, and when sent in at number three the next day against Sri Lanka hit 11 sixes in a hundred off 37 balls.

The best example of the latter, meanwhile, is England. In the Pommy cricket vernacular, 'versatile' translates as 'does nothing particularly well'. Since Ian Botham's retirement they have trialled no fewer than seven *soi-disant* all-rounders – Andy Flintoff, Chris Lewis, Mark Ealham, Ronnie Irani, Craig White, and Adam and Ben Hollioake – for a total of 2283 runs at 19.02 and 164 wickets at 37.4 in seventy-nine Tests. The record of a decade's underachievement is bad enough; the flow-on effect, which has been to push the search for batting depth in other directions, has been worse. Chief victim of the lack of balance in English Test teams has been Alec Stewart. Though his record as a batsman/fielder is vastly superior to his record as a batsman/keeper, Stewart has been forced to carve out a hybrid role as stop-gap-back-stop – the cost of the sacrifice of a potential match-winner to the cause of defeat-prevention is unquantifiable but probably significant.

Not that the prevention of defeat, it should be said, is an altogether unworthy role. Consider the player who is, the feats of the aforementioned Cairns, Pollock, Kallis and Gilchrist notwithstanding, arguably an even greater all-round cricketer, and certainly the individual who has the greatest sway over his country's fortunes. Andy Flower has played every one of Zimbabwe's Test matches since it entered international cricket, has been involved as a keeper in more than a fifth of their Test wickets, has scored nearly a quarter of their Test runs, and has a Test average (56) nearly twice the next best among his countrymen. After his 142 and 199 not out against South Africa at Harare in September, Flower displaced Steve Waugh at number one in the PwC Test Ratings: there isn't another Zimbabwean in the top fifty.

Flower's strengths are his mental toughness, derived from a diet of books on sports psychology, and a technique against spin bowling that is arguably the best in world cricket. When he batted two days to compile an unbeaten 232 against India at Nagpur early this year – the highest Test score by a keeper – spectators were treated to the rare sight of fieldsmen on both square boundaries, for the sweep and the reverse sweep. In Flower's case, the need for action and involvement is even more compulsory than for most all-rounders; without him, the match is probably over.

Inside Sport November 2001

TEST CRICKET

125 Not Out?

This year marks 125 years of Test cricket. Haven't heard much about that, have we? The International Cricket Council must have been busy handing out plastic bats to Eskimos as part of their globalisation program, or coming up with a new protocol for the logos on thigh pads. Or have they not wanted to draw attention to the uncomfortable reality that Test cricket, World Championship and all, is in a bit of a hole?

Not, of course, for the first time: few sporting concepts have been written off as freely as the idea of five-day cricket. And we live, generally, in godless times: a whole generation is growing up that thinks of James Bond merely as Austin Powers without the jokes. But if you're finding it hard to be stimulated by another death-or-glory duel between New Zealand and Zimbabwe, then you're not alone. 'International cricket feels flat, undramatic, even dull,' observed Scyld Berry, English cricket writing's guru, recently. 'Everyone is playing too much. Australia's pre-eminence in the Test and one-day game has become predictable ... "Cricket goes in cycles" is an adage only a fool will cling to.'

Worst of all, the standard of the game may be in decline. Australia walks tall in cricket these days – but maybe it only seems that way because everyone else has shrunk. Few Tests go the distance. Many end inside three days, even those involving established Test nations: this year's England–New Zealand series featured only ten days' play in a scheduled fifteen. Smitten with spontaneous celebrity, cricket seems nonetheless to be producing fewer outstanding players. Of those in the modern game with legitimate claim to greatness, only Adam Gilchrist has emerged in the last five years. Warne, Lara, Muralitharan and Andy Flower have been around for a decade; Tendulkar, the Waughs, Wasim and Waqar for longer. Bowling ranks appear especially bare: not since 1989 have there been as few as five bowlers with PwC rankings of 700.

This had always loomed as a torrid period for Test cricket. During the first half of the 1990s, an entire generation of great cricketers signed off: Indians Sunil Gavaskar, Kapil Dev, Dilip Vengsarkar, Kris Srikkanth; New Zealanders Sir Richard Hadlee, the Crowes, John Bracewell, John Wright, Ian Smith; Englishmen David Gower, Ian Botham, Graham Gooch and Mike Gatting; Pakistanis Imran Khan and Javed Miandad. Luckiest were Australia, where Allan Border's valediction occasioned sentiment rather than sadness. Worst hit were the world champion West Indies, who saw the last of Viv Richards, Jeff Dujon, Gordon Greenidge, Desmond Haynes, Gus Logie and Malcolm Marshall. In hindsight, it's scarcely surprising that the Windies should have been bearded in their own den by ... Australia.

The new order emerging, though, involved more than the champions changing: these retirements represented a bend in cricket's river. Most of the aforementioned masters had been earmarked as emergent talents during the late 1970s. They'd learned their cricket the old-fashioned way, rising through the established grades, and playing at state, county and provincial level before higher honours. Their Test graduations were mostly complete, moreover, before it became necessary to compress one's skills to the specifications of one-day international cricket.

The generation that succeeded them has been different. First-class cricket has only been part of their education. They also came via youth teams and academies, mixing and matching short and long forms of the game, and spending more time in tracksuits than whites. Above all, their expectations have been different. They grew up knowing that cricket could be their living; they have never had to live for cricket. If cricket today seems more routine, perhaps it should not surprise us. Has anyone paid money to watch you work lately?

*

So what's going wrong? As anyone who's watched county cricket will tell you, too much cricket jades palates, for players as well as spectators. Batsmen don't dig in, as Steve Waugh noted last year, because another match is round the corner anyway: 'People aren't prepared to bat long periods the way they used to, or that's what it seems like. Indian players still get big hundreds but that's generally on their own soil where the pitches are flat and the outfields are quick.' Bowlers bowl within themselves for the same reasons, because another match always impends, and because opponents will tend to get themselves out anyway. Purveyors of red-hot, red-blooded pace, like Shoaib Akhtar and Brett Lee, struggle to survive whole series. Smart bowlers, like Shaun Pollock, have extended their careers by shortening their runs and husbanding their energies, although the attrition among even ordinary medium pacers is alarming: New Zealand's bowling has been opened by a dozen different bowlers in the last three years. Coaches are concerned primarily with uniformity of procedure and predictability of outcome.

Another alarming sign is how hard it's becoming to win an away Test. Only three teams have won more often than lost away from home in the last six years: Australia comfortably (twenty wins and thirteen defeats), South Africa just (eleven wins and ten defeats), and Pakistan, somewhat misleadingly (their fifteen wins, against eight defeats, include only six victories outside Asia and the Gulf). Everyone else is finding that travel, though it might broaden the mind, diminishes the chances. Bottom of the class is India, without an away series win since 1986.

Teams tour so much these days, you might think, that they would be more adaptable than in days gone by. But, to keep the bean-counters happy, tours have been getting shorter: Australia's 1993 Ashes trip spread thirty days of international cricket across three-and-a-half months; last year's visit squeezed five Tests into fifty-four days. And with the opportunities for acclimatisation so circumscribed, immediate adaptation does not come easily. When India visited South Africa a year ago, both its warm-up matches were rained out. They proceeded to lose the First Test by 9 wickets.

For some, that seems just fine: Australia walked into its First Test against Pakistan recently without any preparatory game at all. And home ground advantage, of course, is a familiar concept. Some sports even nod to it, like soccer – thus the extra weight attached to an away goal in World Cup qualifiers. Cricket doesn't: an away team can't be gifted a fifth more runs, or ask their hosts to bat two short. If anything, in fact, the game is magnifying the advantage that being the host confers. Thus, perhaps, more money in the short term, but also the likelihood of more and more unequal Tests, and more teams that are lions at home and lambs away, like the West Indies, which over the last six years has lost only seven of thirty-six Tests in the Caribbean, but twenty-six of thirty-two Tests abroad.

*

The flag of Bangladesh features what looks like a cricket ball on a green background. This doubtless provided a powerful rationale for their admission to Test cricket – because others aren't entirely obvious. And the ignominy of their record – they've lost twelve of their thirteen Tests and already chewed up four captains – is matched only by its complete predictability.

Five years ago, on Bangladesh's only significant tour before their Test *entrée*, they lost all four games to provincial teams in New Zealand, three of them by an innings; the local chairman of selectors called them 'district standard'. They've still won only one game against a Test nation, and that was during the 1999 World Cup when Pakistan, as they are wont to do at times, showed all the cool aplomb of lemmings confronted by a cliff.

Opportunities for further evaluation were limited. When the ICC inspection team arrived in Dhaka in January 2000 to assess Bangladesh's cricket credentials, seven of the country's best players had been suspended by their board, and the rest were on strike.

But the other Test nations were unable to resist the push for Bangladesh's promotion from its Asian neighbours.

It didn't take long for other countries to sus the Bangladeshis out. In their first five Tests, their batsmen eked out 21.3 runs per wicket, while bowlers paid 64.3 for theirs. Even after losing the first two days to rain at Hamilton in December 2001, New Zealand's Stephen Fleming expressed confidence about winning the Test there – rightly. Only three of the sixty-six individual innings on that tour lasted more than two hours. Nor has a youth policy paid off. Bangladesh capped the third youngest Test cricketer last year against Zimbabwe: fifteen-year-old Mohammad Sharif made three ducks in four innings and took 3 for 256.

Bangladesh stands a chance of improving: they have the population; they also have the pent-up enthusiasm. Chances are that for Zimbabwe, where per capita incomes have halved in the last five years of Mugabe misrule, more means worse. In that luckless land, as the *Economist* commented recently, 'the thieves are in charge, and the victims face prosecution.' And among those victims are the nation's cricketers: touring England two years ago, players found that they were being paid less than their bus driver.

Zimbabwe have been playing Test cricket for a decade, but haven't won since knocking off Pakistan in Pakistan four years ago. Two of their best batsmen, Murray Goodwin and Neil Johnson, have opted out in favour of county cricket; a third, twenty-four-year-old Trevor Madondo, his country's first black batsman of quality, has died. In a country that can't muster more than two first-class teams, the cupboard now looks as bare as Old Mother Hubbard's. At one stage late last year, they had five captains in six weeks. A jobbing leg-spinner, Brian Murphy, inherited the role on the basis of 18 wickets at 58 each. He lasted one Test.

Yet it's not only the two newest Test nations who drag the chain. A year ago, South African fans were giving their tub an almighty thumping, in anticipation of six Tests with Australia. They've been quieter since losing five of those encounters, one at New Wanderers in February by the second greatest margin in Test history. And president Thabo Mbeki has warned specifically against expecting too much from the national team, which is his way of insisting on more black players: 'For two to three years, let's not mind losing international competition because we are bringing our people into those teams. Let's build a 100 per cent South African team rather than a thirty per cent.'

Which may not be all bad. South African cricket was at a crossroads anyway. Only one of the top ten bowlers in its average tables over the last six years made their last XI; the rest have retired, been dropped, or cremated (that's you-know-who). But for the attractiveness of Test cricket, South Africa's eclipse is grim news. Comparing the present team to the accomplished ensemble coached by Bob Woolmer four years ago is like comparing *Star Wars* and *The Phantom Menace*: one is an original, the other a cobbled-together imitation.

Cricket's chief enigma is India, capable of routing Australia at home, but barely the equal of Austria away. No clearer index of this exists than the records of their chief luminaries: Sachin Tendulkar averages 64 at home, 52 abroad; Anil Kumble's bowling average is 21 at home and 40 overseas. India can be relied on only to confound predictions. Having beaten Zimbabwe at Bulawayo in June 2001, for example, they allowed a tied series by surrendering 7 wickets for 37 on the last morning at Harare.

The enigma of India contrasts with the known quantity of England, bordering on competence at several stages since Nasser Hussain's appointment as captain after the last World Cup, but having provided him with only fourteen wins in thirty-seven starts. The problems aren't far to seek: churn-and-burn selection policies that have turned over fifty-eight players in the last six years (compared to Australia's thirty-six). At Mohali last December, England's opening attack (Matthew Hoggard and James Ormond), frontline spinner (Richard Dawson) and keeper (James Foster) numbered three caps between them. Nor is England the classiest team on the park at present. In India, England eked out 2.9 an over, and kept the home team to 2.5 an over by bowling endlessly into the footmarks outside leg stump. 'Thank God it was a three-Test series and not a five-Test one, for Indian cricket would have lost a great number of spectators seeing the fare dished out,' the peppery Sunil Gavaskar claimed afterwards in the *Hindustan Times.* 'For without the slightest doubt they [England] are the most unattractive and boring side to have played cricket in India.'

The question hanging over English cricket is not how dull it might appear at present, but how dodgy it might be in three to five years. Hussain is thirty-four, Graham Thorpe and Andy Caddick thirty-three, Darren Gough thirty-two, and Alec Stewart thirty-nine. The best of the next generation, all-rounder Andy Flintoff, still averages 20 with the bat and 45 with the ball. And the country that produced Jim Laker and Derek Underwood hasn't fielded a spinner worth the description in decades. Over the last six years, English slow bowlers have paid 43 runs each for their wickets. English cricket has great advantages, which it still might learn to use; the way it has frittered them away in recent years can only be marvelled at.

*

Ultimately, Test cricket's malaise can be distilled to two words: West Indies. They had the furthest to fall: twenty years ago they held the World Cup, Worrell Trophy and Wisden Trophy simultaneously. And they have fallen furthest: their trophy cabinet is now emptier than political rhetoric. For several years, Curtly Ambrose and Courtney Walsh covered their inadequacies. No longer; even New Zealand exposed them in June, recovering from 5 for 117 to post 337 at Bridgetown, then routing their hosts for 107 in 42 overs.

Which is nice for the Kiwis: they're an improving side. But who wants a sport for which New Zealand provides the pulsebeat? At their best, the West Indies are world cricket's most exciting combination. Yet when they are as bad as the present rabble, international cricket's whole equilibrium of entertainment and excellence is disturbed. And this is more than a question of a few weaknesses; the West Indian team since the start of 1996 has been more chink than armour. The batting order has lacked continuity (no fewer than seventeen players have opened) and depth (a third of the players picked have averaged in single figures). Lara remains its touchstone: in three Tests against Sri Lanka late last year, he made forty-two per cent of the runs. The abiding West Indian dependence on speed, meanwhile, has returned to haunt them. They have no masters of reverse swing to make use of the ball once the shine goes off it. And, like their English counterparts, West Indian spinners have been paying 43 for each wicket.

The falling-off, however, has been acutest in leadership. Where Clive Lloyd mooched and Viv Richards swaggered, successors have tripped, slid and stumbled. Walsh and Richie Richardson were undermined by disunity. Brian Lara, focus of much of that disunity, then lost interest in the job, while his successor Jimmy Adams could not justify a place in the team on ability – which is saying something. Then, in March last year, the West Indies Cricket Board took its strangest step yet, conferring the captaincy on prodigal Carl Hooper, a truant in Australia for the preceding two years after falling out with the same body. Roughly the equivalent of the ALP offering Simon Crean's job to Mal Colston, the appointment provoked a storm of criticism from West Indian greats including Sir Garry Sobers and Michael Holding – who vowed not to commentate games involving Hooper. The appointment has done nothing to remedy West Indian inconsistency: they have won four and lost nine under Hooper's leadership. WICB president Pat Rousseau recently admitted his fear that his team would be 'underprepared and embarrass ourselves' at the forthcoming World Cup. One suspects it's unavoidable. In the West Indies' embarrassment, however, international cricket is sharing fully.

Inside Sport November 2002

AUSTRALIA IN 2004

Success and its Discontents

Late in 2004, Australia's national broadcaster screened a documentary series produced by Lincoln Tyner entitled *Rookies, Rebels and Renaissance*, reliving the tempestuous cricket summers of the 1980s, revelling in the beards, body shirts and boofy hair. For the uninitiated, one aspect of the narrative must have been especially arresting. Throughout the period, it was recalled, the Australian cricket team lost Test matches – by its standards, quite a lot.

Never mind the uninitiated: it was a surprise for the initiated to be so reminded. For as the tenth year of this baggy green and golden age unfolded, the chance of challenge seemed as remote as ever. South Africa and Pakistan, second and third on the ICC Test Championship when the year began, had stumbled. England, currently second and fantasising freely, have taken one 'live' Test off their oldest rivals in eighteen years. India, now third and briefly touted as a serious rival, had just been convincingly beaten on their home soil.

In 2004, in fact, Ponting sponsored a most unusual phenomenon: a revival following what was barely a decline. Steve Waugh's farewell series against India had been a two-cheer affair. Without the injured Glenn McGrath and the ineligible Shane Warne, Australia's attack had looked all thrust and no cut. Runs had come, as usual, in plenty – but, unusually for a home series, from both sides. By year's end, however, Australia seemed to have acquired new life; it says much of Ponting's assurance that even Steve Waugh had virtually dropped from view.

Not everyone, however, was happy; as Randall Jarrell once observed: 'No matter how golden an age, there will always be someone complaining that everything looks too yellow.' Success without a sense of struggle being a paltry thing, some critics, including an administrator as respected as Malcolm Gray and a past master as venerable as Greg Chappell, wondered aloud if Australian dominance risked alienating the public. A review of its strategic plan completed in November by the tony management consultants McKinsey's then provided Cricket Australia with some empirical evidence that it already had: flat attendances, diminished ratings, only so-so growth in participation. 'The game is not growing,' conceded CEO James Sutherland, 'or certainly not at the rate we would like it to grow.'

Most countries, of course, would kill to have the dilemmas posed by a surfeit of success, and some saw publicity for the report performing a subtler role, as a *ballon d'essai* ahead of the renegotiation of Cricket Australia's memorandum of understanding with the Australian Cricketers' Association; the current four-year deal between the board and the players' trade union is due to expire on 30 June 2005. For some time, directors of Cricket Australia have been muttering *sotto voce* about the players' revenue rake-off. When *Business Review Weekly* magazine published its annual estimates of sporting incomes in December, half of the Australian XII were said to be pulling down seven figures: Ponting ($2.24 million), Gilchrist ($2 million), Warne ($1.45 million), Brett Lee ($1.3 million), Matthew Hayden ($1.11 million) and McGrath ($1.11 million). These numbers do not seem so extravagant given the public fame and recognition these players enjoy. The administrative argument runs, however, that without a healthy infrastructure, there is no fame to bestow.

There are strains in Australian cricket, too, that are deeper and longer-term. For much of the country's cricket history, for example, the first-grade or district club has been the game's principal organising unit, talent nursery and social institution – something implicitly recognised by the system under which board members of Cricket Australia are still chosen from club delegates elected to their associations. But the reality is that Test players now have precious little to do with their clubs, and nor, increasingly, do promising juniors, given the sophistication of youth cricket programs designed to identify and incubate talent. The implications of this steadily attenuating connection between cricket's higher and lower levels, with a concentration of riches and resources in the elite game, may not be apprehended for a generation.

Pressures have been discerned in the Australian set-up before and prophecies issued that it would pull itself apart like the House of Atreus: the successes have always kept coming. One of the most provocative lessons of *Rookies, Rebels and Renaissance,* nonetheless, was how strategically motivating failure can be. Australian cricket's challenge will be recognising the need for change without the mandate that failure confers.

Wisden Cricketers' Almanack 2005

INJURIES

Please Try Harder

Only one achievement stands between Monty Panesar and the status of bona fide, gilt-edged English Test star: a long-term injury. After all, it's done the job for Simon Jones: never a greater match-winner than since he stopped playing matches. Michael Vaughan, meanwhile, has become cricket's Moby Dick, occasionally rising from the depths to scare the willies out of people with talk he may have played his last.

The psychological war is clearly getting to Ricky Ponting, who last week conjectured that perfidious Albion was at work, and that Vaughan and Jones were malingering deliberately: 'It's a long time to get over any sort of injury. I'm pretty sure they will want Vaughan and Jones here if they can get them here. We are preparing to play a full-strength side.'

On the eve of the Old Trafford Test, Bob Woolmer demonstrated why he is among the game's subtlest psychologists with the proposition that Freddie Flintoff's absence was a plus for England: 'It would have given our team a psychological boost to play against a player of his quality. It is not a positive for us that he is missing.' Given the psychological boost that Monty's quality will now be giving Pakistan, England's only hope at Leeds is that he scalds himself at the tea urn on Friday. When the specialists move in to recommend everything from brain surgery to botox treatment, this indisposition can probably be prolonged sufficiently to preclude his playing in Australia at all.

Victory at Manchester may mislead England in its speed. Two home players took wickets; two made serious runs. Pakistan, a momentum side, can be stopped by such body blows; Australia, more resourceful and adept at regrouping, will not be so straightforwardly thwarted. That leaves plenty of work for what is laughingly called England's injury management program, where men enter what looks like a St John Ambulance caravan and somehow end up needing the services of *House MD*, and from which Geraint Jones will probably emerge with a plaster cast up to his shoulder on the wrong arm.

What has gone wrong this summer? Perhaps the question should be turned on its head: what went right in 2005, when England had to make one forced change in five Tests? This, one suspects, was more than simply luck. The Ashes last year was a series to die for; it was also one to hurt for. How else to explain Flintoff's 18 consecutive overs of brazen hostility at the Oval, more significant even that Pietersen's hundred to the final outcome, after a summer of unremitting toil?

So much about 2006 has been about jockeying for position ahead of the Ashes rematch that it must have influenced the priorities both of players and officials. There's been over-caution and over-eagerness, with an eye on the royal road to the Gabba for 23 November. Had a winter tour to Pakistan been in the offing, different attitudes may have prevailed. Given recent history, when some England players have looked decidedly leery of playing Australia, this constitutes a welcome change.

In some ways, the increasing profusion of injury is an outcome of professionalism. There are further, deeper and longer-term considerations than simply getting on the park for tomorrow's game, while central contracts have softened the immediate financial impact of short-term unavailability. But the prospect of being part of history still makes a sportsman's sap rise. Monty is bound to sustain an injury at some stage – no-one who fields like him can avoid it indefinitely. For the sake of the Ashes, it would be well if he could stave off this rite of passage for at least six months.

*

Is cricket more gruelling than it was? A pity such discussions usually deteriorate into biomechanical gobbledegook about fast-twitch fibres versus tales of Alec Bedser bowling 50-over spells in a pair of clogs. In the current climate of unnatural attrition, though, an anniversary is worth nodding to. It is a hundred years since Yorkshire's George Hirst attained the unprecedented and unequalled feat of 2,385 runs and 208 wickets in a first-class season. Perhaps cricket was not then so physically extentuating; certainly it was not so varied in its forms. But a pitch was still 22 yards, grounds then perhaps larger than today, and Hirst had to bat fifty-eight times and bowl 7838 deliveries: the accomplishment of an athlete who understood the strengths and limitations of his own body – in a way Liam Plunkett, for example, who against West Indies A should obviously have been carried to the crease in a sedan chair with a dialysis machine on standby, does not.

The Guardian August 2006

JAQUES V KATICH

Lightweight Clash

The announcement of the composition of a one-day team is not usually the subject of much comment. Someone always seems to be announcing a one-day team somewhere, carefully arbitrating on the quality of one dibbly-dobbly purveyor over another when a game of rock-paper-scissors might be just as definitive. When Phil Jaques was overlooked for his New South Wales team-mate Simon Katich in Australia's one-day team for South Africa, however, it was as though Frank Ward had been preferred to Clarrie Grimmett all over again.

To recap, Jaques got his chance at Docklands last month when Katich was ruled out by a groin strain; he slathered 94 off 112 balls against South Africa before giving up his place again. Then something interesting happened. Paul Reiffel once observed that his reputation grew whenever he wasn't playing; likewise, the long diminuendo of Jaques' innings seemed to make him a better player each succeeding day. Incanting Steve Waugh's soundbite that Jaques could be 'the new Gilly' like an election slogan, journalists turned him into Australia's new one-day saviour and World Cup secret weapon. When he did not make the cut for South Africa, it was Mark Waugh's turn to provide the soundbite for repetition: 'I think his performances have been outstanding and I think it's a bit of a lame excuse to say his fielding isn't up to scratch.' Jaques' reputation will now be further enhanced by Australia's defeats in the Twenty20 international and the first one-day match in South Africa; at this rate, expect him to be mentioned as a possible CEO of Cricket Australia if the Proteas win the series.

Katich, meanwhile, a thoughtful cricketer who's known his own selection misfortunes, is suffering the burden of incumbency, which he'd probably just prefer, although maybe not by much. His century against Sri Lanka at the Gabba on 15 February was accompanied by one of the most histrionic celebrations this side of the Oscars. Sooner or later, I grant you, a player scoring a century is going to vault the fence and plant a kiss on every member of his entourage. But Katich threatened for a moment to become the Mark Latham of Australian cricket; at his emotional press conference afterwards, one half-expected him to say: 'Say anything you like about me. Just leave my family out of it.' Except that he brought his family into it, dedicating the innings to them.

This rivalry, however, is more than a selection controversy du jour. It is a reflection of the direction of the game's technology and regulation. Jaques is a beneficiary of the era of high-performance bats and ever shorter boundaries. Katich suffers for the same reasons: his *métier* of finding space through the field is passing out of fashion because it has become so easy to hit fours and sixes. The tide of Twenty20, a game about power where bowlers toil as hopelessly as galley slaves, is set to expedite the trend. If Jaques is not at the World Cup next year, he will only have himself to blame; if Katich is not, he probably shouldn't blame himself too much.

The Googly April 2006

CHAMPIONS TROPHY 2006

According to Taste

A trip to Cricket Australia's headquarters in Melbourne can sometimes seem like a visit to one's wealthy but tasteless in-laws. Set into walls all over the buildings are the spoils of the Australian cricket team's decades of success: trophies, cups, plates, bowls, shields, and other tokens that might be cooking pots, astrolabes, sundials and exotic retro lamps. The temptation is to come up with tactfully non-committal responses usually reserved for unrecognisable family bric-a-brac. Well, isn't that ... eye-catching? Hmmm, wherever did you find that ... thing? So, where do you ... plug it in?

At the end of the entrance foyer, there's even the trophy denoting Australia's status as World Test Champion. It is a mace. At a pinch you might use a plate for hors d'oeuvres, a bowl for punch, the Ashes urn for an ashtray. But has your neighbour knocked on your door lately and asked if they could borrow your mace? Because they are, you know, in the embarrassing position of being one mace short.

Of course, trophies are minted for their symbolism, not their utility. But let's face it. There have been 2422 one-day internationals. That's an awful lot of silverware to have dispersed. If it was really worth winning in the first place, where is it now? And, it seems pertinent to ask on the eve of the Champions Trophy, why bother adding to it?

The Champions Trophy started life as the ICC Knockout in Dhaka in October 1998: eight matches, ostensibly to raise funds for Jagmohan Dalmiya's missionary activities, teaching Hottentots the leg glance, handing out plastic stumps to Kazakhs et cetera. In its fifth iteration, it has bloated, for reasons that may have something to do with money, to twenty-one games over a month. It has no distinctive quality and no particular innovations; it contains no especial rivalries or particular traditions. Its format is dull and its name is meaningless: the current champion, the West Indies, gets a harder ride than anyone, having to qualify in order to defend its crown by beating Bangladesh and Zimbabwe. Its trophy, meanwhile, resembles an art deco cocktail shaker. It's a shame it's not an *actual* art deco cocktail shaker. That would be more use, and more fun.

What are the implications of playing cricket so instantly – in fact, inherently – forgettable? For one thing, it breeds contempt among players. The outcome of that contempt in the late 1990s was match-fixing, where meaningless cricket so abounded that it seemed a trifling matter to manipulate scores and results. For another thing, it drags other attempts at innovation down to the level of humdrum. This time last year, the ICC tried to stage its Super Series: a dismal failure in execution, but not without conceptual promise, that could have been validated by performances worthy of the personalities selected. Yet it struggled to define itself as something other than just another one-day tournament, because the public finds that genre so utterly familiar.

Among administrators, it inculcates a sense of routine manufacture, the idea of feeding a conveyor rather than fostering a contest. The DLF Cup in Kuala Lumpur featured the quaint spectacle of Mitchell Johnson collecting a man-of-the-match cheque one day and a boarding pass the next, because he was immediately to be sent home under a pre-ordained rotation plan. Against India, Brian Lara nonchalantly slipped himself down to number nine; against the West Indies, Ricky Ponting gave way to Michael Hussey in order to savour a rest break. At KL, it did not matter overmuch. But the spectator is entitled to the assumption that the best available team will take the field save in extraordinary circumstances. Having perhaps paid for a ticket months in advance to see Lara or

Ponting, how galling to be told simply that it is time for them to 'rest'; 'rest' being spelt 'g-o-l-f'.

For the Champions Trophy to matter, it really needs a distinctive quality. Perhaps it could be played for charity, or as a testimonial fund for past players – that would lend some credibility to its name. Maybe the time is ripe for a version of one-day cricket in which bowlers can bowl overs without limit, or without field-restriction circles, or with a proper cricket ball that actually swings, or on proper cricket fields where the ropes haven't made sixes cheap. After all, Twenty20 cricket will shortly be making old 50-over cricket appear full of longeurs. Why not take 50-over cricket in the opposite direction, by giving it more subtlety, more texture and more variation?

At the moment, the Champions Trophy simply proves that cricket is like life – in the sense of Edna St Vincent Millay's observation that life isn't one damn thing after another but the same damn thing over and over. The only difference between the Champions Trophy and life, it seems, is that the former puts you in the running for an art deco cocktail shaker.

Ekdin October 2006

WORLD CUP 2007

Runneth Over

Cricket's World Cup is a collection of anti-stories. Its coverage has concerned all the stuff *not* happening: the scintillating world-class cricket *not* taking place, *not* being witnessed by crowds that have *not* shown up to occupy arenas that are *not* finished. Plus, of course, the apparent murder that has *not* been solved.

The revelatory form, meanwhile, has been shown by two teams *not* making it through to the tournament's Super Eight stage – actually 'stage' seems a trifling word to describe what has lasted so long it feels like an era. Pakistan and India, who won a match each, against Zimbabwe and Bermuda respectively, have returned home to the usual resignations and recriminations; the official effigy supplier to the World Cup – and there is bound to be one – will have done a roaring trade.

In days of yore, these rituals used to be regarded as quaint eastern exotica – my word, they are *passionate* out there, aren't they? If vestiges of this attitude persist, they should be put to flight at once. India is cricket's financial hub, providing seventy per cent of its global income; its most lucrative franchise is its rivalry with Pakistan. Over the last five to seven years, under Sourav Ganguly and Rahul Dravid, India has achieved on-field success to complement its off-field stature: it has been worth playing India in a cricket sense as well as a financial one. But what are the implications if the world's richest cricket nation and its competitor of choice should rank among its poorer teams?

The gravitational pull of Indian money is now keenly felt in Australia. In 2006–07, Cricket Australia had apparently the best possible summer. Its Ashes series was a sell-out in advance; it obtained handsome sums from domestic and international broadcasting rights; it can expect a fat distribution from the ICC after the World Cup. Yet Cricket Australia will still make less money in 2006–07 than it anticipates in 2007–08 from hosting India for four Tests, when its arenas will be bedecked in advertisements for Indian products, and thronged with Bollywood stars.

The modus operandi of the Board of Control for Cricket in India (BCCI) is an unruly blend of hypercapitalism and feudalism, mixed with the entrepreneurial ebullience of Don King. It has just booted Australia from a one-day round robin in Ireland, and demanded a restructuring of the Australian summer to accommodate its plans for yet another series with Pakistan. On present indications, however, Australia's games against India will make the recent Ashes series look like the closest-run thing since Waterloo.

And if the jet-propelled bullock cart of Indian cricket remains incapable of producing a team worth the country's cumulative talent, what then? What seems to happen when a superpower is checked and thwarted is that it seeks to remake the world along more congenial lines – lines that show it to best advantage. It is no longer bad news for India, for instance, if it is uncompetitive in Test cricket; it is bad news for Test cricket itself.

In fact, if the World Cup has illuminated anything about international cricket, it is the difference between getting and spending. The game has never been richer, and never felt flatter. India, with its byzantine politics, opaque finances, antique infrastructure and risible domestic competition, is merely the most extreme example of a cricket governance system through which money pours to little visible effect. Nor is it alone. As Matthew Engel put it in *Wisden* a couple of years ago, one of the reasons for cricket's complaisance where Zimbabwe is concerned is a fear that action might reveal the double and triple standards elsewhere: 'Pick on them for maladministration and where do you stop?' Heavens, someone might even look at the ICC itself.

*

ICC member countries wore big fat grins last year when they sold the broadcasting rights to their next suite of events for something in the region of US$1 billion. Here are some of the gloating quotes. India's I. S. Bindra: 'Much of the money that comes from this deal can be ploughed back into the development of the game, and that will strengthen cricket even more.' The West Indies' Ken Gordon: 'This agreement ... will put the ICC in an extremely strong financial position and allow us all to develop cricket on a much wider front.' HRH Tunku Imran, President of the Malaysian Cricket Association: 'The revenue received by the ICC can be used for a new era of development, as it will have an impact on all of our eighty-seven members below Test level.'

But how much 'ploughing back' is there really? What width 'wider front' are we talking? How much should junior countries be benefiting anyway when only India, Australia and England among the Test nations operate profitably? And how much bang is being obtained from the development buck? Whither the quadrennially-remembered Kenya and the Netherlands, fleeting and faded presences at the World Cup, and the USA, not only absent but suspended from the ICC for a governance implosion almost as bad as Zimbabwe's? The ICC gives a whole new meaning to the phrase 'glorious uncertainty'.

*

A major sporting event can seldom have worn a more ironic name than Super 8, the Cup's interminable interim stage. Who uses Super 8 any more? It might as well have been called the Betamax round. You'd have thought the ICC would have learned their lesson from the Super Series that wasn't, and the Super Sub that never did.

Perhaps it is time for a worldwide moratorium on the use of the word 'super' in a sporting context. The Superbowl demands respect. But after watching Superbikes duke it out for Superpole in the Supersports competition, even rugby Super 14s seems rather prosaic, endurable only with the aid of Superbeer and

Supercigarettes. It is surprising that football, scarcely prudish where hyperbole is concerned, has so far eschewed going Super. When it does, watch out.

The Guardian April 2007

WORLD CUP 2007

The Dying Game

The 2007 World Cup will be remembered for its ridiculous ticket prices, and quite so: they were not nearly high enough. Another fifty per cent and no-one would have attended the games at all. As it is, there are now people who have partaken personally of its protracted tedium, and seen with their own eyes what a sorry state international cricket is in. And they will talk. At least, they should.

The International Cricket Council and the local organisers have borne the brunt of criticism for the interminable nature of the competition, which proceeded with the same stately drabness as a Victorian family's timetable of mourning. But for the sterility of the spectating experience, they are not entirely to blame: it's not as though the addition of a few conch shells and a steel band or two would have turned the tournament into a pageant of galacticos. The real problem in the World Cup was on the field, where a great deal of the cricket, involving ostensibly world-class teams, drawing on greater coaching resources than at any stage in the game's history, brought to concert pitch by psychologists, physiotherapists, sports scientists, ghost writers and spiritual gurus, was ... well ... rubbish.

One-day cricket is a batsman's game: people go to watch big hitting, innovative placement, quicksilver running. But in only five games did both sides score more than 250. The *sine qua non* of the limited-overs format, meanwhile, is the close finish. Yet only six games were decided by a margin of 10 runs, 2 wickets or fewer. And while it's thought a bit *infra dig* to comment on absolute standards in this resolutely relativist world – we prefer assessments that are more exercises of taste, like 'interesting' or 'boring' – many players seemed to be struggling with the game's basics.

There were batsmen propping on the front foot who couldn't cope with the merest sideways movement, who struggled when they couldn't simply hit through the line and rely on their beefed-up bats to get them out of trouble. There were bowlers who couldn't observe the basic tenets of line and length, incapable of moving the ball on a consistent basis, and going through their variations as if by rote. There were tactics so stereotyped as to make Stephen Fleming, merely a quite good captain, look as inventive as Thomas Edison. There were players in general so anonymous, so joyless, so self-involved as to be unable to communicate, by a deed, or a gesture, or even a smile, that they were playing for any reason other than to make a living.

Sometimes, the standard was almost laughably poor. In New Zealand's game against Canada, for example, the new ball was taken by Anderson Cummins, who bowled fast in the 1992 World Cup for the West Indies, but whose physique now testifies to his years in IT, and will only bear him jogging in off a dozen paces. His first ball was a slow-medium outswinger; likewise the second, and the rest of the over. New Zealand's Lou Vincent, dutifully prodding forward, did not lay a bat on the ball. He finally got off the mark after a painful quarter of an hour with a panic-stricken flail that just cleared cover, and hacked and hoicked his way to an undistinguished hundred.

The second semi-final through which Australia coasted then involved ritualised public humiliation of *Big Brother* intensity. According to their coach Micky Arthur, South Africa intended asserting themselves early to disrupt Australian momentum. Against an opening attack bowling a disciplined line and doing just enough with the ball thanks partly to a stiff cross-breeze, this became as intelligent a plan as trying to stop a train by standing in front of it. South Africa's CEO, Gerald Majola, denounced his team for lacking 'mental strength' – and this, he couldn't understand. Why, the team had a support staff of twelve – including, presumably, an expert mental strengthener. 'We are dealing with these issues at the High Performance Centre,' he concluded. And maybe that's part of the problem.

This event has, I suspect, exposed the effect of a secular shift in the way cricket talent fructifies. Bowlers especially, but also batsmen, are arriving at international level with relatively little first-class experience: elite junior competition, high performance hothouses, and specialist coaches are expected to equip them with the kind of common-sense knowledge that used to be instilled by playing alongside experienced team-mates in state, county, provincial and club cricket. Too much learning and skill-acquisition is being done after players graduate to international level. The result is batsmen with biomechanically perfect stroke-production inexperienced in building an innings, bowlers with every conceivable variation who struggle to organise a spell, and plans like South Africa's that, as they say in the military, don't survive contact with the enemy.

Fans in the West Indies know their cricket; they don't sit there waiting for the next beach ball to bounce along or Mexican wave to wash over them. Maybe it wasn't only exorbitant ticket prices that kept them away. Maybe they saw this spectacle for what it was: a bunch of overcoached, overcooked look-alikes providing third-rate content for Rupert Murdoch. Perhaps the idea all along was to soften us up for the inexorable advance of Twenty20 cricket. It has never looked better.

The Guardian May 2007

MALCOLM SPEED

The Case for the Defence

Malcolm Speed has proven a very unpopular chief executive of the International Cricket Council. But Malcolm Speed was never a very popular chief executive of Cricket Australia. Many of the complaints are the same now as then: too cold, too hard, too aloof, too commercial. In Australia, nonetheless, he's as effective an administrator as we have ever seen, vastly more accomplished and organised than any of his predecessors. Which suggests that if Speed is being judged negatively in his present position, it says as much about the position as about its occupant.

Make no mistake, what we saw in the Caribbean was dire. John McEnroe would have called it the Pits-of-the-World Cup. Wracking your brains for a redeeming feature just gives you a headache. It was too sanitised, too corporatised, and *way* too long. Mind you, it was *way* too long from the moment the ICC directors signed off on it, when everyone fondly imagined that India and Pakistan would cruise straight through to the Super 8s. And the main problem was that the cricket itself was rubbish: there's a few people to blame for that before you get to Speed.

At times like these, people go all wistful about sport being turned into a business. Leading this push at the moment are administrators from India, which is a little like a bunch of tobacco company CEOs speaking in favour of corporate social responsibility. 'My board is of the belief that cricket is a simple, enjoyable game, but that is not how it appears at present,' said the secretary of the Board of Control for Cricket in India this week. Oh, spare us. The BCCI is ill-placed to be giving advice to anyone on the game's management, incapable as they are of producing a world-class team from a population of a billion cricket-crazy people, and with a bureaucracy themselves that is an international byword for incompetence.

How much of a business is the ICC anyway? It has no power to elect its own directors: these are sent by the sovereign boards who compose it, who judge them chiefly on the benefits they deliver to their own countrymen. It has no authority to choose its president: the presidency is meant to rotate every three years, but the directors pathetically deadlocked at their last vote. It cannot bind its directors to vote in the interests of the organisation itself: essentially, everyone votes in order to get their own way, and usually *en bloc*. Its members routinely flout its policies anyway: the Betty Ford Clinic has nothing on the Pakistan Cricket Board when it comes to rapid rehabilitation from drug use.

The ICC's main purpose has become to make money. This it has done quite successfully. But it has very limited power over how the money it earns is spent: the surplus is distributed to sovereign boards, who spend it on whatever takes their fancy. Ostensibly, it returns to cricket's 'grass roots'. But I wonder on what Zimbabwe Cricket will be spending their World Cup dividend, given that in Zimbabwe grass roots are something you eat.

In other words, the ICC breaches just about every principle of good corporate governance. And who keeps it that way? Not Malcolm Speed, but its members. Why? Because everyone thinks they can work the system to their own advantage. Those complaining about the ICC being 'too corporate', then, miss the point. The ICC is less a commercial organisation than a political one; the attacks on Speed from India are, in the main, politically motivated. Which is not to say the ICC has no problems. On the contrary, they are queueing round the block. But axing Speed would solve none of them; in fact, it would simply provide a pretext for continued inertia.

The Guardian May 2007

MANAGEMENT AND MISMANAGEMENT

JAMES SUTHERLAND

Taking Charge

Cricket, a resolutely nostalgic game, loves its centenaries, but one forthcoming on 6 May 2005 seems barely to have been noted. Some would think the anniversary of the inaugural meeting of the Australian Board of Control for International Cricket barely worth celebrating; it is nonetheless certainly worth marking.

To be sure, nobody remembered when the board turned seventy-five in 1980, although that was perhaps because not much had changed. The Australian Cricket Board was still more an address than an organisation. Its senior executive officer was its secretary, the Dickensian figure of Alan Barnes, who answered correspondence from a dusty office in Cricket House and was nicknamed 'Justa' for his regular response when asked for a document: 'Just a minute, just a minute.' The files he could not fit in his cabinets – sometimes because of the cartons of cigarettes and bottles of scotch stored in there – were stacked on the floor, in places as high as the ceiling.

The centenary will probably slip by now for the opposite reason, because what is now Cricket Australia is rooted so firmly in the present. Presiding over that first meeting, at Wesley College, was Lawrence Adamson, the school's forty-five-year-old headmaster, an old boy of Rugby and lifelong bachelor whose role was of a piece with other *pro bono* works like chairmanship of the lost-dogs' home. Its chief executive officer since June 2001, James Sutherland, is a thirty-nine-year-old schoolmaster's son with three young children who doesn't look much less fit than in the four first-class and nine one-day games he played for Victoria in the early nineties.

Mind you, if a Melbourne establishment can verifiably be said to exist, Sutherland is a scion of it. He is married to Heidi *née* Asimus, daughter of former chairman of the Australian Wheat Board and BHP director Sir David, while his maternal grandfather was Sir James Darling, legendary headmaster of Sutherland's *alma mater* Geelong Grammar.

Sir James told the story of how, on coming to Grammar from Charterhouse in 1930, he was at first disconcerted by the earnestness with which Australians pursued their recreations. His sportsmaster seethed at him through gritted teeth: 'The trouble with you Englishmen is that you don't know the difference between games and sport.' James Sutherland, it would seem, could tell the difference, and came down on the side of games. He was serious about cricket but never entirely wrapped up in it. 'There were two reasons for that, really,' he says. 'One, I never had enough belief in my cricket ability to think that I could bank on it. Two, while as a cricketer I wanted to be the best I could be, I knew there was a lot more to life than playing cricket.'

Broad-shouldered and standing 194 centimetres, Sutherland had all the physical gifts to be a fast bowler, but lacked perhaps the necessary loose screw. His reputation was as a reliable medium-paced workhorse and a rock-ribbed team player, who found his main cricket mentor when he left Melbourne CC for Melbourne University CC in 1985 in the latter's coach, Peter Spence. 'University's reputation had been of a club that was well-run off the field, but a bit of a chopping block for others,' Sutherland recalls. 'Peter Spence brought about a real cultural revolution there. The thing I learned was that success breeds success. When we got to the finals in my first year [1985–86] and players got the feeling that we could compete, things changed. When people start believing in themselves, they begin to take pride in everything around them. They begin to want to take responsibility for committee roles, to organise social functions. The club mag goes from being a sheet that comes out a couple of times a year to fifty pages a month.'

Sutherland also recalls his sense of connectedness to the rest of cricket: 'I remember the feeling I got from the fact that Malcolm Gray was on the Victorian Cricket Association, and chairman of the Australian Cricket Board while he was vice-president of the Melbourne University CC. That resonated with me, that connection to the whole. And I think while it can be argued that it's a weakness of Australian cricket that it has principally been made up of volunteers, there's also a sense in which it's been a great strength that a grass roots cricket administrator can serve cricket at the highest level.'

This was, however, unaccompanied by an illumination that he might one day himself rise to the top of Australian cricket: 'I had no idea what I wanted to do. All I wanted was to put myself into a position where I had the best possible choice.' Work and cricket ran in parallel. His undergraduate degree was in commerce and he spent five years at Ernst & Young after qualifying as a chartered accountant; in the meantime, he won flags at University in 1990–91, then at his old club Melbourne in 1992–93, before returning to University, leading it to another premiership and obtaining life membership. This is not by the way; the experience was formative.

'The culture twenty years ago was very supportive of players who worked,' he says. 'It was accepted. People went: "Well, we don't pay you a wage as a cricketer that is sufficient for you to get by. You need to work. And on that basis, we'll start training at 5 p.m." If I was a cricketer like me now, I actually think I would have faced some tough decisions about work and cricket. I hope I would have made the right ones. And I've got a problem with that. The fact is that very few cricketers get through to a level where they earn sufficient income to set themselves up for the rest of their lives to justify the sacrifices they have made. Ten to twenty at any one time. So that means there are 120 to 130 players making significant sacrifices that mean that their transition when their cricket career is over will be difficult. We haven't got it right yet.'

Colleagues whom I told I was going to interview Sutherland warned me to expect a sort of Bismarck, who proverbially could say nothing in seven languages. I didn't find him so; on the contrary, he was personable, candid, sometimes humorous, and on one occasion decidedly unimpressed. This was when I recounted to him a recent conversation with a talented teenage cricketer, the member of a Pura Cup squad, who told me that he did not feel he had time to work or study in winter because he was 'so busy' going to training and keeping fit. 'That's absolute crap,' Sutherland scoffed: 'These guys, they do not know what busy is. That's a great pity. Players at state level shouldn't go round thinking themselves in clover to the extent that they can simply fritter the winter away not furthering themselves, whether that's study, improving their qualifications, getting work experience.'

GH: I think this bloke knows that. But he needs someone he respects to give him that advice.

JS: That's the trouble. We send mixed messages. We tell players: 'We want you to be the best you can be. You need to do this, this and this to improve. We've got a training session at 6 a.m. and we'll be back together at 3 p.m.' But if it prevents players developing in other ways, what is that doing for them in real life?

An earlier form of this dilemma plagued the ACB when Sutherland was recruited in November 1998 after six years as the finance director at the Carlton Football Club. Although the ACB had signed its first Memorandum of Understanding with first-class players, the dust was still to settle on the industrial unrest caused by the irruption of the Australian Cricketers' Association. 'When I was hired, there wasn't really a job vacancy,' says Sutherland. 'It was a created role, because the ACB needed someone with commercial background who could understand the MOU, but also the cricket experience to talk and deal with the players as a cricketer. The relationship at the time was pretty average. There was a lot of animosity. There were a lot of "players" in the mix [an allusion to the involvement as consultants of former ACB CEO Graham Halbish and IMG's James Erskine], which I suspect created an uncertainty about the ACA's position.'

Sutherland can take credit for an altogether calmer industrial relations environment than that bequeathed him by Speed, but his reservations about full-time professionalism remain, and he is comfortable thinking about them aloud.

GH: The current MOU expires in June 2005. Will the concerns you've expressed be on the agenda?

JS: They're certainly on my agenda. And I think they're on Tim May and Ian Healy's agenda too. I'd like to think we're like-minded on that. It's just that we haven't found the magic recipe to get it right. Because you can't really make people, take them and tell them they're going to do this and this. Well, perhaps you can. Perhaps you can make it part of the contract: that in return for getting paid, there will be an expectation that they will do boom-boom-boom to further their career or set themselves up later. Ideally, I wouldn't want to get to that stage. But in the absence of other solutions, that might be an extreme we have to explore. It's what I grapple with. Ultimately, people have a choice in the way they choose to live their lives. But in five or ten years' time, when they're not prepared for a transition, what happens?

GH: How much do professional cricketers have to be told today? How much guidance do they need?

JS: That's a tough question.

Sutherland has been prepared to answer it. The initiative probably most associated with him has been the Spirit of Cricket charter to which Australia's contracted internationals signed last year. Sutherland got there, he explains, by degrees. The bad-tempered Sydney Test of 2003, in which both Adam Gilchrist and Matthew Hayden were fined for ICC code of conduct breaches, disturbed him. Glenn McGrath's contretemps with Ramnaresh Sarwan at St John's five months later infuriated him, to the extent that he rang Steve Waugh from Australia. Interestingly, perhaps, Sutherland does not refer directly to the *politesse* of cricket; his concern was that these incidents clashed with the first of four 'strategic priorities' in the

ACB's 'From Backyard to Baggy Green' strategic plan, which is 'to strengthen and protect the spirit of cricket'. He might well have been recruited to the ACB because of his cricketing background, but he now speaks very like a manager.

JS: It was starting to get to me. I thought: 'You're saying that this is important. But how bloody important is it?' If you're going to hold the game up as special, then you've got a problem if your leaders and role models aren't buying into that. Might as well not have it.

GH: Why did we need a process for what used to be thought of as common sense?

JS: The game's different. There's huge amounts of personal income involved. I'm not saying people try any harder than they did. There's just more at stake, commercially and financially at least.

GH: You're not telling me that Glenn McGrath was thinking about his income when he threatened to rip Sarwan's throat out, are you?

JS: No. But for whatever reason, there has been a stigma attached to the way the Australian cricket team played the game. And that wasn't consistent with the strategic plan.

GH: That's surely not only a matter of financial stakes.

JS: No you're right. I think one of the factors was that ICC referees, for whatever reason, perhaps because of the law, or because of a lack of support, had not been policing the code. Nor, I think, was the code itself clear enough. I think our code of conduct now is very clear. It says you can do this but not that. And that's what players need. Players need battle lines to be drawn because when you get out there, in the heat of battle, you've got a job to do, you want to know where your boundaries are so you can just go for it.

GH: But it's not a battle. And these aren't battle lines. It's a game. The very words that we use these days, I think, complicate the determination of what constitutes suitable aggression.

JS: That's probably the case. But you can't snap your fingers and change that. It's how it is. Let's take 'battle' out of it. Lines have been drawn. That's important, because people in their uncertainty were pushing the lines and not being pulled up.

Sutherland's approach seems to have paid dividends. The Australian team was recently awarded the 2004 Ausport Prize by the Australian Sports Commission for their contribution to the 'integrity, good sports and fair play of Australian sports' through last year's Spirit of Cricket campaign. The misbehaviour of players has probably been less of a concern recently than that of administrators, particularly those at the Zimbabwean Cricket Union. Engulfed by the despot Robert Mugabe's ruling ZANU-PF, the ZCU triggered a crisis in world cricket in May by sacking its leading (mostly white) players in favour of more tractable junior (mostly black) players – a crisis into which Australia reluctantly wandered on a short but embarrassing tour.

The visit proceeded largely because the ICC's Future Tours Program threatens those who do not tour with fines and suspensions. Sutherland defended this policy strongly in Cricket Australia's *Insight* magazine: 'Cricket clearly does not exist in a vacuum. It is affected by and in turn has an impact on all sorts of other aspects of local and global life. However, Cricket Australia has the task of promoting cricket as its core purpose. The only authority we have from our owners, who are ultimately the cricketers at a community level, is to focus on that task.' The reasoning, I have to confess, did not impress me: the concession that cricket does not take place in a vacuum was accompanied by confirmation that this is the way it would be treated. I questioned Sutherland in a detail that seems worth quoting at length.

GH: It seems, to me anyway, that the role of Cricket Australia expands and shrinks according to what you want to get involved in and don't. Cricket is a *national* game. 'Promoting cricket' might be Cricket Australia's 'core purpose', but it also has the purpose of representing Australia. The Test team is called 'Australia' not

'Australian Cricketers'. How can we be national representatives one minute and just a group of cricketers the next?

JS: I understand your argument. It would have been easy for us to say: 'We're not going.' But the effect of that is a compromise that would have far-reaching consequences in lots and lots of ways. It's a really difficult issue. One of the simple things for me to say is the Australian government should just have said: 'You're not going. We don't want you to go.' And if they'd said that ... then we wouldn't have gone. If the government was serious about that and about the issues in Zimbabwe and an association by Australia as a country ... then clearly it should have taken a much stronger stance.

GH: But surely that's the essence of our protest about Zimbabwe, that the government of the country shouldn't be bossing the cricket board around. Look, it's fair enough, I think, to deplore it when cricket and politics mix; but surely by going to Zimbabwe, which involved an act of recognition of our parallel authority, you were helping it mix. You were saying: 'Fill your board with political cronies. Turn your team into an arm of state propaganda. Plunder your exchequer. Do as you please. After all, it's only a game of cricket.'

JS: I think you're drawing conclusions about Mugabe having representation on the board.

GH: He *is* the patron. And haven't there been a host of appointments in the last year with ZANU-PF connections? Isn't that clear?

JS: It's not clear to me. In fact, nothing on the Zimbabwe issue is clear to me. The lead-in to this tour was extremely frustrating because we just weren't getting a clear view of the situation. I don't know whether that's because the people at the ZCU didn't know or what it was. But on a daily basis, we were getting advice to the effect that the players were back, then they were sacked, then they were back, then sacked again. If we'd known what was going to happen a long way out, it may well have been easier to make a decision. But, I mean, we were always going to go, weren't we? We telegraphed that by going to the World Cup.

GH: Hadn't things changed somewhat since the World Cup?

JS: There's some speculation about the inner workings of Zimbabwean cricket.

GH: Isn't it more than speculation?

JS: If you ask the ICC, and they've done far more on this investigation than we have, then I don't think they've drawn any conclusions about that.

GH: Everything I've seen coming out of Zimbabwe has suggested that the game has been intensely politicised in the last year: systematically, at the levels of selection, administration and finance, in domestic cricket, club cricket and coaching. And every political event in Zimbabwe since the last election suggests that this is of a piece with what's happened in the country. I understand that sport and politics mix more freely in some countries than others. But it can only be seldom that boards are actually taken over in full view of other countries, as ZANU-PF has devoured the ZCU. If the Australian government demanded control of Cricket Australia, sought a balance of power on your board, took control of your selection, and opposed the involvement in the game of a racial minority, what would you want other countries to do? Would you want them to keep playing with us?

JS: That's very much a hypothetical question, and I suggest my answer may vary in the case of extreme circumstances. Generally speaking, however, given member countries' collective commitment to the Future Tours Program, we would expect other Test-playing countries to support the game in our country by continuing to play against us ... Anyway, is this a position that a member country should have been placed in in the first place? Or is it an issue for world cricket? One of the things we've not mentioned, of course, is that the Future Tours Program says if a country does not turn up and play without a good reason, specifically related to security, then they get a US$2 million fine as a minimum plus any damages ... You're saying to me that we shouldn't have gone, but I've also got the commercial consideration that it's going to cost us two million dollars plus.

GH: Isn't that to imbue the Future Tours Program with the status of the Ten Commandments?

JS: (smiling) That's what it is to us, Gideon. Look, if there is a key plank of the financial arrangements of world cricket, it is the knowledge, comfort, security of who is going to be playing here this summer. Without that, we're frantically trying to organise whoever we can get …

GH: … and you're back to the old days of bilateral arrangements.

JS: Which weren't all bad, but the positives of the Future Tours Program far outweigh the negatives.

GH: Is that primarily because cricket has obligations to sponsors and broadcasters?

JS: It's certainly that.

GH: So isn't that the tail wagging the dog?

JS: No, it's broader than that. We've got obligations to the cricket community which includes broadcasters, it includes sponsors, it includes grounds, members of cricket associations, fans and players who expect cricket every summer. And that has a negative impact on the level of interest in the game and the status of the Australian cricket team.

GH: But doesn't it have a negative impact at least on the status of the Australian cricket team that we're prepared to go to Zimbabwe under present circumstances?

JS: The reality is we're in a no-win situation with Zimbabwe. And we chose the lesser of two evils. There was obviously a lot of public comment. A lot of people thought very hard about it round here.

GH: What did you think, James? Not answering as CEO of Cricket Australia but as James Sutherland, private citizen?

JS: (pause) I don't think it matters what I think.

GH: It doesn't matter what I think either James. But I'm sure you've got your own thoughts on this. I'm giving you the opportunity to take your Cricket Australia hat off and express them.

JS: It's hard for me to do that, because I've been to Zimbabwe,

I know some of the people involved in Zimbabwean cricket, I know the game. What I can say is I'm not uncomfortable with the action Cricket Australia took.

GH: You won't take it off will you?

JS: (smiling) I try to take it off when I go to the footy and watch the Cats. One thing I will say is that I don't think countries should be placed in those difficult situations, where they're even more compromised in their decision-making by the Future Tours Program.

GH: Do you object to the idea of the program being a regulation, and entailing the possibility of fines and suspensions?

JS: It does seem rather drastic. But when you see the importance of the Future Tours Program to some countries, you can understand the rationale. There are some countries for which an Indian tour is the main source of revenue [because of television rights]. If India does not tour, Zimbabwean cricket is dead meat for five years. It's that significant.

Sport and politics, of course, sometimes mix in Australia – specifically when prime ministers get involved. It seemed worth asking Sutherland's view of John Howard's infamous gaffe, and Muttiah Muralitharan's decision not to undertake the subsequent Top End Tour. Sutherland's remarks were rather more nuanced than Shane Warne's 'I-cop-it-sweet-so-should-he' response.

JS: I think it [Howard's comment] would have been better left unsaid. Needless to say, a prime minister's comment will inevitably get airplay, and those about Muttiah Muralitharan especially so. But I'm not sure that the comments were directly responsible for Murali not touring. I don't think he wanted to come.

GH: Was it beyond the wit of man to find some way to make touring here a little easier for Murali?

JS: We tried. Not on a formal basis, but we wanted to give him some comfort about playing. The players were encouraging about him coming. I made public comments to the effect that I wanted him to come, and I also spoke to Duleep Mendis [CEO of the Board of Control for Cricket in Sri Lanka] about it too. But it was pretty clear that he wasn't coming.

GH: In Murali's position, I doubt I'd've wanted to come. There was nothing in it for him.

JS: I agree.

GH: I think he's had a very rough time out here.

JS: He has. And he gets a lot of coverage. Yes, I agree.

Zimbabwe, meanwhile, presents the ICC with other problems. The Future Tours Program may be next to godliness, but it is also leading to an awful lot of lacklustre, low-intensity cricket being miraculously imbued with Test status. The glutted cricket calendar, like the weather, is a subject we all discuss but no-one seems to want to do anything about. I asked Sutherland about this in the light of the whiz-bang ICC Super Series pitting the world's number one Test nation against a Rest of the World XI which Australia in June won the right to stage.

GH: It seems surprising to me that there would be any question about the number one nation not being the host.

JS: I think you're right. I think that, while the ICC initially favoured South Africa, they eventually came down on our side for that reason. For the event to be successful you need good crowds and atmosphere, and you can't guarantee that in a country not supporting the national team.

GH: So what's the point of it? Every year we sit down and say that cricket is cheapened by its proliferation. Every year we find we have more cricket than ever.

JS: My personal view is that the amount of cricket being played is about right. The problem has been the amount of mediocre cricket, which has grated on everyone. This goes the other way. This is the best against the best. People can't get enough of the best cricket. You saw that last summer. India and Australia played one of the best summers of cricket that the country's ever seen, and whilst the Australian public have enjoyed the success of the Australian team, they also enjoyed last year seeing them under the pump, having to come from behind to equalise then go one-all to Sydney.

Cricket Australia is both a very new and a very old institution. The idea of a serious permanent executive and staff is really no more than ten years old, dating to the end of the board's post-World Series Cricket relationship with Kerry Packer's PBL Marketing. But the concept of the board composed of members elected by the state associations is as old as the body itself: that is, a hundred in May 2005. Is it time it was revisited?

GH: Australian cricket's structure is historic, but unusual, almost as though the paramount body is owned by its subsidiaries. Is it improvable and how?

JS: (smiling) That's a prick of a question. Depends on the side of the fence you're on. Sometimes we think we run Australian cricket. But if you go to a state association, they'll say: 'Well, we own you.'

GH: So that's the difference between the board and the associations? The board *thinks* it runs Australian cricket, the associations *know* they do?

JS: They know they own the people who think they run it.

GH: Cricket Australia is governed by fourteen directors: three each from New South Wales, Victoria and South Australia; two each from Queensland and Western Australia; one from Tasmania. So the founder states have nine votes. Yet in interstate cricket, the most successful states for the last fifteen years would almost certainly have been Queensland and Western Australia, and they have four. Why?

JS: (sigh) Next question. Well, it's historical, you know that.

GH: That doesn't mean it's optimal.

JS: That's true ... Look, I'm a big one for worrying about the things I can control and not about those I can't. We executives don't have any input in that. It's for the members. If they believe it's an issue, they'll address it.

GH: How do you know when you're doing a good job, James? The CEO of a listed company knows: it's in his profits and his share price and P/E ratio. That doesn't get you far here. What are your performance indicators?

JS: I'm appraised in a formal sense by the chairman, which is also based in part on assessments by other people. I would be judged in line with the strategy, how my performance has been on achieving strategic goals. I know that sounds very corporate, but the reality is the outcomes of our policies on the community are very hard to measure.

Just how hard is illustrated by one of Sutherland's key initiatives last year: a major census of participants in Australian cricket. Setting a stricter definition of participation than most previous censuses have used, it revealed 281,000 club players, 90,000 school players, 64,000 reduced numbers: a total of 436,000. While not itself of great use until a comparative census is done in a few years, it does illustrate some of the complexities of the issues confronting cricket at community level.

JS: What do I feel about that number? I'm glad we have it. Is it a performance indicator? Yes and no. Say you have a club turning over about eighty players in a season. If suddenly they have 120 in one season, they're going to suffer capacity constraints. Where do they play? Where do you find grounds? There's no point in us attracting more people to play the game if there aren't the grounds, the facilities, umpires, the coaches, the volunteers. Grounds especially are harder to come by than ever, and more expensive. Housing estates are being built where developers think about pathways for people to walk their dogs, but not ovals to play cricket on. If they have some spare space, they might build a little soccer pitch, which is not big enough for cricket or footy. So it's much more of a challenge than incremental increases in participation rates.

Cricket Australia's resources have their own capacity constraints. In seasons 2001–02 and 2002–03, Cricket Australia reported operating surpluses totalling $77 million, about eighty-two per cent of which was distributed to the states. Is the status of Cricket Australia as a partnership of state associations to which it immediately disgorges its surpluses one that will work in its second century? All that Sutherland would say on the subject was: 'In any organisation owned by its members there is a debate about the right amount of retained earnings.' The associations, he was quick to add, were 'doing a very good job' and 'running a tight ship'.

GH: Would you like Cricket Australia to lead a more independent, more autonomous existence, with less reference to the states?

JS: In an ideal world, you'd be in a position where you could manage on a needs basis rather than having to juggle from year to year. But we're just not in that position. We *are* trying to build our reserves, but that's in a context of a level of distributions to states that means the growth is minimal. So we're squirrelling a bit away, but whether there's enough there to deal with a disaster is highly debatable.

Nothing has changed very quickly in Australian cricket administration, but perhaps we should give it time. In some respects, it's hardly begun.

Wisden Australia 2004–05

MATCH-FIXING

Fallen Idols

Five years ago, on the commission of a sports magazine, I rang Mark Waugh to ask him for an interview. To my bemusement, he asked how much he'd be paid for it. When I said I couldn't offer him anything, and that the magazine concerned probably wouldn't, he murmured dejectedly that things he did never seemed to lead to money.

For the record, Mark went ahead with a brief and bland interview on the phone a week or so later. I was grateful and, thinking that I'd probably led a sheltered life, rationalised his remarks as a momentary lapse from one I'd hitherto regarded as a model of courtesy.

But it's true to say that – as an admirer rather than a journalist – I did not look at Mark in quite the same way for a long time. Now it's turned out he found other ways to make a little cash on the side, I know how hardcore Democrats felt when it was demonstrated that President Clinton didn't only smoke his cigars.

To be sure, there are a variety of mitigating circumstances to the disclosures of the last couple of days. Mark Waugh and Shane Warne betrayed no significant confidences in their transactions with the Indian bookmaker in question, paid the fines for their misdemeanours promptly, and have been exemplary advertisements for cricket in this country. Warne, in particular, I have admired both as a player and an unfailingly obliging and generous media subject.

Yet it is precisely because of those outstanding reputations that the sense of disillusionment will be so profound. These were not inexperienced junior cricketers anxious about their financial futures, but worldly and well-rewarded international athletes. Warne, in fact, demonstrated an awareness of the stakes in his autobiography last year: 'The whole betting scene in India and Pakistan is illegal so the people running the betting are basically gangsters. Not the sort of people to trust or play around with.' He wrote as much knowing that he had already done precisely that.

The implications of the affair go further. Australia's international cricketers assured us last season that they were campaigning for better pay in the interests of all first-class players. I didn't doubt their sincerity and don't now. But some will be tempted – given the casual and heedless way that two have subsidised their incomes – to perceive those remarks as disingenuous. Reputation, so hard won, can be the very devil to restore once tarnished.

During an Ashes Test at Adelaide Oval in January 1925, the great Australian leg-spinner Arthur Mailey once related, he and his captain Herbie Collins were visited by a bookmaker offering them money to throw the game. They threw *him* – down a flight of stairs. History will now record that nearly seventy years later, another legendary Australian leg-spinner and his experienced colleague contentedly parlayed with a bookmaker for personal gain. In time, this will be forgiven, but it won't be forgotten.

The Australian December 1998

MATCH-FIXING

The Fix is In

It was a sure thing. Worth putting money on, in fact. Sooner or later, an international cricketer would fry for his dealings taking cash in return for influencing the outcome of a game. You'd scarcely have imagined that it would be South Africa's flinty skipper Hansie Cronje, sacked by his country's board of control on 11 April after he and three team-mates were charged by Indian police in connection with an allegedly rigged one-day match against India four weeks earlier. But then, nobody could believe that 'Shoeless' Joe Jackson was among the eight Chicago White Sox players implicated in gifting the 1919 World Series to Cincinnati. Such is the nature of sporting conspiracies.

No, you could see it coming. Cricket has had a seedy odour for at least ten years, maybe longer: one former Test player, Pakistan's Qasim Omar, has spoken of pay-offs to international cricketers dating back to 1984. Two separate inquiries, in India and Pakistan, have generated plenty of heat, if little light. The stakes were large enough a decade ago to cost a man his life: leading Bombay bookie Jitu Bhai poisoned himself rather than meet losses incurred in – by an eerie coincidence – a match involving South Africa and India. And the stakes now boggle the mind: up to $400 million can change hands on a single limited-overs international.

So don't be misled by any platitudes you read over the next few weeks about cricket's good name being under threat, about how the game synonymous with fair play and a straight bat has suddenly been sullied. The slide into sleaze has been steady, perhaps even inevitable. And in some respects, it reflects aspects of cricket even older than its reputation as the *soi-disant* 'gentlemen's game'.

Cricket first achieved widespread popular appeal during the general upsurge in English sport after the Restoration. This was a gambling age, and the first references to bets being taken on matches date back more than 300 years. In the eighteenth century, bookies were as much a feature of Lord's, cricket's holy of holies, as Epsom and Ascot; as the crack batsman of the era, Billy Beldham, remembered it: 'If gentlemen wanted to bet, just under the pavilion sat men ready, with money down, to give and take the current odds.' Most early sets of cricket laws contain provisions for the fair settlement of bets. It has even been contended that the publication of the first average tables was motivated by the need for a reliable 'form guide'.

There is, however, even more to the relationship between cricket and gambling than historical coincidence. The fact is that cricket is a great game to bet on. Unlike horse racing, in which betting is concerned purely with the final outcome, cricket offers a plenitude of punting opportunities: from the winner, loser and margin of victory, through spread bets on the performances of individual competitors, to minutiae like the number of extras conceded and the scorer of the first boundary (nor is comparison of horse racing and cricket idle: much of the growth in cricket betting in India has been at the expense of racecourses, where attendances have halved in the past decade).

Where goes gambling, of course, corruption is bound to follow: by the early nineteenth century, matches were being routinely fixed, gamblers frequently swindled. So pervasive was the practice, indeed, that the whole rotten system ultimately collapsed under its own weight. As William Fennex, a leading cricketer of the day who publicly repented his crooked ways, put it: 'Matches were bought and matches were sold, and gentlemen who meant honestly lost large sums of money, till the rogues beat themselves at last. They overdid it; they spoilt their own trade.' Administrative action also played a part: William Lambert, generally acknowledged to be the finest player of his time, was excommunicated from big cricket in 1817 when it was revealed that he had thrown a game between England and Nottingham. But perhaps the overriding consideration was that cricket had by now also become a lucrative spectator sport, and that its popularity was now endangered rather than enhanced by the influence of gambling.

The decline of gambling in cricket had a curious effect. It was in celebrating its wane that cricket lovers first began to place their game on a lofty moral pedestal. In his famous book *The Cricket Field* 150 years ago, Rev. James Pycroft remarked: 'The constant habit of betting will take the honesty out of any man ... It is no small praise of cricket that it occupies the place of less innocent sports. Drinking, gambling, cudgel-playing insensibly disappear before a manly recreation, which draws the labourer from the dark haunts of vice and misery to the open common.' It is to Pycroft in his paean of praise to the summer game, in fact, that we owe that ever-popular expression for the unethical and mean-minded: 'Not cricket'.

Yet the possibility that cricket matches might be fixed never entirely vanished. At a 1921 meeting of the Imperial Cricket Conference – forerunner to the today's International Cricket Council – Australian captain Warwick Armstrong suggested to the English cricketing grandee Lord Harris that the appointment of Test umpires be delayed until the day before their engagements commenced, explaining: 'The umpires are paid little for their services and, as there is a lot of betting on Tests, it would be wise to remove them from temptation.' Harris made enquiries – apparently as superficial and half-hearted as those of the ICC today – and advised the meeting the following day: 'I can find no evidence of betting on cricket – people don't do it.' Armstrong replied: 'You don't think so, my Lord? If you'd like £500 on the next Test, I can get it on for you.'

At times, money was even waved under the noses of players. In January 1925, with an Ashes Test match in Adelaide on a knife edge, Australian skipper Herbie Collins and leg-spinner Arthur Mailey were approached by a bookmaker who offered them money in return for allowing England to win. There was also always talk. Even Sir Donald Bradman heard it. England won the opening two Tests of his first series as Australian captain in 1936–37, before Bradman's team rallied memorably to capture the next three and the rubber: a result that to some looked a little too stage-managed. Bradman told the writer Ray Robinson: 'My own father told me those [First and Second] Tests must have been rigged to ensure better gate takings at the last three Tests. I told him you can't rig a game of cricket but I can't say I convinced him.'

For once, however, Bradman was wrong: you *can* rig a game of cricket – one-day cricket in particular. It takes little to upset the competitive equilibrium of a limited-overs match. A few sloppy and misdirected deliveries from a bowler, a few overs blocked out by a batsman, can at the pivotal moment be the difference between winning and losing – both for players and for punters. Nor is it difficult in the hurly-burly of a one-day international – where crude methods and clumsy mistakes are commonplace – to lose one's wicket to a wretched shot or mismanage an easy run-out. The spectator will nod sagely: 'Pressure'. Even if, in a guileless assumption that both teams are playing for keeps, that spectator is unaware that the pressure is from bookies who want a certain batsman to achieve a pre-determined number of runs.

If you're an international cricketer offered a financial incentive to bowl a few wides or deadbat a few overs, moreover, it must be inordinately tempting. After all, what's another one-day slogathon? Especially if you're a South African cricketer, whose relative rate of pay has dwindled drastically over the past two years with the shrinkage in the value of the rand. And perhaps not least if you're a South African captain who has been at loggerheads with his board over the past year.

Yet Cronje should not bear all of the odium to come. Cricket authorities also bear a degree of responsibility for the affair; not only because of the glacial pace of their response to the growing number of allegations about match-fixing, but because of the way that their schedules have fostered the climate for corruption. Some will shortly be professing indignation about the venality of international cricketers who accept cash from bookies on the grounds that: 'These are men playing for their country. National pride is at stake.' Yet what patriotic sting was there to the one-day international in question between South Africa and India at Faridabad on 15 March, one of almost 600 played during the last five years? The answer is next to none: the games were staged for gate and television revenue, and in effect if not design the convenience of bookmakers.

It is now almost proverbial to say that too much cricket is played these days. The idea should be refined: what exists is a surfeit of meaningless cricket on which nothing hinges. These are the conditions under which corruption flourishes: when tired, bored, apathetic professionals are compelled to go through the motions for money.

The Eye May 2000

MATCH-FIXING

Who Fixes the Fixers?

Facing the press after an Australia v Pakistan match during the one-day CUB Series three months ago, Steve Waugh unconsciously offered a telling insight into the nature of modern cricket.

'What about the next game, Steve?' asked one journalist. 'Who are we playing?' responded the Australian captain. Chuckles all round. Waugh continued: 'We just get on a plane and go somewhere and find out who we're playing.'

This moment of candour from the game's most earnest professional set one wondering: if a player as compulsively competitive as Waugh was feeling bored and surfeited by cricket's glutted calendar, what of others involved in the if-this-is-Friday-it-must-be-Faridabad world? We now know the answer in at least one case: South Africa's captain Hansie Cronje, so blasé, so greedy that he thought nothing of turning snout for the thieves of Bombay bookmaking.

Cronje is alleged to have conspired with bookies to rig a series of one-day matches in India last month, which would have been forgotten by now had they not become the subject of police investigation. He has admitted receiving cash for passing information to bookmakers during a triangular one-day series in South Africa a few weeks earlier, which likewise promptly faded from the collective memory but is now being minutely examined.

In all likelihood, his career is over. Yet in the hurry to scapegoat Cronje, let us not forget how exquisitely administrators have served the interests of the $16-billion-a-year industry that is cricket gambling on the sub-continent. Over the past five years, one-day internationals have been scheduled at a rate of one every three days. As Graham Halbish, former CEO of the Australian Cricket Board, put it: 'We're in the entertainment business ... we believe that one-day international cricket is a form of pure entertainment and provided for the enjoyment of the public.' And it so happened, of course, that this 'pure entertainment' also provided the likes of Halbish with a geyser of cash from television broadcasting rights.

From time to time during this period, the various boards of control have gathered at the International Cricket Council and agreed: 'Well yes, we're probably playing a tad too much; it's rather cheapened the game.' But, like state governments who publicly deplore the social costs of gambling but can't get enough of those fat gaming revenues, nobody wanted to spoil the party. Occasionally the result has been something akin to *Cricket's Funniest Home Videos*. In September last year, for instance, the boards of control in Australia and India sent Second XIs to play five limited-overs games in Los Angeles, ostensibly to promote the game in the United States. The games were played on crummy pitches and in front of empty stands, but no matter: sponsor AXN, the broadcasting arm of Sony Pictures, was beaming them back to India, where they were watched by numberless thousands. And their bookmakers.

For everyone knew that bookmakers on the sub-continent were getting fat, and that the preposterous amount of meaningless cricket being scheduled was playing into their hands. Indians bet more on a single one-day international than Australians throw at the Melbourne Cup every year and, so far as the bookies were concerned, the more matches the merrier. Everyone knew, too, that players were getting bored, jaded, cynical. As tough a competitor as South African fast bowler Allan Donald commented last year: 'I've hardly had time to draw breath since we got back into international cricket ... It's simply been a matter of getting on with the schedule, wondering where I was when I woke up some mornings' (Donald has since taken a sabbatical from international cricket). Yet all this was strangely lost on administrators. When allegations of match-fixing by Indian players were first raised three years ago by the *Pioneer,* for instance, Indian board secretary Jagmohan Dalmiya dismissed them as 'absurd' and an attempt to 'malign the name of Indian cricket for the sake of a juicy story'. This is, of course, the same Dalmiya who as ICC president now piously insists: 'We have said before that any attempt to interfere with the fair conduct of our sport is totally unacceptable.'

The cricket glut continued to be regarded as someone else's problem: more than 200 one-day internationals have been staged since 1999 began, with Cronje's team seemingly never out of its coloured motley. As the *Wisden Cricketers' Almanack* pointed out: 'The South African board ... seems incapable of turning down an invitation. Rare is the triangular or quadrangular tournament that does not include South Africa. Probably the only person who has done more touring than Cronje in the past few years is Bob Dylan. How many roads must a man walk down, before you give him a break?' Time has proved this a prescient remark.

The Australian Cricket Board, meanwhile, presents every season a one-day tournament in which fifteen fixtures are scheduled to decide which of three teams is best. The risk is that this narrows quickly to a two-horse race, as occurred last season, with the third team condemned to a series of games whose purpose is no more elaborate than keeping the ads apart on Channel Nine. And, of course, providing something for Indians to bet on. It is curious that, while players are dropped, captains sacked, selectors replaced, coaches and managers fired, administrators are never held to account. But perhaps, in this case, that is as it should be; that having helped create this Augean stable, they should have the task of cleaning it.

Australian Financial Review April 2000

MATCH-FIXING

So Far, So Bad

The most distressing aspect of cricket's corruption crisis, it was generally agreed after the first allegations were made about a fortnight ago, was that it threw the integrity of every international match into doubt. As this was regarded as such a depressing development, one wonders why it has become such a media sport to do so.

On Thursday 20 April 2000, the *Australian* ran on its front page what was promoted as an interview with UCBSA chief executive Ali Bacher in which a string of allegations were made: that two World Cup matches last year had been fixed, that doubts had been raised about 'more than one umpire', and that one international team was 'throwing and manipulating matches'. Writer Malcolm Conn reported that Bacher 'declined to be more specific', but proceeded to be so on his behalf, citing Pakistan's World Cup defeat by Bangladesh as 'the match that raised most concern', and Javed Akhtar's officiation in South Africa's deciding Test against England twenty months ago as 'the umpiring that has raised most eyebrows'.

The story was picked up round the world, and repackaged as though the match and incident specified had emanated from Bacher himself, forcing the administrator to issue a clarifying statement. But this was not the only example, since the crisis began, of conjecture being made concrete: 'questions' have been raised over England's recent Test win at Centurion Park, over England's defeat by New Zealand at Old Trafford last year, and over any number of games in Sharjah. Three 'famous' English Testmen have been accused by former team-mate Chris Lewis in the *News of the World* of accepting cash from bookies. Other reports suggest that India's Mohammed Azharuddin and Ajay Jadeja will shortly be in the firing line.

Perhaps all these speculations have foundation. But perhaps they do not. Pardon such a 'naïve and stupid' observation, but I had always imagined cricket's unpredictability to be part of its charm. I had also thought it generally accepted that umpires occasionally erred, and that players did not always perform at their peaks. Unfortunately, we are now moving in a realm where rumour and fact have become all but indistinguishable.

Where does this process cease? Bangladesh's defeat of Pakistan was a turn-up for the books, and perhaps also for the bookies, but so was Zimbabwe's thrashing of South Africa a couple of days earlier. And surely no result was so bizarre as that in the preceding World Cup when Kenya mauled the mighty West Indies. How long before a crusading journalist casts doubts on the courageous Kenyans' proudest cricketing day?

Javed Akhtar's familiarity with the LBW law did seem remote at Headingley in August 1998, but it impacted on both teams, and by far the most influential decision in the series had occurred in the Trent Bridge Test a week earlier: the reprieve granted match-winner Mike Atherton, then 27 going on 98 not out, from an appeal for a catch at the wicket. If you're searching for umpiring that 'raises eyebrows', meanwhile, what of Sachin Tendulkar's recent run of luck with our own officials? A few Indian punters would have been looking for tall buildings to jump off after that LBW in Adelaide, don't you think?

You see, it's the simplest thing in the world to raise 'questions' by inverting the burden of proof, implying guilt through rumour and hearsay, then leaving it to the injured party to establish his innocence. For innocence frequently relies on nothing more than an individual's word and, in an age where the vogue is for cheap cynicism, that counts for little.

This climate of reckless allegation and imputation, however, endangers cricket's good name as much as Hansie Cronje may or may not have. If everything unusual, unforeseen, unworthy and even incompetent is to be deemed suspicious, cricket faces extinction sooner rather than later.

Wisden Online April 2000

MATCH-FIXING

Caught

When Hansie Cronje testified before South Africa's commission of inquiry into match-fixing in June 2000, Judge Edwin King offered him the advice of St John's gospel: 'The truth will set you free.' Alas, as Oscar Wilde commented: 'The truth is rarely pure and never simple.'

It falls to another Wilde – the industrious Simon of the *Sunday Times* – to demonstrate how well this applies to cricket's dirtiest secret in his new book *Caught.* Several writers have already tackled the breaking stories of match-fixing in their own countries: South Africa's Deon Gouws and India's Pradeep Magazine, not to mention the indefatigable website tehelka.com with its *Fallen Heroes.* But Wilde's is the first truly global panorama and, given the breathtaking speed with which it has been produced, it is excellent.

Cronje's disoriented confession in April last year is Wilde's embarkation point, and Cronje's is the case that most consumes him. He does an admirable job of picking up the pieces from the sadly-truncated King Commission, demonstrating the evasions and inconsistencies in Cronje's testimony; anyone countenancing Cronje's cricketing rehabilitation will now find it very hard to do so.

Only one aspect of the story eludes him, concerning M. K. Gupta's now infamous approach to the South Africans to play dead for dollars in a Mumbai one-dayer in December 1996. The game was organised under bizarre circumstances. Originally designated as a benefit for Mohinder Amarnath, it was for no obvious reason

---

Review of *Caught* by Simon Wilde (Aurum, 2001)

reclassified as an official international: the tour's eighth. The South Africans were peeved, Cronje particularly so. It suddenly became his hundredth one-day international, a landmark he'd hoped to achieve at home. I suspect that this sense of being a pawn of self-interested administrators played a part in Cronje's slide into malpractice, as indeed did the involution of South Africa's cricket community after decades of sporting isolation.

Caught then widens to encompass the various reports on match-fixing now in such plentiful supply, reinforced by some intelligent original reporting. We are left to gawp at the deceptions, the hollow denials, and the crass hypocrisies, as pious Hansie, devout Azha and sundry Koran-clutching Pakistanis happily lie their heads off. Wilde follows it all studiously, only occasionally, in the odd infelicity of expression and unchecked fact, showing the strain of the incredible haste with which *Caught* must have been composed.

The only real shortcoming of Wilde's book – doubtless also from haste – is a general lack of context. What of the massive (legal) gambling apparatus that now surrounds cricket, and indeed all sport? What of the mistrust between the old and new cricket worlds that has so hampered investigations? What of the affair's implications for cricket's industrial relations? As it is, we are left to take FICA's Tim May at his word when he says: 'It [match-fixing] was the only way they could make the game pay them a reasonable wage ... you can draw some sort of relationship between pay and conditions and corruption.' Some sort of relationship, perhaps, but surely not a linear one. Many people feel under-rewarded; only an infinitesimal proportion are so devoured by grievance that they turn to malfeasance.

The speed at which *Caught* has been produced, however, is also among its virtues. It is almost a shock to find between a book's covers what newspapers have reported so recently. Occasionally, too, Wilde shows how raw these events truly are. He reflects that there was a time when cricket journalists could 'go through their entire careers without writing a "news" story of any description', then gives an insight into how discomfiting this can be. When Alec Stewart was implicated in the report of India's Central Bureau of Investigation this year, Wilde was an uneasy observer: he was Stewart's *Sunday Times* 'ghost'. 'Though I had spent so much time on the match-fixing story, I could not bring myself to quiz him doggedly,' Wilde relates. 'He was going through hell and I had to be sympathetic rather than critical; the idea of probing seemed indecent and disloyal. Besides, we both knew that after Cronje's exposure, protestations of innocence counted for little. At one point, he said to me: "I don't know whether you believe me or not."'

This is a candid reflection. And imagine how much more difficult it is for players, so close to one another for such long periods, so detached from the outside world, to guess at and judge one another's motives and actions. For this is the match-fixing affair's most understandable, and at the same time abominable, aspect: that it remained such a well-kept dressing-room secret so long. The Proteas are especially culpable. As Wilde comments: 'No South African players were punished in connection with match-fixing, despite most of the team sitting on information relating to the issue for years.' In a way, *Caught*'s most telling remark belongs to Pat Symcox, whom Cronje consulted after he received his first inducement during the Mandela Trophy in January 1995: 'My advice was not to worry about it and just get on with the game.' Evil triumphs when good men do nothing; evil has a veritable field day when good men prevent anyone doing anything.

Wisden Cricket Monthly October 2001

THE LAWS OF CRICKET

Spirited Debate

Even John Howard – perhaps especially John Howard – would agree that the Goods and Services Tax was not the year 2000's only raft of life-changing legislation. The Marylebone Cricket Club greeted the new millennium with a substantial revision of the Laws of Cricket, particularly at each end: from a preamble concerning 'The Spirit of Cricket' to a vastly-expanded Law 42 delineating circumstances under which an umpire may penalise a team runs for 'unfair play'.

This caused consternation, some of it not without foundation. It would seem contradictory to on one hand remind players of the game's immanent spirit, then on the other to propose sanctions to police it; spirit is spirit, law is law. There's reason, too, to believe that many of the proscriptive additions will never be invoked. How often, for instance, has one seen a batsman trying to steal a run during the bowler's run up, as foreseen in Law 42.16? Not even Dr Grace had that one up his sleeve.

Just because a law is seldom applied, however, is no reason not to have it. Some very effective cricketing statutes are never used. Law 31, allowing for batsmen to be 'timed out' should they make insufficient haste to the crease at the fall of a wicket, works a treat. The mere threat of such a mortifying method of dismissal is quite enough to ensure cricket's expeditious conduct. Those who always seem to be asleep or on the toilet when it's their turn to bat, incidentally, should be aware that Law 31 is one of those that MCC has fine-tuned; you must now be 'ready to face the next ball' within three minutes of the previous batsman's fall, rather than having two from the wicket until you enter the field.

Local attention centred on Laws 42.4 and 42.5 involving 'deliberate distraction' of a batsman by 'word or action'; aka 'sledging'. Both Australian captain Steve Waugh and Australian Cricketers' Association secretary Tim May expressed reservations, fearing a blunting of cricket's competitive edge. Yet it's unlikely any international umpire would wish to interfere with the natural hurly-burly of competition. Nor are Test players the MCC's only constituency; the Laws concern every cricketer, however humble, who would prefer to enjoy his weekend rather than listen to a chorus of effing and blinding from his opponents. In all, it's quite a workmanlike effort. Just a pity about that preamble – as the prime minister might also say.

Wisden Australia 2000–01

THE AKHTAR CASE

Thrown to the Wolves

Imagine if a magistrate returned a licence to a banned driver on the grounds that his future conduct would in any case be inhibited by the speed limit. For that is approximately what International Cricket Council president Jagmohan Dalmiya has done in sanctioning Shoaib Akhtar's inclusion in Pakistan's side for the CUB Series, and why all heaven is resultantly in a rage.

Dalmiya's pretext for the remission – that only Akhtar's bouncer, which would perforce be no-balled in limited-overs cricket, is at issue – is one of the feeblest *post hoc* rationalisations that cricket's community has ever been asked to swallow. Especially given its prompt contradiction by members of the ICC's own Advisory Panel on Illegal Actions, it may also prove equivalent to Dalmiya taking careful aim at his foot and blowing off both kneecaps: once again, debate rages about the ICC's credibility and competence.

Global cricket governance is one of those issues that, as Mark Twain said of the weather, everyone talks about but nobody does anything about. A spirit of *sauve qui peut* prevails. In an interview with ABC radio a few weeks ago, ICC CEO David Richards was quizzed about the proliferation of one-day internationals. He commented that national delegates had actually agreed to a one-day: Test ratio, but that their boards had essentially paid it no heed, and continued scheduling hit-and-giggles like there was no tomorrow.

Perhaps the ultimate hypocrisy was Sri Lanka's a year ago. Having carried on piously about the ICC being the only possible forum in which the legality of Muttiah Muralitharan's action could be decided, it turned around and disputed the application of the

ICC's code of conduct to the misbehaviour of its captain Arjuna Ranatunga at Adelaide Oval: an act of the most egregious bad faith.

This is not to say that Akhtar and Murali infringe the laws; indeed, my personal opinion is that neither does. But unlike some cricket administrators – who shall remain nameless in accord with their facelessness – I don't assume that the ICC is wrong whenever it does not reflect my views. If in a democracy the party you vote for does not win power, that does not entitle you to ignore its laws.

Nor is it to say that cricket does not need the likes of Akhtar and Murali, exotic talents who are ornaments to the game. Once again, I would concur. But by this argument, South Africa would never have spent twenty years in its deeply-deserved political purdah: the pleasure forgone in depriving the public of Pollock, Richards, Procter et al would have been deemed too great.

No, the argument here is that the whole concept of a body running international cricket is undermined whenever short-term national expedients intrude. Dalmiya, and those with his ear who presumably sought his fiat, have done little more than bring a system they helped create into disrepute. Not even Australia can hold its head up in this shabby mess. As Robert Craddock pointed out in a perceptive commentary on 10 January: 'Australian cricket officials love to bag the ICC, but in doing so they are effectively bagging themselves for the ICC will only ever be as strong as the member nations allow it to be.' That's so true, it hurts.

Wisden Online January 2000

CROWDS

Patriot Games

On the biggest day of the international cricket summer, at least part of the limelight falls on the Melbourne Cricket Ground crowd. Usually, this involves awe at its dimensions and tributes to its carnival atmosphere; this year, it may entail conjecture about its character.

Ugly incidents involving racist abuse and threats have marred the first two Tests in Brisbane and Adelaide. The *Herald* has reported several cases of heckling and jostling of Indian spectators and officials, including one in which an immigrant Indian businessman 'feared for his safety for the first time in fifteen years of living in Australia'.

Sambit Bal, editor of the Indian cricket magazine *Wisden Asia*, reports that the standard term of abuse of the racist baiter in Adelaide was 'coolie', and that the harassment sometimes went beyond the verbal: 'While walking past the group of Australian fans sitting below the scoreboard, we found ourselves pelted with empty water bottles. Then I had a chewed bone thrown at me from close proximity with the words, "here, take it".'

With the national reputation for plurality and tolerance under threat, such reports are enough to make any self-respecting liberal cringe. The infamous Nicky Winmar incident forced Australian football to acknowledge the racist blight in its bleachers; should we worry about something similar in Australian cricket?

Worry, of course, is cheap. And in a world with so much to legitimately concern us, it is easy to lose perspective. International sport is probably this country's chief forum for overt patriotism, and it is a reality, however unpalatable, that patriotism mutates quite easily through nationalism and into xenophobia. Perhaps 70,000 people will attend the MCG on Boxing Day. Some will harbour racist thoughts; a subset of those may vent them. When senior politicians under the influence of alcohol behave so stupidly, should it surprise us that spectators, judgment similarly impaired, turn from barracking for their own country to barracking against its rival?

What's unusual about this summer is not necessarily the extent of Australian jingoism, but the fact that it has a focus. Indian spectators, local and visiting, are present in unprecedented numbers – and are unprecedentedly vocal. Professor Richard Cashman of the University of New South Wales, author of the seminal work on Australian cricket crowds *Ave a Go Yer Mug*, says this is a confronting shift for local fans: 'Because the Indian community is more physically prominent than they're used to, that tends to generate a response, especially when India are doing well.'

Television, Cashman believes, plays a part in generating that response: 'The media has a way of focusing on oppositional groups, suggesting, for instance, that all the visiting spectators are in one part of the crowd, which tends to play up the idea of there being a "spectator war".' Australian crowds have always had a reputation for volubility. Now, television turns their sporting passion into a commodity and sells it back to them, offering in return a nanosecond of notoriety and narcissism. Cameras that search for outpourings of allegiance, crowd catches, clever banners and pretty girls encourage a kind of competition in exuberance and exhibitionism. And, of course, it's not just us. Like England's boisterous Barmy Army, the Swami Army is turning up in order to be seen as well as to see.

It is arguable that it is this competition, rather than a straightforward racism, that pushes behaviour to extremes. Nor should the significance of context be ignored. Australian fans who hectored Sri Lanka's Muttiah Muralitharan with cries of 'no ball' were somehow more offensive than the Barmy Army's similar cries when

Brett Lee was bowling last season, because the Australians were part of a majority and the English were not.

In coming years, however, the issue may become more pressing. This summer's Indian spectators form part of another emergent trend. Where international sport has tended to be played in front of audiences solidly behind the home team, increased prosperity and a greater consciousness of sport as a potential source of inbound tourism have made the modern fan more mobile. Decades of migration have also altered crowd composition. At the 1998 Barbados Test between England and the West Indies, for example, there were more English fans in the ground than locals. We have constructed our cricket crowds as pageants of uninhibited patriotism: the freedom to scorn and ridicule opponents seems to be regarded as almost an inalienable right. In future, however, it won't only be *our* patriotism on display.

The Sydney Morning Herald December 2003

LORD'S

Cricket's Fawlty Towers

I first came to Lord's twenty years ago as a wide-eyed Australian teenager. The Tower, the Palace, Earl's Court: they could all wait until I'd seen what Sir Robert Menzies once called the Cathedral of Cricket. One of my most vivid cricket memories is of getting off a plane in April 1989 and heading straight for Lord's to watch MCC v Worcestershire, and especially the youthful phenomenon Graeme Hick of whom I'd heard so much. Hick made a power-packed hundred, but my overpowering recollection is of the whispered news that swept the ground of the horrors of Hillsborough. It seemed such an English affair: there we were, a handful of spectators in this quiet county cloister, while, to the north, scores were perishing in an overcrowded football ghetto.

I love Lord's. I hate it too. Marylebone Cricket Club remains a law unto itself, wrapped in ritual, cobwebbed in custom. Over a drink a few weeks back, my friend David Studham, librarian at the Melbourne Cricket Club, told me a story about a visit to Lord's a few years ago when he overheard a nonagenarian in the Long Room spluttering to the members around him: 'I say, d'ya know there's a bally woman talking to Swanton in the committee room? What's the world coming to?' Errr, yes, murmured one of his fellows: it was ... well ... the Queen.

MCC also remains a state within a state in English cricket. Journalists, for example, must obtain separate accreditation for games at Lord's in addition to their ECB pass. If they can. Clare Skinner, the deputed authority, moves in her own sweet way, impervious to emails and phone messages. When I finally make contact with her, she issues an airy promise to leave said pass at the East Gate – and, of course, it's not there. 'No accreditation here,' says the resident jobsworth.

'Well,' I suggest helpfully, 'perhaps you could call Clare Skinner and find out why it's not.'

'No,' he says simply.

'Why not?' I ask.

'You call her.'

'That's going to be difficult. I don't have a phone.'

'You've got a problem,' says the attendant, smirking at his mate.

Actually, it's Lord's that has the problem. The rudeness of its personnel is legendary, yet it seems perversely proud to be the Fawlty Towers of English cricket, where everything would be fine if it wasn't for the deuced public wanting to watch cricket there. Looking in another direction as he does so, the attendant finally pushes a piece of paper to me, on which is handwritten a telephone number. I presume that I'm meant to call someone. I find a payphone and call it. It is someone's voicemail. The day is going swimmingly.

Of course, it's nothing personal. They'd stop W. G. if he didn't have the right pass ('Where do you think you're going, beardy?'). The truly baffling thing I learn, however, is that, although the Australians are practising this morning, the public is not allowed into the ground. Two Aussie friends of mine, who have decided to take time off from work this morning to come and watch their countrymen, are disappointed; I am baffled. At the Confederations Cup in Germany recently, 30,000 people turned up to watch the Brazilians practise: the tournament's organisers turned it into a major event, selling merchandise and laying on food and drink. I suppose when the tickets to your Test match sell themselves – and would half-a-dozen times over – you probably don't have to think too much about 'promoting the game'. I finally get some assistance from a more helpful attendant at the Grace Gates. But grace, I fear, is a word I find hard to associate with Lord's.

Cricinfo July 2005

COACHES

Moores: The Pity

No wonder the England Cricket Board is getting a right ticking-off from the media for its prompt appointment of Peter Moores as national coach. Months of fun beckoned speculating about Duncan Fletcher's successor. Warnie. Moody. Buchs. Boycs. Becks. Posh. It's so crazy it might work ...

There could have been a long list, a short list, a pointy-headed technocrat, a gruff but warm-hearted paterfamilias, and a professional motivator skilled in neurolinguistic programming, with the final choice between a Mitteleuropean savant like the one who takes the Steeple Sinderby Wanderers to the FA Cup in J. L. Carr's novel and Jeffrey Archer. Instead, we have Moores, who, according to the *Cricketers' Who's Who* I just yanked from the shelf, has seven O-levels and three A-levels. All that can be said authoritatively is that twenty years ago he had a very bad haircut.

Critics of the appointment have been concerned about what it says about English cricket. The essence of their criticism says something perhaps just as interesting. Corporatist thinking so pervades sport that an appointment process not involving headhunters, multiple interviews, strategic plans and psychometric tests now seems hopelessly lacking in rigour. One involving orderly succession must, by definition, be a case of 'jobs for the boys'.

Is that right, though? Such thinking in the corporate world is now rather outmoded. According to Jim Collins, easily the world's most influential management thinker, 'larger-than-life, celebrity leaders who ride in from the outside' are 'negatively correlated' with commercial outperformance. The best leaders are 'humble but ferocious': something like a cross between Charles Pooter and Vlad the Impaler, apparently.

There's no disputing that Tom Moody would have been an outstanding candidate. All the same, one objective in running an organisation – any organisation – is to limit upheavals to those that are genuinely unavoidable. What is the point of grooming successors to important jobs if you do not then permit their succession? Is there nothing to be gained from instilling the feeling in aspiring English coaches that one day, they, too, might coach their country?

In any event, the evaluation of cricket coaches is very far from an exact science. Fletcher's departure satisfyingly suggests that it's all about results. But were that the case, a path would surely have been beaten to the door of the most successful national coach of all time – who, it so happens, is about to become available. John Buchanan – for it is he – stands down as Australia's coach next week after almost eight years. He has just turned fifty-four; the leathery Bob Simpson coached Australia until he was sixty.

The truth is that Buchanan, compared to the charismatic Warne or the articulate Moody, is a faintly ridiculous figure. After his last Test as coach, Ricky Ponting was asked what Buchanan had advised on his final morning in charge. Hmmm: there was 'control the controllables'; there was 'play in the moment'; and ... well ... actually, the last one might have been 'make poverty history' for all Ponting could remember.

But something is to be learned from Buchanan, at least in the philosophy behind his appointment. Australia appoints its coaches with its captains and its anticipated teams in mind. Simpson inaugurated the position twenty-one years ago as a tough-talking taskmaster, as the taciturn Allan Border struggled beneath his unwanted burdens of captaincy.

Simpson was not so happy a fit with Border's more confident successor Mark Taylor, and was replaced by the low-profile Geoff Marsh. Taylor was content to rely on the cumulative cricket wisdom of Steve Waugh, Shane Warne, Ian Healy and Glenn McGrath, and had no use for an *éminence grise*.

Buchanan took over as coach for Waugh's first home series as captain. In his diary of that series, Waugh recalls that Buchanan instantly made him 'very confident about the future' because 'many of his ideas and goals are similar to mine'. In other words, he enhanced Waugh's feeling of control over his own side. It's arguable that Australia's team of the talents would have won everything in sight whoever was coaching; but Waugh without Buchanan, I suspect, would not have been nearly so effective a captain.

Similar considerations suggest it is now time for Buchanan to go. Ponting has grown in his job; the advent of Troy Cooley as bowling coach has bolstered the Australian back room; generational turnover is in progress and Buchanan's successor Tim Nielsen has spent the last two years at Cricket Australia's Centre of Excellence working alongside many of the young players who will be competing for Test places in the next two.

Similar thinking seems to underlie the appointment of Moores, whose last two years have been spent as director of the ECB Academy. The likelihood is, in fact, that the Ashes of 2009 will be contested by teams whose coaches are English-born keepers turned first-class coaches (Nielsen was born in Forest Gate). Ultimately, though, Moores' effectiveness as coach will hinge on how he works with whomever captains England. This suggests that the really important appointment is still to come – even if it won't be nearly so much fun to speculate about.

*

A quality assuredly unwanted among cricket coaches is boorish exhibitionism. Which brings us to Geoffrey Boycott. Last week, as Exhibit A in his prosecution of Fletcher, Boycott revealed he had not so long ago received a private request for Tyke-to-Tyke technical advice from Michael Vaughan.

Private? Boycs was having none of that: 'This winter *I* had a captain of England requesting to have dinner with *me* to get *my* help on his batting but he said he must not be seen with *me* ... Because *I* have been critical of the coach, an England captain is now frightened to have dinner with *me*.' Italics mine – well, his really. Yet is it so surprising that Vaughan should have approached Boycott confidentially? A batsman with technical concerns is hardly likely to advertise them. A captain of England seeking help from an individual who is altogether a stranger to the sensation of quiet satisfaction from a job well done knows he is not entering into a conventional coaching arrangement. If Vaughan wanted to keep his contact with Boycott low-key, it may have been because he feared becoming grist for the mill of a professional controversialist; Boycott's shameless narcissism in revealing the approach is Exhibit Z5473 in the case for having nothing to do with him. Boycott once complained that the cricket establishment wanted his expertise but didn't seem to want *him*. It's odd he should so consistently illustrate why.

*

The new *Wisden* arrived last week, to be pored over, then set aside. To my mind, *Wisdens* improve with the passing years. After twenty, they are full of enchanting memories; after fifty, they are rich with half-remembered facts; after a hundred, no source more reliably reveals how much and how little has changed.

Recently, as you do, I was reviewing Yorkshire's 1896 season, when they were 'batting in wonderful form' and 'showed some very brilliant cricket' – this being before Neville Cardus reimagined the county's cricketers as a cross between the Amish and the Plymouth Brethren. Against Notts on June 1–3, *Wisden* recorded, Yorkshire's hard-hitting opener John Brown was bowled for 107 'in foolishly hitting back-handed at a lob'. Sounds like a prototype of the reverse sweep, executed so majestically by Paul Nixon at North Sound three weeks ago. Technical advice from Yorkshire's opening batsman 110 years ago might have been more interesting than popularly assumed.

The Guardian April 2007

ZIMBABWE

Out of Africa

In the 1960s, one of the catchcries of the anti-apartheid movement seeking the boycott of South African athletes was 'no normal sport in an abnormal society'. So judgemental. Surely, that should have been 'differently abled' society. And hey, what's 'normal sport' any-way? Curling. Zorbing. Cheese Rolling. You can't tell me *those* are normal.

Similar thinking seems to underlie apparent indifference to the prospect of the Australian cricket team touring Zimbabwe in September. Oh, it's such a shame about Zimbabwe, isn't it? Millions starving and not so much as a pop concert. But, well, it's *hardly* as important as Kevin Rudd's 4WD, is it? There's bound to be a 'root cause' or two in there somewhere; probably a few 'double stand-ards', too. Say what? John Howard and Alexander Downer don't think they should go? Well, there you are: would you buy a used foreign policy from these men?

Ricky Ponting, meanwhile, agrees it could be a tad dicey – but you never know, do you? 'It's such a long way away yet,' he told jour-nalists during the World Cup. 'Anything could happen between now and then in Zimbabwe. We'll see what happens.' If he batted like he talked, Ponting would be timed out in every innings. When Australia bravely flew in and out of Zimbabwe for their World Cup fixture in 2003 inside twenty-four hours – security reasons, you understand – Ponting declined to say whether he would shake Robert Mugabe's hand on the grounds that it was a hypothetical question. Perhaps they didn't tell him how to answer those at the Academy.

Yet in terms of the general situation regarding the evolving scenario vis-à-vis on-going long-range optimisation Mugabe-wise, Ponting has a way to go before he out-wimps Thabo Mbeki, South Africa's serene prime minister, advocate of dealing with his old chum Mugabe by 'quiet diplomacy'. Mbeki's perspective? 'The point really about all this from our perspective has been that the critical role we should play is to assist the Zimbabweans to find each other, really to agree among themselves about the political, economic, social [and] other solutions that their country needs.'

Alas, the only Zimbabweans that Mugabe wishes to find are members of the Movement for Democratic Change, the country's endlessly persecuted opposition coalition. And it doesn't need diplomacy, quiet, noisy or otherwise, to determine that what Zimbabweans mainly agree on is that they're hungry. Mugabe's ruinous 'land reforms' have reduced a hearty agricultural exporter to a country that can barely cover a third of its grain needs. We'll deal with the human rights violations, the crushing of the free press and independent judiciary, the GDP that has halved since 2000, the 2000 per cent inflation, the eighty per cent unemployment, the unofficial exchange rate of US$1 to Z$25,000, the three million refugees, the national median age of nineteen and the life-expectancy of thirty-seven for males and thirty-four for females ... well, later. Much, much later.

Against all this, of course, a cricket tour is a trifle. But in Zimbabwe, the old chestnut that sport and politics should not mix doesn't have a lot of traction – if it ever did. Zimbabwe Cricket (formerly the Zimbabwe Cricket Union) is now hardly more than a ZANU-PF front: after a long period of exercising increasing suasion, the Sport and Recreation Commission officially took over its offices in January last year to break a deadlock between ZC and recalcitrant provincial boards. 'Reform' began – using, that is, its Mugabe definition. New national and provincial boards were constituted, composed in the main of malleable cronies of the regime. Their zeal to serve may have something to do with the expectation of big payments from the International Cricket

Council for Zimbabwe's participation in last year's Champions Trophy and the recent World Cup.

Mugabe, of course, famously declared in 1984: 'Cricket civilises people and creates good gentlemen. I want everyone in Zimbabwe to play cricket.' On present trends, everyone who wishes will enjoy the opportunity to play *international* cricket. Not a single member of the last Zimbabwe team to play a Test against Australia remains in the XI. Their able young captain when last they met Australia in a one-day international, Tatenda Taibu, fled Zimbabwe eighteen months ago after being threatened by a ZANU-PF hardliner and having had the police turn up at his home to repossess his Zimbabwe Cricket car.

Zimbabwe's benighted cricketers, in fact, are regularly humiliated by absurd, pettifogging rules, like last year's ban on dreadlocks: three complied under sufferance; a fourth left the country. They are barely paid. Their previous coach has recently revealed that he wasn't paid at all; their World Cup squad were forced to sign their contracts on the spot on pain of omission, and their fees have been withheld until June to prevent an immediate exodus. Three players were even briefly jailed on trumped-up foreign exchange violations. Not surprisingly, Zimbabwe are a shadow of the half-way decent team they were a decade ago, and now rate behind Ireland in world one-day rankings. Fortunately, perhaps, the Zimbabwe Broadcasting Corporation did not telecast any matches; apparently it was unable to afford the US$50 for a satellite technician to obtain the signal from South Africa. The act of touring Zimbabwe, then, is effectively doing business with a branch of a government that is an international pariah. Even if Ponting and co want to stick to their 'no-morality-please-we're-sportsmen' shtick, there is an argument that Zimbabwe Cricket is no longer an administrative body with whom Cricket Australia should have reciprocal relations.

Yet it should never have come to this. Perhaps the International Cricket Council should have done more. Because – prepare to be amazed – they have done squat. Perhaps the Australian government could have provided firmer guidance; perhaps more information should have been made available to the public. But – well – why? So professional sportsmen should not have to show an ounce of curiosity and exercise their consciences? The Australian rugby player Tony Abrahams who declined to play against the Springboks in 1971 was once asked how difficult it was for him to speak out. Difficult? 'It wasn't that difficult,' he said. 'I mean, it seems to me, looking back on it, but even then, that it was probably one of the clearest issues you could make a stand on.' Australian cricket shames itself every day it dallies.

The Monthly June 2007

TWENTY20 2005

The Shape of Things to Come

The last time I saw a county cricket match at the Oval, spectators could have been allotted a stand each. Today each of those stands brimmed with boisterous, partisan supporters. Admittedly, there were four counties involved; admittedly, too, the fixture's resemblance to cricket could have been disputed. The occasion was the semi-finals of the Twenty20 Cup, contested between the Lancashire Lightning and the Surrey Lions, then the Somerset Sabres and Leicestershire Foxes. The Sabres ended up conducting and earthing the Lightning by 7 wickets during the final.

For the uninitiated, and that includes Australians, whose states will not compete in the inaugural domestic Twenty20 tournament until January, the phenomenon is essentially 50-over cricket with its unseemly midriff liposuctioned away. There was some efficient slogging, with the biggest blow, from Ali Brown, almost in need of a Zone 1 and 2 Travelcard. There was some effective fielding with probably a bit too much falling over, some rather unambitious running, and some generally forgettable bowling. The whole thing coasted along at about 10 runs an over. Defensive shots – and there were a few – seemed heretical. In the abbreviated game, everything is somehow magnified. Perhaps the day's deftest stroke was a reverse sweep by Mal Loye off Doshi, sweetly struck for four; by far the worst was a reverse sweep by Rikki Clarke off Crook, the ball in perfect position for an orthodox sweep and hitting leg stump half-way up. Such, I suppose, is the nature of the shot, which seems the most brilliant *jeu d'esprit* when it succeeds, the most humiliating *faux pas* when it fails.

With 23,000 present, the whole affair was a big straight six for the marketeers let loose by the England Cricket Board. The games were interrupted by a steeplechase involving the county mascots over inflatable obstacles attended by scantily-clad npower girls. You may wonder who this is aimed at, but it certainly held Andy Flintoff's attention during his man-of-the-match press conference, and the crowd was indubitably entertained.

Today may not have been the best opportunity to judge the format. Rain interruptions made it a very long day for the cheery, chirpy, steadily-getting-pissed audience. One of the rationales for Twenty20 is that it brings in children; whether families would have felt completely comfortable around 9 p.m. as the effects of a day's drinking took their toll on behaviour is another matter.

Personally, I didn't mind it. I've no doubt it will sweep the world. My reservations remain the same. My fear is that, as in indoor cricket, where you play basically every game that can be played within a few years, it will run short of variations and begin repeating itself. There already seem basically two kinds of innings: one where your top four get runs, the other where they get out and you have to hold on to wickets in order to use the full complement of overs. And ... errr ... that's it. I wonder, too, whether anyone in authority has thought through how this game will work in lower levels of cricket. One of the joys of the grass roots game – and one of the advantages that cricket enjoys at grass roots over the various football codes – is that it can accommodate so many different styles and characters of player. Twenty20 defines the cricketer narrowly; it excludes many for whom the game has been a welcoming home. I don't know why I'm wondering, of course, because no-one in authority gives a twopenny damn about much that happens below first-class level. The same boneheads who insist that they must 'give the people what they want' are seldom if ever around when the people actually want something.

Cricinfo July 2005

TWENTY20 2006

The Excitement Machine

Last week in Australia may in hindsight be seen as a historic turning point. Monday night brought the first home Twenty20 international, won comfortably by Australia in front of a record crowd for the Gabba of 38,894 patrons – who left slightly deafer than when they came in thanks to an atmosphere more reminiscent of a disco than a cricket ground.

But this was not the historic event: everyone has known for some time the potentialities of Twenty20 cricket and their implications, not so much for Test cricket as for one-day cricket, whose humdrum nature it displays in even more stark relief. The truly fascinating development was the role of the Channel Nine commentary team, who abandoned all pretence of being disinterested critics and turned into carnival barkers: 'Hurry hurry hurry! Step right up and see the AMAAAAZING cricket match!'

During South Africa's insipid and incompetent reply to the Australian total, viewers were told repeatedly that what they were watching was the most exciting innovation since penicillin. One expects this from Tony Greig, of course, who has been selling ghastly gewgaws for years. But here were Mark Taylor, Ian Healy, Mark Nicholas and Michael Slater, almost tumescent with excitement, essentially doing the same: selling us a one-sided one-dayer as though it was the Tied Test. No wonder Rich and Chappelli had the night off; George Galloway on *Celebrity Big Brother* was a model of parliamentary dignity compared with Slater's desperate attempts to endear himself to his temporary bosses. This reinvention of cricket commentary as infomercial raised some provocative questions. Is the commentator there to call the game, or to sell it? Is his duty primarily to the viewer, to his employer or – strange anachronistic notion, this – to the game of cricket? The commentators here are on a slippery slope, but they look determined to slalom down it.

It was almost a relief to watch the comparative dignity of the opening VB Series game on Friday evening, another damp squib thanks to the serene inertia of Sri Lanka's Martin Van Dotball, but with a soundtrack neither so hysterical nor hyperbolic. It was possible to savour instead the restoration of heart-warming traditions like the sound of Murali being no-balled by one of those famously knowledgeable and hospitable Melbourne crowds – something, of course, to which the commentators were far too polite to refer. But ho! What have we here, with Nicholas and Healy at the microphone? Mr Smooth and Mr Shrewd wearing false moustaches as part of a beer promotion involving a talking Boonie doll! Pure ruddy gold. Kerry Packer might have gone to his reward, but his spirit is alive and well. If you can bear to sit through the eye-glazingly dull games, there's some veeeeerrry interesting stuff going down in Aussie cricket at the moment.

The Googly January 2006

TWENTY20 2007

The Balloon Goes Up

It starts on 11 September. It finishes on 24 September. On its bigger brother World Cup, the inaugural World Twenty20 Championship is an advance before a ball has been bowled. Where the Cup runneth way, way over, cricket's hot new ticket will not be overstaying its welcome.

What else might be said in its favour remains to be seen, although there are plenty who want to see it. The cricket world is on the brink of one of its rare innovations of significance. It promises to alter not merely cricket but its economics and politics at the same time.

Twenty20: the very name belongs to the acronym- and abbreviation-crazy culture that gave us eBay, Boyz2Men and L8R G8R. It is the first form of cricket designed exclusively by marketers, specifically those of the England Cricket Board, who devised it after consultation with thirty focus groups and in 4000 fifteen-minute face-to-face interviews.

Forty years earlier, the first domestic one-day competition, the Gillette Cup, had followed a recommendation of a sub-committee of the Marylebone Cricket Club in November 1962. The first Twenty20 championship in 2003 sprang straight from the whiteboard of the ECB's marketing chief Stuart Robertson, whose objective was to drag in not cricket lovers but the far larger group of cricket 'tolerators': young men, young women and children. It surpassed all expectations: when Middlesex hosted Surrey, the crowd of 27,500 was the biggest seen by counties at Lord's for half a century.

It took twelve years for one-day cricket to go from English county competition to international championship: the World Cup of 1975. It has taken four years for Twenty20 to move the same distance. That's slower progress, however, than it might have been. The first Twenty20 international wasn't staged until February 2005; Australia didn't host its own until January 2006. The reason is simple. Cricket was potentially cannibalising its own market. The limited-overs international is a lucrative franchise; in fact, the cash cow of the modern game. How would it withstand a snappier, slappier rival?

India and Pakistan, for whom one-day internationals have been a veritable horn of plenty, actually resisted the idea of a global Twenty20 jamboree when it was first discussed in March last year. 'We feel it dilutes the importance of international cricket,' said BCCI boss Sharad Pawar piously. But their preference for jazzing up the 50-over format has been a squib so damp as almost to need a Super Sopper.

Shorter boundaries, wilder uniforms, Super Subs, Power Plays, and official status for contrived teams like World XIs and Africa XIs – they have had much the same impact on cricket as leaving a pie in the microwave a bit too long. When the abject failure of these steps was revealed by the World Cup in the Caribbean, which moved at torpid pace to an inevitable conclusion, reality dawned: if the ICC didn't develop Twenty20, someone else would.

In fact, someone else already has: Texan billionaire Sir R. Allen Stanford. Stanford Financial Group, an asset management and financial services conglomerate headquartered in Houston, is the largest private investor and employer in Antigua and Barbuda, its investments including the regional airline Caribbean Star. He has been called 'haughty, arrogant and obnoxious' by the tiny nation's prime minister Baldwin Spencer; so capacious are his moneybags that everyone else calls him 'sir'.

Last August, Stanford won the adulation of Antiguans by staging an eponymous regional Twenty20 championship, Guyana's Narsingh Deonarine blasting a six off the penultimate ball of the final to secure victory over Trinidad and Tobago. Winning alone was worth US$1 million; the whole affair was valued at US$32 million. This would be big money in Australia; the Caribbean hadn't seen such plunder since the days of Jack Sparrow. In a reversal of the traditional theories of sponsorship, Stanford has *since* agreed to pay the West Indies Cricket Board about US$2 million over five years to have the tournament officially recognised.

Stanford's next trick is a US$23 million week-long round robin involving Australia, India, South Africa and Sri Lanka in 2008, with the winner to take on his own Stanford Super Stars: an ensemble chosen from the best players in the inter-island domestic Twenty20 tournament. He has already offered terms to Cricket Australia, which has publicly advertised its interest. The plan is evidently to follow the same route: moot the event, *then* have it made official.

Stanford worries the ICC; so does such a precedent. The 'official' stamp is not one used indiscriminately: not even Kerry Packer could buy it. Thus the rush: a successful official Twenty20 tournament will occupy the space that might otherwise be annexed by privateers like Stanford, and also Subhash Chandra's Zee Television, which has foreshadowed a breakaway Indian Cricket League involving all-star teams 'later this year'.

As for the playing of Twenty20, competitors are still working on it. Australia isn't tampering overmuch with its one-day formula. Retirement having spared Glenn McGrath the transition, there seems no pressing need to alter the line-up that carried off the World Cup (and then, during their celebrations, apparently dropped it a few times). Far from slow bowling being a liability, Brad Hogg appears an asset, his 16 wickets in the KFC Big Bash having cost 10 runs each.

Interestingly, India is taking the opposite approach. Its three senior batsmen, Rahul Dravid, Sachin Tendulkar and Sourav Ganguly, have sidelined themselves. Their places in the thirty-man squad have been taken by the high achievers of India's inaugural domestic Twenty20 tournament, including the uncapped Karan

Goel and Niraj Patel who were its top scorers. The selectors have proclaimed their belief that Twenty20 is a game for youth, strength and elastic athleticism.

The biggest obstacle for the Australians, however, might be their own dislike of the format. Ponting has dismissed it as 'a lottery', and confessed in his latest diary: 'I don't think I really like playing Twenty20 international cricket.' The philosophical antagonism between cricket and its newest variant is obvious. Cricket proper is a game designed for players; Twenty20 has been devised with the crowd, sponsors and television in mind. With cricket proper, people have traditionally come to spectate; with Twenty20, they are encouraged to regard themselves as part of the spectacle. For all its success in attracting crowds, in fact, Twenty20 in England has done a mediocre job of supervising them. In the spiritual home of binge drinking, umpire Peter Willey has already warned of trouble: 'There might be some clubs who will be reluctant to employ security guards, but how expensive is a life? Those clubs would not want to be sued. And we don't want the kids to hear foul and abusive language.'

Ultimately, what's being tested in South Africa is not so much the players as the game, with the awareness that both failure and success prelude potential problems. Failure, after the fiasco of the World Cup, would make this a genuine *annus horribilis.* But success would also be a mixed blessing. Taking a whole day to play a game of cricket might suddenly seem rather twentieth century, while Twenty20 arguably has as much to do with Test cricket as graffiti on a toilet door with an Old Master on the wall of the National Gallery. Regardless of who wins the final at New Wanderers in Johannesburg on 24 September, chances are that the face of the game is about to change. It will be cricket, Ricky, but not as we know it.

Inside Sport September 2007